JIHADI TERRORISM

JIHADI TERRORISM
Making of a World War?

Shashi B. Sahai

GYAN PUBLISHING HOUSE
NEW DELHI-110002

Jihadi Terrorism
Making of a World War?

Rs. 540

ISBN: 81-212-0905-6

Published in 2006 in India by:
Gyan Publishing House
5, Ansari Road, Darya Ganj,
New Delhi-110002
Phones : 23282060, 23261060
Fax : 011-23285914
E-mail : books@ gyanbooks.com
Website: www.gyanbooks.com

Lassertype Setting by: Rudra Computer Graphics
Printed at : Salasar Imaging System, Delhi

To my life partner Shashi Prabha, ailing and yet a live wire, but for whose support, care and attention, I couldn't have undertaken this nerve-wracking exercise in the sun-set years of my life.

Prologue

There is no finality in the affairs of man and human endeavour. And you cannot call it a day until the last day of your life. I did not realize it until, despite my physical handicaps consequent upon advancing years, I took the plunge to unpack the poisonous baggage of thoughts overloading my mind over the past few years. It was extremely difficult, if not impossible, to weild the pen and eject the poison corroding my system on paper in this last phase of life. In the circumstances, the completion of the heart-rending exercise in the shape of this book has come as a great relief.

I had a similar feeling of relief after completing my last book "South Asia: From Freedom To Terrorism" in 1997. I would like to recall what I wrote in the preface to that book: "Going down the memory lane step by step through all the horrors of the last 50 or 51 years, beginning the 'Great Calcutta killing' and the partition riots, has been like wading through rivers of blood or orgy of fire, enough to mentally exhaust or 'burn out' any normal, same human being completely. In the bargain, I have not only burnt my fingers but burnt myself out as far as the affairs of my country are concerned. No more of any further forays into the realm of Indian reality for me. The affair with India in my writing exercise ends with this book, which is kind of a valedictory presentation to my country. I have unburdened myself of my last load".

As it has turned out, that was a premature goodbye to my writing endeavours on the affairs of India. Not really on account of the fact that writing is kind of an addiction which it is difficult to give up. If I am addicted to writing on current affairs, there is no dearth of outlets, with periodicals and magazines soliciting papers and articles on a regular basis. What made my itch to venture into this book –writing project so late in life irrestible was an agonizing search for answers to some pertinent questions tearing my mind.

Jihadi terrorism is in the air today the world over. It has come to grip large parts of the world, and more so India, in its blood-spilling fangs posing a grave threat to civilized life. Hostility between Islam and the West, which had started surfacing in 1990's, has reached a level which could not be imagined even in mid 1990's. It found its most macabre manifestation in the Jihadi terror strike against the leader of the western world on Septemnber 11, 2001. If Jihadi terrorism was the outcome of 1400 years old animosity between Islam and Christianity, which defines the western civilization, or a 'clash of civilisations' coming on for the last fourteen centuries, why has it emerged as such a Frankestein now ? What has brought it about at this point of time in the chequered history of the world ?

Is it the arrogance of western powers vis a vis the Muslim world ? or the running sores of

Palestine and Kashmir, for example ? But after the end of western imperialism around the mid-2oth century, Muslim countries of the Middle East have never been more free and vibrant as today. Palestine and Kashmir problems have been there since 1948, but there was no terrorism of the kind and on the scale as it is today. How come Jihadi terrorism has emerged as a major threat to world peace now ? What are the ultimate objectives of Jihadi terrorists? So much was being said and written about'Islamic Jihad', but these vital questions have not been touched upon. That leaves a vacuum in the growing literature on the subject.

Being deeply concerned about the magnitude and ravages of Jihadi terrorism devastating India and the world, I could not help burying myself deep into a study of the history and dimensions of Jihad to find answers to the questions raised above. They kept racking my mind no end. The agonizing search continued until somewhere in the process of churning of the brain and oceans of books, I stumbled upon the answers, which put my harried brain to rest. The result is this book.

According to our mythological story, when the gods churned the ocean at the time of the universal deluge, both ambrosia ('amrit' or nectar) and poison, among other things, came to the surface. The ambrosia could give eternal life to the gods, but poison could kill them. While they were happy about the ambrosia, they were mighty scared of the poison. They prayed Lord Shiva to save them from the evil effect of the poison. Lord Shiva drank the poison which made his neck blue (Neelkanth). For me, the book, which has come up as a result of the churning, is nothing short of ambrosia as it has relieved me of a killing obsession. If some find it to be a poison, I cannot help it. As the saying goes, one man's meat is another man's poison.

Shashi B. Sahai

1

War, Jihad and Terrorism : Historical Background

War

War is as old as human history, or recorded history to be precise. Even some famous epics of pre-historic times, which constitute the source material for construction of proto-history, are tales of one deadly war, or another. The Indian 'Mahabharata', the oldest and longest poetic work in the world, is a all about a devastating war between 'Kauravas' and 'Pandavas' at 'Krurkshetra' to the north of modern Delhi. And the well-known Greek epic "Illiad", attributed to Homer, narrates the story of the capture of the Greek beauty Hellen by Paris and the siege of Troy by Greek Kings and chieftains to recover her.

Of all ancient civilizations that flourished in Egypt, Mesopotamia, Hoang Ho Valley in China and Indus valley in India, it is the ancient Greeko-Roman or Hellenic civilization which is best known.

And it is precisely because of its consistent record of parennial wars and conquests. The first recorded history in the world is an account of the protracted wars fought by the Greeks against the invading Persians. And the recorder-Herodotus-is acknowledged as the first historian of the world.

The recorded history of ancient, medieval and modern world is all about a ceaseless chain of wars in pursuit of tribal, regional, dynastic, religious and nationalist goals. It started with the migratory movements of marauding tribesmen from central Asian steppes, generally known as Aryans, in early second millennium B.C. They moved west-wards and south wards conquering indigenous peoples and settling down in Europe, Anatolia, the Iranian table land etc. From the new habitats, their descendents kept up the momentum of migration to new areas. In the process, they migrated to more areas in the Middle East, round the shores of the Black sea, the Mediteranean, and eventually as far as the Atlantic coast of North Africa through centuries of wars. It was in course of this onward march that the Greek Aryans conquered and destroyed knossos in Crete, the capital of the Mycenaean rulers and center of the Minoan-Mycenaean civilization which preceded the Hellenic civilization. That marked the end of the oldest known civilization in the Aegean Basin.

The advent of Greek Aryans in the Aegean Basin was followed by anarchy for about 400 years. There were relentless conflicts between high-land shepherds and low-land farmers among the Greek migrants themselves. These were ultimately resolved by clear victory of low-land farmers over the high-landers in the 8th century B.C. This brought about the re-establishment of ancient peace and order in the Aegean basin which had been shaken when the Mycenaeans were swept off by the Greek Aryans. And with restoration of order, the Hellenic civilization was born in 8th century B.C. which profoundly influenced the growth of modern western civilisation during its formative stages.

The mid-wife which brought about the birth of Hellenic civilization was war. This "early marriage of war with Hellenic History", in the words of Arnold Toyanbee, made war a basic institution of Hellenic life. So much so that an early 5th century B.C. Greek philosopher, Heracleitus of Ephesus, observed : "War is the father of all things."

The next spurt in the Greek surge came in the 4th century B.C when Alexander the Great (also known as Sikandar in India) took up the mantle of the Greeks to settle scores with their long lasting adversaries, the Persians. Although not exactly a Greek but a Macedonian—a close neighbour—he was acknowledged as the leader of the Greek armed assault on Persia in view of his vigour and strength. His chief claim to fame was that it was under his leadership that the Greeks ventured out of the Aegean basin to conquer other parts of the known world or the world that mattered to them.

In a blitzkrieg, Alexander conquered Egypt, then a part of the Persian Kingdom, quickly and went on to attack Persia itself. He occupied Babylon and captured Persepolis, the grand capital of the Persian King Darius III, with lightening speed. From

Persia, he carried on his conquering campaign through Herat, Kabul and Samarquand entering India via the Khyber Pass in the north west. It has here that he met with heroic resistance from the legendry Indian king Porus. Although he defeated Porus, he did not carry his Indian campaign any further due to fatigue and exhaustion of his soldiers. He returned back to Babylon where he died a premature death at the age of 33 years only.

After the lightening military triumphs of Hellenic arms under Alexander's leadership in the 4th century B.C, the Greeks started declining. Eventually, they were superceded by the more militant Romans in the Hellenistic world towards the close of the pre-christian era. With the Romans, war was glorified in to a cult. After conquering the Mediterranean world, Roman warriors went ahead with their campaigns of conquest in western Europe. Julius Ceasor, the most celebrated Roman General, conquered Gaul (modern France) and Britain. He fell a victim of conspiratorial killing in the year 44 B.C. His adopted son Octavion succeeded him and became the first Roman monarch, ending the republican character of the Roman state, just on the eve of the christian era.

With the birth of Christ and advent of Christianity, the Greeko-Roman war-mongering started tapering off. In its hey day, Rome ruled over Italy, Spain and Gaul (France) in the west, Greece and Asia Minor in the east, with Egypt in North Africa being its progectorate. But peoples of central and northern Europe beyond the Rhine, like the Germans, were outside the pale of the Roman world. It is these tribes from central and northern Europe—the Goths, a Germanic tribe, Vandals and Huns who in turns struck the Romans and eventually eclipsed the warring Romans early in the Christian era.

As a territorial empire, Rome was destroyed by the above North European "barbarians", as they came to be called, but Romanism as a cult of war was decimated by Christianity. Christ's humanitarian message of compassion, brotherhood of man and peace had a tremendous appeal among the war ravaged subjects of the Roman Empire. As a result, starting with the Roman Empire of southern Europe, Christianity spread to central and northern Europe and as far as Iceland and Greenland during the first thousand years of its birth.

In the event, the addiction to war of the western peoples in modern times cannot be attributed to Christianity which is their dominant religion. It is a hang-over from their pre-christian past, a legacy of their ancient Greeko-Roman ancestors to whom war was "a father of all things." No wonder that the western world had the dubious distinction of indulging in two mega wars of the 20th century and is not averse to engaging in another, if it comes to that, to defend itself. Ironical for the followers of Christ, universally acknowledged as the apostle of non-violence and 'Prince of Peace'. War has come to be the special trade mark of western civilization in spite of christanity which defines it.

Jihad

Islam is a different proposition. Even as Hellenism with its glorification of war was giving way to the peace message of Christianity, the desert people of Arabia were being stirred by a new religion to come out of their isolated sleepy existence. It was Islam preached by Prophet Mohammed who was born in the year 570 A.D. in Mecca. As a religious faith, Islam transformed the inconsequential tribes of Arabia, feuding and quarrelling among themselves and worshipping numerous Gods, beyond recognition. It brought peace, order and brotherhood among the Arab people. After facing initial resistance by the people of Mecca, Mohammed succeeded in instilling in the Arabs absolute faith in one God, Allah Almighty, whose Prophet he was.

What is more, the Prophet sent messages to the kings and emperors of the world to acknowledge the one God, Allah, and himself as his Prophet. Heraclius, the Constantinopole Emperor got the message, the Persian king got it and it is said that Tai-Tsung of China also got it.

Islam filled the Arabs with a new kind of vigor and strength and, more importantly, made them conscious of it. As long as they kept confined to purely religious pursuits, the world at large was not concerned. As a religious faith, Islam was one thing, pious and holy as all other religions. But as Islamic Umma or Quom, that is, a politico-religious entity, it turned out to be quite different. Once the Arab followers of Islam stepped out of the domain of pure religion and took to sword in pursuit of power in the name of Islam, they shook the world.

It marked the beginning of the era of pan Islamic polity which has re-emerged as a major factor in the 21th century.

It all began with Abu Bakr and Omar who became Khalifa or Caliph of the Islamic world in quick succession after the Prophet's death in the year 632 A.D. With them as Caliphs or chiefs, politicization of Islam was completed. For they combined both the offices of religious heads and political chiefs, kind of "king and pope in one" (Jawahar Lal Nehru in his "Glimpses of World History.") And during the dozen years that they ruled, they set about to conquer the world around them. They fought and defeated the Eastern Roman Empire as well as Persia, and occupied Jerusalem, the holy city of Jews and Christians. The whole of Syria, Iraq and Persia became parts of the new Muslim Arab Empire embracing Islam.

Once the Arabs armed with their new found faith of Islam took to the path of war, there was no stopping for them. They marched on from conquests to conquests both in east and west, spreading Islam all the way. In the east, they captured Buddhist Afghanistan and marched up to Sindh in Hindu India converting them to Islam. In the west, they pushed right across northern Africa conquering Egypt in the way and reached the Atlantic ocean on the western coast of Morocco. It is said that the conquering Arab general named Okba rode as far as he could into the sea and then expressed his regret to Allah that there was no more land in that direction to conquer in His name. The spirit of Jihad, which implies holy war of Muslims against

Kafirs or non-believers, was unmistakable in Okba's reported observation.

From Morocco and northern Africa, the Muslim Arabs crossed the narrow sea to enter into Spain and Christian Europe. They conquered Spain rapidly and poured into southern France. It is here that surging Islam came in direct class with Christianity for the first time. The Christian Europe panicked and formed a coalition of Christian Europeans which defeated the Muslim Arabs at the battle of Tours (France) in the year 732 A.D.

In his "Glimpses of World History", Nehru writes : "There can be no doubt that if the Arabs had won at Tours, European history would have been tremendously changed — Instead of Christianity, Islam would have become the religion of Europe ————" Who says Islam was not spread by the might of the sword ? It was the sword of the Arabs that in only in a hundred years from the death of prophet Mohammad in the year 632 A.D, the Islamic empire spread right across northern Africa to Spain and southern France in the west and Afghanistan, Persia (Iran) and central Asia up to the borders of Mongolia in the east.

The next surge in Islamism came when old Turks of central Asia got converted to Islam under the influence of ruling Muslim Arabs, known as Seljuq Turks. They took up the cause of Islam with the extra zeal of new converts. So when thousands of Christian pilgrims from Europe journeyed to the holy city of Jerusalem on the eve of one thousand years after Christ, they suffered badly at the hands of the Muslim Turks,. Even as they returned to

Europe with tales of horrors and sufferings, Constantinople, the seat of Greek orthodox church, was threatened by the Muslim Turks.

Although the Greek orthodox church based at Constantinople and Roman catholic church were separate and rivals, they combined at this stage to fight the Islamists. Pope Gregory the Seventh of Rome convened a great church council comprising all of Christendom, both Greak and Roman, in the year 1095. That marked the beginning of a period of religious wars between Christianity and Islam, the cross and the crescent, which rocked Europe and west Asia for over a century and a half.

For the Christians, it was crusade, for the Muslims, Jihad. They fought bitterly for control over west Asia in which millions perished. At one stage, the Christian crusaders succeeded in capturing the holy land of Jerusalem, but 75 years later it was retaken by the Muslims. The last crusade was led by King Lous IX of France. He was defeated by the Muslims in the year 1249. The net result of "Crusades", as these wars were called, was more or less a stalemate between Christianity and Islam on the religious front.

The Islamist jihadis being thoroughly exhausted and, additionally, devastated by fearsome Mongols of central Asia, there was a lull on the Pan Islamic front for over half a century. The lull was broken by another Turkish tribe which took up the cause of Islam with renewed vigor. These sturdy people from the deserts of Turkistan in central Asia had migrated to Muslim West Asia in large numbers. In course of time, they got converted to

Islam which was the religion of the people among whom they had settled.

Around the year 1300, the chieftain of one of these Turkish tribes named Osman or Othoman assumed the title of Emir or prince of the Muslim Turks. Those owing allegiance to him and his successors came to be called the Ottoman or Osmanli Turks. It was these sturdy Muslim converts who took up the baton of Islamism from where the Arabs first and Seljuq Tturks later had left. And that started a protracted series of most bitterly fought religious wars or jihad launched by the Islamists against the Christian world which lasted for well over 200 years.

In the first half of the 14th century, the Ottoman Turks undid the work of the Christian crusaders and wrested all of Asia Minor from the Greek Christians. In the second half, they began their onslaught on South Eastern Europe and conquered nearly the entire Balkan Peninsula except Constantinople, the seat of the Greek orthodox church, by the end of the 14th century. The Ottoman Sultan Mohammad II completed the process by capturing Constantinople in the middle of the 15th century (year 1453). A combined Christian contingent, including priests and monks fought the rampaging Muslims to the bitter end "for the glory of God and safety of Christendom." They were all killed, including Constantine XI, the last of the Greeko-Roman Emperors. The victorious Sultan Mohammad II went on to conquer Romanian lands at the mouth of the river Danube and Russian and Mongol lands north of the Black sea.

The Muslim push continued in the first half of the 16th century. In the year 1521, another Ottoman Sultan captured Belgrade, the capital of latter day Yogoslavia (present day Serbia) and crossed the river Danube. In 1526, he defeated the king of Hungary and occupied Budapest. In 1529, he laid siege to Vienna. Though he could not take Vienna, he forced the Holy Roman Emperor to agree to a partition of Hungary, the smaller portion going to Christian Austria and the larger one passing on to the Muslim Ottoman Empire.

There is no scope for any doubt about the thoroughly Islamic character of the Ottoman Turkish expansionism from 14th to mid 16th century. Only Muslims could be full-fledged "citizens" of the Empire in which Jews and Christians could only be "subjects". They were taxed more heavily than Muslims and excluded from most public offices. The Sultans converted the historic Christian cathedral of Saint Sophia in Constantinople into a Muslim edifice. Wherever the Ottoman armies marched, they took over the principal Christian churches and converted them into mosques.

Incidentally, it was around this time that Baber, another Muslim adventurer of Turkish origin, conquered north India and got the Ram temple of Hindus in Ayodhya transformed into a mosque. It was part of a pattern followed by all Muslim conquerors in all parts of the world. Kind of a jihad against 'kafirs' or non-believers.

A bird's eye view of the history of Islamic expansionism since the times of caliphs Abu Bakra and Omar would show that whenever the followers of Islam have acquired muscle and strength, they have set out to conquer the world. It is a bid to impose their own way of life, value-systems, codes and mores based on Islam, upon others by force. That is the core of pan Islamic Jihad, rumblings of which are being heard all over the world today.

In this sense, Islamic Jihad is not merely a by-product or hang-over of Muslim history. It flows out of the Islamic scriptures which make a clear cut distinction between 'dar-al-Islam' (the home of peace) and 'dar-al-herb' (the home of war). More of it later, but here is what an important functionary of an Islamic Seminary based in Pakistan told a noted French writer in 2003. "Osama, I repeat is a good Muslim. He is our brother in Islam..... when he distinguishes between dar-al-Islam (the home of peace), which unites all Muslims of the world, and dar-al-herb (the home of war), which encompasses all the rest, he is right". And further, "war against the infidels is not war, it is a duty." (Bernard Henri Levy – "who killed Daniel Pearl" – 2003) That is what jihad is all about.

Terrorism

Terrorism, pure and simple, is the cult of ruthless violence and blood-spilling to cause intense fear or terror among its target group or groups. The idea is to coerce or subdue by creating terror in society. Terrorism is in the air, today in India and the world over, as never before. It is the most widely publicized and sensationalized phenomenon of our times. And yet there is so much confusion about the true import of the term, sometimes deliberately created to cover up or side track the gravity of the threat terrorism poses to civilized existence in present day world.

Many academic luminaries stretch its meaning to include even the extra-legal violence or injury caused by the state to its dissenting citizens. They cite the example of brutal atrocities including mass murders perpetrated by such notorious dictators like Hitler, Mussolini, Stalin, Mao, and Pol Pot. One writer goes to the extent of observing that "in the twentieth century, terrorism has been overwhelmingly practiced by the state apparatus." (Terrorism : History and Facets in the World and in India, N.S. Saxena 1985). Stretching it further, some talk about international terrorism practiced by some big powers in war, like nuclear bombing of Hiroshima and Nagasaki by the U.S. forcing Japan to instant surrender. In a seminar on the Iraq war, some left inclined speakers dubbed U.S. military intervention in Afghanistan and Iraq against Taliban and Saddam Hussain respectively as acts of terrorism. Such a contrived perception to suit one's ideological inclinations is not only wide off the mark and misleading but also suspect regarding its motive.

Apart from landing one into endless controversies involving finer points of national and international law, this kind of over-stretching to advance one's political agenda or fit in with one's ideological leanings shifts the focus from the real thing— the current terrorist threat. It leads to fruitless arguments about such ethical issues as ends and means, rights and wrongs etc., which should better be avoided in order to understand the actual nature of the problem the world is facing today.

Shorn of all academic hair-splittings and ideological twists, terrorism, as commonly understood, is nothing more or less than indulgence in raw violence and meaningless killings by a militant minority to pressurize the society by creating terror. This more or less is in conformity with the Declaration on Measures to Eliminate International Terrorism adopted by the U.N. General Assembly in 1994. It states that terrorism includes: "Criminal acts intended or calculated to provoke a state of terror in the general public, and group of persons for political purposes" and asserts that all such acts are in any circumstances unjustifiable, whatever the consideration of a political, philosophical, ideological, racial, ethnic, religious or other nature may be invoked to justify them."

By all accounts, killing or assassination is the center-piece of terrorism. The origin of this cult of killing or terrorism can be traced to an Arab Muslim religious teacher, Hassan Ibn Sabab, of the 11th century. He founded a fanatical Muslim sect of 'Fedavi' (devoted ones) who were made to believe that killing bad people on the command of their leader was a sacred duty-which ensured their place in heaven. It is said that in his headquarters at a castle in the Nosairi mountain in Syria, he had created the ambience of Zannat (heaven), with fountains and 'hoors' in tandem, to tempt his followers with the vista of life after death if they killed people at his command and got killed in the process. On top of that, they were treated with doses of hashish which created an aura of hallucination. This earned the name of "Society of the Hashasins" for the sect. It was from the name of this sect of killers that the English words "assassin" and "assassination" have been derived.

Two cardinal practices of this sect were — (1) an oath of secrecy among the members, and (2) propanda to convince the general public about the righteousness of their cause. Both these practices, particularly the latter, are the principle mantra of terrorists down to this day. Secretive conspiratoriality and wide publicity which are the hall-mark of terrorism in modern times can be traced to this religious sect of the 'assassins'. They continued to operate spreading fear and terror among their targets till around the middle of the 13th century when they were eventually demolished by the Mongols.

They, however, left an impact on many 16th and 17th century political ideologues who were debating weather killing was always murder. Many European secret societies of the early 19th century were more concerned about the political effectiveness of killings. Political terrorism emerged as a systemic creed towards the second half of the 19th century among the Russian anarchists, Irish, Armenians etc. But terrorism in its modern version which has snow-balled into such a major threat to world peace started from the Middle East in late 1960's.

Terrorism, like Jihad, originated in the Muslim world of the Middle East. Perennial warfare is a legacy of the pre-christian Greeko-Roman or Hellenic past of the west. The world today is being tossed around by the interplay of the triple factors of war, Jihad and terrorism. Of these three, Jihad and terrorism being structural neighbours, both originating in the Arab Muslim world, have now merged into one, giving rise to jihadi terrorism. This is pitted against the war addiction of the western world. The result is the frightful spectre of a new world war, which posterity could perhaps brand as the Third world war.

2

Jihadi Terror at the Center-stage

Their Hour of Fame

It was the Jihadis' tryst with destiny. Their hour of fame (or notoriety ?). 9 September 2001. They had done it, carried out the biggest, most lethal attack ever mounted by any terrorist outfit anywhere in the world. Sky was the limit. Literally. And the target was America, the flag-bearer of the developed world, the lone Super power in the unipolar world of early 21st century. Leaving around 3000 Americans dead in one stroke and the rest psychologically devastated. It was almost like the Japanese of early 1940's who had lived under the blissful belief that Japan was invincible until Hiroshima happened in August 1945.

For hours together, Americans, and the world at large, watched on their TV screens the twin towers of the World Trade Centre in New York, the mascot of America's developed economy, collapsing in flames, one after another, having been struck by hijacked planes used as missiles. They were dismayed, horrified and numbed. The myth of inviolability of U.S air space was broken, not by any enemy missile but its own passenger air crafts being converted into deadly missiles by terrorists stalking the land. No, they were not quislings or fifth columnists of an enemy state at war, but jihadis hidden in America's own courtyard and trained in its own technological institutions, even though remote-controlled by a shadowy enemy safely ensconced far away in the Islamic world.

Ramming of the two hijacked planes into the twin towers of the World Trade Centre in New york, though causing large number of human casualties, was primarily symbolic. A third hijacked aircraft hit the Pentagon—the citadel of U.S. defence establishment. And a fourth hijacked plane was flying over Pennsylvania, evidently heading for Washington, the national capital. The target could have been the White House itself, the seat of U.S. Presidency, or the Capitol, that of the American legislature, in order to decapacitate the government by killing its top leaders. That it did not happen was due to the passengers on board who fought it out with the Jihadis inside the air-craft and sacrificed their own lives in the process to save their country.

President Bush was relaxing down south in Florida and the Secretary of State Collin Powall attending a meeting of the Organization of American States far away in Lima, Peru. There was great confusion in Washington with signals of further attacks pouring in. The Vice President Dick Cheney, who was present in Washington, was whisked away from his office into the emergency bunker beneath the White House grounds. Even as President Bush was rushing to the national capital in the Presidential aircraft, Dick Cheney advised him not to return to Washington as grave threat persisted. The President agreed to get his plane diverted to an Air Force Base in Louisiana. As Washington was still not considered safe by the security agencies at around 1.30 PM, Bush reluctantly agreed to another diversion of his flight from Louisiana to the Air Force Base in Nebraska, fretting and fuming all the time at not being able to reach the capital. It was finally at 6.30 P.M. that the President was back at the White House, nearly 9 hours after the jihaids had struck America on 9 September, 2001.

Never in its history, America had faced a direct hit like that on its main land. The only time in the past when it felt gravely threatened, though not actually hit, was during the Cuban nuclear missile crisis at the peak of the cold war in October 1962. As picture after picture of nuclear missiles and launching pads installed by Soviet Russia in Cuba unfolded before the U.S. President Kennedy, the Americans realized the gravity of the situation. The threat of nuclear destruction was right at their doorstep. What was more, Soviet vessels carrying more nuclear missiles were already in the high seas moving towards Cuba. The situation was grim, the threat immediate.

The American response was quick. Congressonal leaders vacationing at far away pleasure resorts were picked up by helicopters and otherwise and flown over to Washington. After harried and hectic consultations, the U.S. decided to impose a naval blockade of Cuba to prevent the

Soviet missile ships reaching their destination and to force the Soviets to remove what had already arrived. American ships moved into the path of the Soviet vessels carrying nuclear war heads. Any confrontation would have led to a nuclear holocaust, shadows of which sent shock waves throughout the world. But in the nick of time, the Soviet President Khrushchev withdrew from the precipice. The Soviet ships first slowed their speed and then turned back. By the end of October, Khrushchev agreed to dismantle the missile bases in Cuba and ship the Soviet missiles back to Russia. The crisis was over. The world heaved a sigh of relief. The event turned out to be cataclysmic, as it marked the thawing of the cold war and beginning of détente between the two Super powers.

But October 1962 was basically different from September, 2001. For one thing, America was not actually hit but was only endangered. More importantly, the U.S. had to reckon with a known, compact and determinate adversary whom it was in a position to confront on one to one basis with all its might. What it was confronted with after 9/11.2001, was an in determinate dark conglomerate which it was nearly impossible to pin point and take on. What was more, the enemy could be here, there and right inside America's own belly whom it was very difficult to detect and locate. To hit the Jihadis back was like firing missiles at a swarm of mosquitoes.

The Jihadi assault on America on 9/11.2001 was not an abrupt development or entirely unexpected, even though its sweep, modality and the scale of revages caused were beyond anticipation. Islamic resurgence accompanied with terrorism had already emerged as a major threat to world peace before 9/11. Sporadic Muslim terrorism was rocking different parts of the world since around late 1980's even as the cold war was tapering off. The infamous blowing up of the Pan Am flight No.103 over Lokerbie in Scotland in 1988 had cost around 270 lives. Jihadi terrorism against India related to Kashmir had assumed alarming proportion by early 1990's. Pakistan, which was sponsoring Islamic terrorism in Kashmir, and India, which was at the receiving end, had both acquired clandestine nuclear capability which posed the danger of a nuclear conflagration in South Asia. According to one assessment, terrorist attacks around the world, an overwhelming majority of which related to Islamism, had increased to a record 5404 in 1992 costing above 10,000 lives (Pinkerton Risk Assessment of the U.S.A).

It was with such a dark scenario in mind that Ronald Reagan, the ex American President, bemoaned in a speech in December 1992 : " If you look around the globe, the new world order looks increasingly like one of disorder..........we might well wonder if we are trading a single, monolithic threat to world's peace for a host of smaller, yet no less deadly flash points..... evil still stalks the planet." (circulated by news agency AP, published in the `Times of India dated December 22, 1992).

Reagon's fulminations turned out to be prophetic. In February, 1993, Islamic terrorists led by Sheikh Omar Abdel Rehman, an exiled Egyptian cleric, set off a bomb in New York's World Trade Centre's basement, killing six and injuring around 1000 persons. That was the first attack on the WTC which was replicated on a much more devastating scale on 9/11. On 12 March 1993, there were serial bomb blasts in Bombay or Mumbai, the commercial capital of India, which ripped through the 29 story Stock Exchange and Air India buildings in the heart of the city. Bombs also went off in the rooms of Sea Rock and Centour hotels in posh Juhu and Santa Cruz localities. Within a space of two and half hours of terrorist assault, several hundreds were killed and over 1500 injured.

Americans across the world continued to be targeted by the Jihadis. In 1996, U.S. army barrackls in Saudi Arabia were hit. A fuel truck detonated outside Khobar Towers, an American military housing complex in Dhahran, Saudi Arabia, killing 19 Americans. In 1998, U.S. embassies in Kenya and Tanzania were bombed in a calibrated manner with a telling effect. 224 embassy personnel lost their lives, most of them being the embassies African staff. In the year 2000, two suicide bombers aboard a small boat in the Yemeni Port of Aden staged a midday attack on the American guided missile destroyer U.S.S. Cole nearly sinking it. 17 American sailors were killed.

Over all, Muslim terrorist organizations across the world were involved in violent clashes between Muslims and Non-Muslims in Bosnia, Kosovo, Macedonia, Chechnya, Azerbaijan, Kashmir, the Philippines, Indonesia, Sudan and Nigeria, besides of course the Middle East involving Palestinians and Israelis during 1990's. The 9/11 strike against Americans inside America was no more than a continuation of the Jihadi onslaught worldwide which was on the ups wing since early 1990's. It is another matter that it touched a new peak never reached before and signaled the arrival of Islamic terrorism at the center of the world stage.

New Dimensions of Jihad

What America's Black September epitomized more than anything else was the open globalization of Jihadi terrorism. It was already so covertly but Jihad went overtly global with a big bang on 9/11 and after. What was earlier sporadic and scattered became an unconcealed and compact monolithic threat. The Islamic terrorists have not looked back since.

In December 2001, they mounted a 'fiadeen' (suicide) attack on Indian Parliament in the highly protected area of Delhi which could have resulted in incapacitating the entire political establishment. It was lucky that they were confronted by the security forces which prevented them from entering the Parliament House and indulging in massacre of government leaders and law-makers. A number of security personnel were killed in the encounter. With Pakistan as the hub of Jihadi terror against India, the event brought India and Pakistan nearly on the verge of war. Since both countries are equipped with nuclear arms, the Indo-Pak face off in the wake of the terror attack on Indian Parliament sent shock waves across the world.

Among the major Jihadi terrorist acts that followed were the devasting bomb blasts in the Hindu populated Bali pleasure resort of Indonesia in 2002, repeated in 2005, seizure of a school at Beslan in Russia in 2004, serial bomb blasts in London underground train system in July 2005, explosion in Sherm-el-Sheikh tourist town in Egypt and bomb blasts in the heart of Delhi in October 2005. In all these Jihadi strikes, a large number of civilians, innocent men, women and children lost their lives. In the two bomb explosions at Bali island in 2002 and 2005 and the one at Sharm-el-Sheikh, the targets were Australian and western tourists who bore the brunt of the attacks.

The Jihad continues. A blue-pring of the Pan Islamic strategy entitled "The International Islamic Resistance call" was prepared in December 2004 by Mustafa Set marian Nasar, a Syrian born Iislamist who had been based in London for many years. It marks out the targets of the Jihadi onslught : "Jews, Americans, British, Russians and any and all the NATO countries as well as any country taking the position of oppressing Islam and Muslims." Osama bin Laden of course has already declared a holy war against the U.S. and enjoined upon Muslims all over the world to kill Americans indiscriminately.

The globalization of Jihad territorially is a matter of record of Jihadi terror across the world since early 1990's. What is more significant is the ideological globilization of Jihad, giving rise to the cult of Pan Islamism. Jihad now encompasses the whole world, not only as the area of its terror operations but also as the ultimate goal of its mission of Islamisation. The non Muslim world is anathema to the Jihadis waiting to be conquered and Islamised.

Francis Fukuyama of the 'End of History' fame observed in the wake of 9/11 : "unfortunately, the basic conflict we face is much broader, and concerns not just a small group of terrorists, but a much larger group of radical Islamists and Muslims for whom religious identity overrides all other political values.... It may therefore clarify things to say that the present conflict is not simply a fight against terrorism, nor against Islam as a religion or civilization, but rather with Islamo-fascism- that is, the radically intolerant and anti-modern doctorine that has recently arisen in many parts of the Muslim world." (Francis Fukuyama in his article, 'Their Target : The Modern World', published in special issue of 'News Week', December 2001 to February 2002).

The U.S. President George W.Bush voiced almost the same feeling when he met the congressional leaders on the morrow of 9/11. He told them that the real enemy was not only the terrorist gang which attacked the World Trade Centre. It was the Jihadi mind-set that promoted hatred against non-Muslims. They hated Judaism, they hated Christianity, they hated everything that was not them, he said. (Quoted by Bob Woodward in his book "Bush At War" Published in 2003.)

For westerners who are not quite familiar with Islamic tenets, this hatred towards non-Muslims, referred to by Bush, might appear to be shocking or startling. But there is nothing so new about it, nor is it the creation of present day radical Islamists. It actually follows from Islamic scriptures, which concede no rights whatsoever, far from equality, to kafirs' (non-believers) in the Islamic scheme of things. The 'Mushriks' (idol-worshippers) do not even have the right to live in the Islamic world. They have either to convert to Islam or be eliminated, failing which the Muslims are enjoined upon to perform the 'Hijrah', that is, migrate from the land of the idol-worshippers. In the circumstances, there is no question of religious tolerance or peaceful co-existence with the followers of other religions in the world of Islam. That is, strictly according to the scriptures.

It is in this light, that the Islamists divide the world into dar-al-Islam' (the home of peace) and dar-al-herb (the home of war). While 'dar-al-Islam' unites all Muslims of the world, 'dar-al-herb' encompasses the rest. Evidently, the two are in perennially adversarial relationship, until the 'dar-al-herb' is obliterated or converted into 'dar-al-Islam'.

What actually has happened is the re-emergence of the old concept of Jihad with the objective of conquering the non-Muslim world which is Pan-Islamism all about.That is the core of the ideology of new Jihad which the world or the non-Muslim world, has been confronting since the last decade of the 20th century and which has surfaced in a big way with the advent of the 21st. It regards the entire non-Muslim world as 'dar-al-herb' (home of war) and as such as its target.

Md. Masood Azhar, a former professor at the Islamic University in Karachi, who was arrested in Kashmir in February 1994, observed in an interview with "India Today". "We fight for religion, for the spread of Islam. We don't believe in the concept of nations". ('India Today' 15 May 1994). That in nut shell defines the ideology of Pan Islamic Jihad.

A word about Mohammad Masood Azhar would be relevant here. He was the Secretary General of Harkat-ul-Ansar, an amalgam of Harkat-ul-Mujahedin and Harkat-ul-jihad-e-Islami, when he entered Kashmir to foment terrorism and was arrested. To secure his release from Indian prison, another veteran Jihadi of international notoriety, Omar Saced Sheikh of Pakistani origin based in Britain, arrived in Kahsmir. He managed to kidnap four foreign tourists-three British and one American-in Kashmir in 1994 to bargain for the release of Masood Azhar, but failed in his mission. Omar Sheikh was arrested and put in Delhi's high security Tihar Jail pending trial in the above kidnapping case. And then the Jihadi network struck in a big way. They hijacked the Indian Airlines Flight No. 814 from Kathmandu in December 1999. Putting at stake the lives of around 200 passengers and killing one on board, they succeeded in securing the release of both Masood Azhar and Omar Sheikh. Masood Azhar went back to Pakistan to found his own Jihadi outfit Jais-e-Mahammad, which is engaged in ceaseless terrorist acts against India.

Omar Sheikh, it may be noted, was a British educated die-hard Jihadi who dropped out of London School of Economics to fight for Islam the world over. He was closely associated with Islamists fighting in Bosnia and having links with Osama bin Laden's Al Quaida. He is reported to have sent Rs. 50 lacs to Moahmmad Atta, one of the attackers of the World Trade Centre in New York on 9/11, out of ransom collected by his associates in India by kidnapping a Kolkata businessman. On top of all that, Omar Sheikh was the prime accused in the kidnapping and brutal murder of the "Wall Street journal" reporter Daniel Pearl at the end of 2002.

The Omar Sheikhs, Masood Azhars, Mohammad Attas and even Osama bin Ladens of today are mere tiny particles in the solid mass of Islamist ideology that came to be formed after the birth of the religion. It was the product of politicisation of Islam which began immediately after the departure of the Prophet. It was reflected in the lightning conquests of the Arab Muslims during the first hundred years after the death of the Prophet. In coming to an understanding of the true dimensions of Jihadi resurgence in the 21st century, individuals do not matter. Ideology does, because ideology is the fountain spring of it all.

It is amazing that the basic thrust of Islamism to engulf the rest of the world, which showed in the Arab and later Turks expansionism, has not abated a bit through the last fourteen centuries, even though the world has changed such a lot in the meantime. The world has traveled far from medieval to modern age. Politics in the rest of the world has been thoroughly secularized. Science and Technology have replaced religion and ideology as prime movers of human development. The world is poised to enter the post-modern era of new economism based on knowledge revolution. And yet the original spirit of Jihad has not only survived among the Muslims but re-surfaced with a new vigor to rock the modern world. It is kind of a puzzle which needs to be explained.

It can be attributed, first and foremost, to the unchanging character of Islam. It is a revealed religion with finality of its tenets and massage which its followers can not tinker with. Islam is not open to change at all. Any attempt or even thought of a change is not only frowned upon but considered outright blasphemous. A believer talking about a change in keeping with the changing times, or even floating the idea, is dubbed as a sinner and risks inviting a 'fatwah' of Islamic clergy calling for his death. As a result, Islam remains unchanged and so does the Islamic view of the non-Muslim world as 'dar-al-herb' waiting to be converted into 'dar-al-Islam'. That is the ideological base which has kept the spirit of Jihad live and kicking.

The other contributory factor is that in the Muslim world, polity is still tagged on to the apron-string of religion. In other words, separation between religion and polity, which is an essential attribute of modern society, has just not taken place in Islamic society. That accounts for the infatuation of the Muslim peoples in general with the idea of Jihad, which is identical with the itch for pan Islamism. For them, Islamisation of the whole world is a cherished goal ever to be aspired for until achieved. That is the primary support base which provides sustenance to modern Jihadis, of whom Osama bin Laden is the most visible mouthpiece and apostle.

Jihad, or new Jihad, is not all about the proselytizing spirit of Islam, though conversion of non-Muslims to Islam is an important component of it. That way Christianity has been an equally, if not more, proselytizing religion, seized with the mission of converting people to the faith. But there is a subtle difference between Christian missionaries engaged in proselytizing all over the world and

Islamic Jihadis committed to subjugating the world to Islam. Missionaries seek to convert people, specially the neglected and deprived sections of society, to Christianity by means of persuasion and preaching for what they believe to be the salvation of the converts. To them, it is a matter of winning the hearts and minds of the people in the interest of their own redemption. The Jihadis, on the other hand, believe in conquering the world to Islam, that is, imposing Islamic faith, codes and mores on diverse peoples of the world in order to expand their own tribe. "Fight for religion for the spread of Islam", in the worlds of Masood Azar, and conquest or victory are key ingredients of Jihad. It is a cult of war and not peaceful persuasion or preaching as in the case of Christian missionaries.

This is corroborated by the history of Christianity and Islam, both revealed religions equally committed to spreading their respective faiths in the world in distinctly different ways. It took Christianity about a thousand years after Christ to bring the whole of Europe within its fold. But it took Islam only a hundred years after Mohammad to bring the Middle East, Northern Africa, Central Asia and Spain in southern Europe under its fold through wars of conquests. Aggression and conquest have historically been integral parts of Islamism. And Jihad is the avowed and garish manifestation of radical Islamism.

The Jihad of the Arabs and Turks was about conquering their known world or the world that mattered to them. The new Jihad of the 21st century is global in dimension aiming at subjugating the entire planet to Islam.

3

How, Why and To What End ?

How Come ?

The emergence of Islamic Jihad in a big way towards the close of the 20th century and beginning of the 21st poses a pertinent question. What has brought it about at this point of time in the chequened history of the world ? Is it the arrogance of western powers vis a vis the Islamic world ? Like the western approach to the problem of Palestine, or lately Iraq, for example ? In other words, is it the increasing strangle-hold of the west over the Muslim countries of the Middle East which has given rise to Islamic Jihad ?

Recent history of the relationship between the western powers and the Muslim world proves just the opposite. It is a history of phenomenal growth of Muslim power in the Middle East at the cost of the west, and not the other way about. The status of Muslim Middle East in the first quarter of the 20th century is quite revealing in this regard.

At the end of the First World War in 1919, virtually the whole of the Muslim world, except Saudi Arabia, was under the imperialist control of Britain and France. Egypt was a British protectorate and as such under the tutelage of Britain. Sudan was governed jointly by Britain and Egypt. Iraq was placed under British mandate in 1920. Similarly, Syria and Lebanon came under French mandate at the end of the First World War. Morocco, Tunisia and Algeria were dependencies of France. Turkey was a defeated country in the process of transformation and Iran was under the occupation of British troops. All of them are totally free and vibrant Muslim States today.

Palestine too was placed under British mandate after the First war in 1919. But its problem was very complicated for various reasons, the most important being the fact that it is the holy place of three religions - Zudaism, Christianity and Islam. The long cherished dream and demand of the Jews for an independent homeland in Palestine evoked considerable support worldwide after their brutal persecution by Hitler in Nazi Germany. There was large-scale influx of Jews from Germany into Palestine during and after the Second World War. This was bitterly opposed by the Arab Muslims resulting in violent riots between Muslims and Jews. A special committee of the United Nations recommended partition of Palestine. It was not acceptable either to the Muslims or the Jews. By now, the mandate in Palestine had become a millstone round the neck of Britain. To get rid of it, Britain unilaterally announced termination of its mandate and withdrew from Palestine in May 1948.

Immediately after that, the Jews proclaimed the establishment of the new state of Israel. It was promptly recognised by Britain and America followed closely by Soviet Russia. Even Muslim countries like Iran under the Shah (before the Islamic Revolution) and Turkey accorded recognition to it. But the Arab countries around Israel attacked it from all sides, resulting in the first Arab-Israeli war. The Israelis beat back the Arabs in the war and an armistice between the two sides was signed in 1949. The Arab Muslims and Israelis fought two more wars in 1967 and 1971 and have since lived in perennially conflictual relationship with intermittent peace initiatives brokered by the U.N and U.S.

The Palestinian problem has thus been there ever since the birth of the Jewish state of Israel in 1948 in the teeth of opposition by Arab Muslims. But there was no pan Islamic Jihad then or later, until the last decade of the 20th century. A distinction must be made here between Pan Islamic Jihad and sporadic acts of terrorism. For instance, there was a spurt in terrorist acts on the part of Palestinians and their Arab allies after Israel's decisive victory in the 1967 war. In this war, Israel made considerable territorial gains at the cost of the Arabs by occupying the West Bank (of Jordan river), the Gaza strip and Golan Heights. In protest, Palestinians and their Arab supporters resorted to a series of terrorists acts against Israelis and their western friends. These included shooting of eleven Israeli sportsmen during the Munich Olympics in 1972, massacre of 26 passengers at the Israeli airport of Lod by Japanese terrorists financed by Arabs and seizure of the French embassy at the Hague in 1974. These acts were scattered, sporadic and demonstrative rather than destructive, like kidnappings of diplomats and dispatch of parcel bombs etc. All these acts were Palestine specific. There was no such thing as Islamic Jihad against the entire non-Muslim world as such.

There was no jihad either when the Muslim countries were kept under some kind of a bondage by the western powers till around the middle of the 20th century. How come the Islamic Jihad has surfaced on a world-wide scale now when the western strangle-hold over the Muslim world lies buried deep under the sands of time ?

For Jihadi terror in South Asia, that is, India, Kashmir dispute between India and Pakistan is commonly believed to be the causative factor. But Kashmir problem has been there right since the birth of India and Pakistan as independent states in 1947. The two countries have fought three wars between 1948 and 1971 over the Kashmir issue. But apart from a few token and sporadic events like hijacking of a plane or some stray terrorist acts, there was no Jihad against India until the beginning of 1990's. The Pakistan hand in the Jihad against India during the 1990s will be dealt with a little later, but first the facts. On 3rd November 1993, over 30,000 Islamists from 20 countries assembled in Pakistan for the annual convention of a fundamentalist organization known as Markaz Dawa al Irshad. The chief of the Markaz announced : "Kashmir is only the gateway to India. We have to tie up with movements in Bosnia and Palestine to rescue 125 million Muslims from Hindu rule" ("Pan Islamic Fundamentalism", India Today; 15 May 1994). This was Jihad loud and clear. How come ?

Why Now ?

Palestine and Kashmir, even Bosnia or Chechnya for that matter, are mere pretexts. The root of the new Jihad, which has come to occupy the center stage of the world, can be traced to the history of Islamic polity since its very inception. It is only a continuation of what started during the caliphates of Abu Bakr and Omar who set out to conquer their known world to Islam since the year 632 onwards. And was followed up with renewed vigour and spectacular victories by the Arabs and Osmanli Turks during the next 900 years.

There was, however, an interval of over two centuries in the Islamic thrust beginning around the year 1100. It was first checkmated by the 'crusades' organized by the whole Christendom (Roman and Greek orthodox church combined together) after Constantinople was threatened and Christian pilgrims to Jerusalem were harassed and tortured by Muslims. This was followed by the raging and tearing Mongols - another tribe of world conquerors emerging from the steppes of northern Asia to shock the world. Chengiz and his successors ravaged the Muslim world, along with parts of North Asia and Europe, through the best part of the 13th century.

The nemesis of the Muslim world at the hands of the Mongols came after the accession of Mangu as the leader of Mongols in the year 1252. His brother Hulagu was the Mongol Governor in Persia when a dispute arose with the Caliph of Muslims at Baghdad. When Hulagu sent a message of protest to the Caliph, his envoys were insulted and the Caliph sent an offensive reply. That was the signal for the end of Baghdad, then the capital of the Muslim world. Hulagu marched on Baghdad, and captured it after 40 days of siege. The Caliph and his sons were executed. A general massacre of the city's inhabitants continued for weeks, taking a toll of about a million and half lives. It is said that the river Tigris was dyed red for miles with human blood.

But the Mongol onslaught on the Islamic world, like the Christian 'Crusades' earlier, proved only to be a comma and not a full stop to the onward march of Islamism. The mantle of Islam was taken up by the Ottoman or Osmanli Turks in the 14th century with greater vigor than ever before. Under the leadership of Ottoman Turks, the Islamic surge continued from the 14th to the first half of the 16th century in full flow. In course of this spurt, not only the whole of Asia Minor but the entire Balkan Peninsula and Russian and Mongol lands north of the Black sea were conquered to Islam, as described earlier. After that, the triumphant march of Islam was stopped, not by counter religious resistance or military might of Christian Europe, but on account of other more mundane reasons.

While the Muslim Turks were rampaging through South Eastern Europe, converting churches into mosques all the way, the west Europeans were exploring uncharted oceans armed with mariner's compass, sailing charts and maps. In the process, they set upon a course which was to change the face of the planet. Even as the Ottoman Turks were resting on their oars after conquests and Islamisation of a part of the known world by the middle of the 16th century, the Europeans had discovered a much bigger world as their playing field.

They had gathered considerable knowledge of the actual shape and size of the world. They had acquired knowledge of the general location of oceans and major continents. All this while, the Muslim world remained stewing in its own juice of religious orthodoxy.

Almost simultaneously during the 15th and 16th centuries, several momentous developments took place, which took the wind out of the sail of Islamic expansionism. A whole New world, that is, North and South Americas, was discovered, Pacific Ocean was crossed, Southern most tip of Africa was reached – all leading to gigantic economic expansion of European peoples. They went through a great religious upheaval known as Reformation, marked by the emergence of many protestant sects opposed to Catholic orthodoxy. It facilitated the process of separation between the church and the state and secularization of the polity. Strong national monarchies emerged in Europe which eventually led to the emergence of nation-state system. All these epoch-making developments were both the cause and effect of each other.

For the next three hundred and fifty years or so beginning the 16th century, the world was totally occupied with breathtaking scientific, economic and political developments which kept the forces of Islamism bewildered and stunned. The Europeans rediscovered their pre-christian, ancient or classical civilization, questioning many Christian traditions, practices and theology. The 'Renaissance', as it was called, had significant effect on scientific enquiry, political thought and economic expansion. Nothing like that happened in the Muslim world which remained rooted in its religious past.

The religious 'Reformation' leading to secularization of polity, Commercial Revolution of 16th and 17th centuries and European 'Renaissance' or 'intellectual quickening' led to the transition from medieval to modern times. The scientific inventions of the 18th and 19th centuries like that of the steam engine brought about the great Industrial Revolution, first in England and then in other countries of western Europe. This combined with their wide reach across the length and breadth of the planet through newly discovered ocean routes transformed Europe into the lead society of the world. Their wide commercial penetration enabled them to thread the static societies of Asia and Africa, including the Muslim world, into their imperial network.

The Industrial Revolution accelerated the process. It brought about a quantum jump in production of commodities which made the European countries hungry for sources of raw materials and markets to sell their products. It enabled them to use new sources of energy like fossil fuels to produce goods and commodities on a vast scale while the Muslim world was still dependent on camels and human muscle as energy sources. As a result, Europe spread its imperial tentacles over non-European peoples across the globe by the end of the 19th century. Shorn of jingoistic rhetoric of men like Edmand Burke and Rudyard Kypling (the 'whiteman's burden' syndrome), colonialism was primarily an economic imperative for the western nations which happened because they had arrived in the modern age well before the non-western world.

By the beginning of the 20th century, competitive colonialism itself became a bone of contention among European powers vying for supremacy over each other. In the race for one-upmanship, they fought two mega wars in the 20th century which involved the non-western world as well and kept the whole world totally occupied with European affairs. At the same time, the rise of communism as a potent force took the world by storm leaving no space for any other ideology to come to the fore. The Marxian vista of a classless society was the most attractive utopia of the first half af the 20th century. It led Arnold Toyanbee to observe that even if Marxism succeeded, it will still be a western political ideology to shape the world.

At the end of the Second world War in 1945, the world appeared to be entering an era of normalcy and peace. For reasons recorded in recent history, almost all colonial or less than fully self governing countries, under some kind of tutelage of western powers, became fully independent in just over a decade or so after 1945. This included Muslim countries of the Middle East and North Africa like Syria, Iraq, Egypt, Libiya, Lebanon, Tunisia, Morocco, Algeria, Sudan, Nigeria, besides Indonesia and Malayasia of South East Asia. But the normalcy in international situation proved to be illusory. The world entered a period of uneasy peace tainted by what come to be called the 'cold war' between two power blocks led by America and Soviet Russia, almost on the morrow of the end of the Second World War.

It was a period of constant confrontation and much muscle-flexing between the two Super Powers during which they lived from crisis to crisis. The so-called cold war came very near turning hot three or four times over Berlin issue beginning 1948 and during the Cuban missile crisis in 1962. Although the cold war thawed after the resolution of the Cuban crisis, the U.S. and Soviets continued confronting each other through their proxies in Vietnam until 1970's and in Afganistan until 1988. The cold war virtually tapeo red off in December 1987 when the U.S. and Soviet Union signed the momentous INF Treaty stipulating removal of intermediate range missiles from Western and Eastern Europe . It finally came to an end with Soviet withdrawal from Afganistan in February 1989.In fact, right from 1914 when the First World War broke out to 1989 when the cold war ended, the world lived under either the shadow of war or fear of war. A columnist, Peter Miller, aptly summed up when he wrote that it was a 75 year war that ended in 1989.

During the period of 350 years, beginning mid 16th century, so much happened in the world as had not happened in course of 4000 years before. The world remained fully crowded with such monumental happenings as the commercial revolution of 16th and 17th centuries, Industrial Revolution of 18th and 19th centuries, growth of colonialism, the two world wars rise of communism and cold war of the 20th century. Such was not the time for Islamism, lying dormant since mid 16th century, to raise its head. Even after the Second World War when the Muslim countries got free from the shackles of European imperialism, the world got too deeply involved in the cold war to leave any scope for Islamists to re-start the thrust of Pan Islamism from where the Ottoman Turks had left in mid 16th century. But it was only a semi-colon, and not a full stop to the Islamic surge. It re-emerged with fresh energy as the cold war started petering out towards the end of 1980's.

Ironically enough, it all began with the U.S.sponsored Jihad against the Soviet occupation of Afganisatn in 1979-80. The U.S. funded, armed and equipped the Jihadis drawn from Arab and other Muslim countries, besides the Afgans themselves, to fight and drive the Russians out of Afganistan. It was a part, and in continuation, of the cold war then on its last leg. And when the Russians withdrew from Afghanistan in 1989, the Soviet Union collapsed and the cold war ended, the Jihadis got the opportunity to come out with full force. The success of Jihad in Afganistan gave a tremendous boost to it. It inspired the Islamists to aspire for world domination which their Arab and Turk ancestors had dreamt of. That is how and why the ideology of Pan Islamism was reborn when it did during the last decade of the 20th century.

To What End ?

The tumultuous events of the three and half centuries that elapsed since the conquests of Ottoman Turks, kept the ideology of Pan Islamism at bay, but did not obliterate or change it. The ideology remained intact, kind of frozen in the cold storage of time, as fresh as ever. And it came out of hibernation, live and kicking, when the world was in sight of sun shine of peace as the clouds of war, hot or cold, looked like disappearing.

As mentioned earlier, the Afgan Jihad acted as a catalyst to de-freeze and bring the Frankenstein of Pan Islamism out of the cold storage. For the non-Muslim world, it heralded the rise of the tide of Islamic Jihad to a new high. Since Pakistan acted as a front-line state in the U.S. sponsored Afgan campain, it would be relevant to look into the mind-set of some key Pakistani military officials closely associated with it. At the peak of the Afgan Jihad, Lt. General Hamid Gul played a prominent role in it as the Chief of Pakistan's Inter Services Intelligence (ISI), the notorious intelligence outfit promoting cross border terrorism in India. In an interview to "India Today" in 1994, he was proud to proclaim : "The Afgan war was the Internationale of the Muslim youth all over the world. It has changed them for ever. And they can change the world around us. They are the jewels and flowers of Islam." The reference obviously was to the revolutionary song 'The Internale' of the communists who once were out to turn the world red.

Another Ex-ISI Brigadier of Pakistan, Mohammed Yousuf, who left the ISI to work whole time with the Jihad in Afghanistan, boasted about the Jihadis; "once these people are convinced that a cause is a Jihad, they will willingly die for it.".

The fortnight observations of two top Pak Army Officials closely involved with the Afghan-Jihad throw enough light on the ultimate goal of Jihadis. "The jewels and flowers of Islam", in the words of Hamid Gul, are out to "change the world". And Mohammed Yousuf's Jihadis are willingly dying for the "cause", as evident from the suicide attack on the WTC and Pentagon on 9/11 and recurring fiadeen attacks in different parts of the world.

It would, however, be a mistake to consider the Afgan Jihad as the cause of Jihadi terrorism that has surfaced all over the world. It only gave a fillip or impetus to a latent phenomenon rooted in Islamic history. A significant lesson of 1400 years of Islamic polity is that whenever the Muslim 'oumma' or 'quom' has gained in strength or acquired enough muscle, it has set out to conquer the world. The Muslim countries have never been more independent, prosperous and powerful than they are today. With the end of colonialism by the mid 20th century, they became fully independent and masters of their own destiny, as described earlier. Their immense oil wealth made them fairly prosperous. The huge induction of petro-dollars helped them to develop tremendous muscle power to flex around And, what is more important, made them conscious of it. Paradoxically enough, it is the growth of Islamic muscle power, and not a feeling of economic deprivation or unemployment among the burgeoning young population as made out by western analysts, which has led to the rise of Pan Islamism on a world wide scale. It is not without significance that Osama bin Laden, the most visible symbol of Pan Islamic Jihad, is a Saudi national and Saudi Arabia is the biggest oil producing country in the Muslim world.

World conquest has been the ultimate goal of Islamic polity since its very inception. That is the cherished dream of Jihadis today for which they are prepared to go to any length. There have been other world conquerors before the birth of Islam and after, but they have become part of history. The remarkable fact about Islamism is that it has survived the ravages of time, coming up at regular intervals to shake the world.

When Mayas, Incas, Azteks and Caribs in American far west, Chinese and Japanese in the Far East, Negro groups in Southern and central Africa were living unknown in glorious or inglorious insulation, the young Macedonian ruler Alexander 'the great' emerged as a first conqueror of the known world, which was of course very small then. Though not exactly a Greek but a neighboring Macedonian, he was catapulted to the leadership of the Hellenic world by virtue of his extraordinary valour.

Interestingly, the myth or ideology that set him on course to his conquests as leader of the Greeks was their belief in the inborn right of the Hellenes to rule over "lesser breeds". The Greek philosopher Isocrates had appealed to Alexander's father, King Philop of Macedon, to unite the Greeks and lead the Pan Hellenic attack against the Asian "barbarians". And Alexander began his campaign of conquests with a sentimental visit to Troy – the symbol of Greek myth. But that was only kind of a cover for his ambition to conquer his known world, which ended with his premature death' at the young age of 33 in the year 323 B.C.

The next in the chain of world conquerors were the Romans who went about conquering the neighboring peoples with their military might and governing them centrally from Rome. Like the myth or ideology of Greek superiority over the "lesser breeds", Romanism also turned into an ideology which inspired the Romans to destroy their rival

Carthaginians on the northern coast of Africa and establish their sway over the Mediterranean countries. By the beginning of the first century B.C., the Romans had conquered Greece, and Asia Minor and established a protectorate over Egypt. Thus originating from a mere city state in the Hellenic world, Rome became a myth, an ideology of world domination. Its sway encompassed only a small part of the planet, the known world at the time, but the Roman Empire epitomized the idea of head ship of the world. Although it lasted longer than Alexander's, the Roman myth was exploded by the invading tribes of Goth, Franks and Vandals in the 5th century A.D.

Among the latter day conquerors of the world were Fascists and Nazis who dazzled the world scene for a while and then were dumped in to the dust bin of history. Mussolini revived the myth about old Roman glory to raise the Leviathan of Fascism and Hitler created the myth of Nordic racial superiority in their bid to conquer the world. But like Alexander's effort to subjugate his known world in the name of Hellenic myth earlier, Mussolini's and Hitler's misadventures were basically individual enterprises of two megalomaniacs which ended with their crushing defeat in 1945. The flitting moments of their success have become the dark chapters of recent history.

The most glamorous and ideologically comprehensive aspirants for world conquest in the 20th century have been the Marxists. Unlike all the earlier bidders for leadership of the world recorded in history, Marxists appeared on the world scene well equipped with a philosophy which had a tremendous appeal among sizeable sections of intellectuals as well as the masses. Its materialistic interpretation of history and theories of social development and class struggle as the harbingers of a new millennium on earth constituted a comprehensive ideology of world domination. The lethal combination of messianic fervour with pre-destinarianism, that is belief in certain victory, invested Marxism with uncommon energy, assurance and purposefulness.

When Marxism succeeded in Russia towards the close of the First World War and in China at the end of the Second, it appeared poised to take over the world. The mood was most eloquently articulated in an editorial in the official Soviet paper 'Izvestia' on January 1, 1950, concluding : "The New Year has come to us as a welcome and dear quest. With faith and hope, the downtrodden people are looking to the great Soviet Union-mighty and spiritually close to the working people of all lands. Around the USSR, the camp of the fighters for peace, democracy and socialism is growing and becoming stronger. The forces of this camp are multiplying day by day. The sun of freedom and communism shines brightly for the world today. Communism is conquering, communism will triumph".

The dazzling success of Marxism in the immediate post-war years was reflected in the spread of communist hegemony in widely scattered countries from North Korea and Mongolia to Poland and East Germany and from North Vietnam in the east to Cuba in the West. Originating in the writings of Marx and Engels around mid 19th century and elaborated by Lenin in early 20th , Communism was a modern ideology of world domination unlike the Hellenic and Roman ideologies of the past, and was expected to sway large parts of the world for a long time to come.

And yet it collapsed like a house of cards before the close of the 20th century. As to how and why it happened is another story which is not a part of this study. It would, however, be interesting to see how Marxism was repudiated by its one-time most loud champion-China. A corporate executive who visited China in June 1986 as a delegation member of Indian Merchants chamber recorded his impression as follows:

" No sooner you enter Kaitak airport of Beijing from the plane and thereafter enter the city you start disbelieving your eyes that you have a totalitarian country where Marxism rules supreme. The new slogans of `Walk away from Marxist Bookism' and 'nothing wrong in embracing westernization' have been given to the people by the Chinese Communist Party (CCP)".

Another observer of the Chinese scene, wrote in 1992 : "Indeed, the joke making the rounds among Chinese intellectuals is this: under the leadership of the communist party, we are advancing from socialism to capitalism. It is true that one can spend days rummaging through the free markets of cities like Guangzhow or Shanghai and find little trace of communism". (Nicholas D. Kristof , 'New York Times' service, in his article China's secret Farewell to communism', October 1992.)

It is no longer a secret or a surprise as the above observers recorded at the time. China as well as Russia, the two erstwhile citadels of communism, have since moved too far away from Marxism to cause any surprise to neutral observers, or dismay to the rump of the faithfuls. What is of significance is the fact that the altar of Marxist ideology, which was supposed to hold the key to the future of mankind, collapsed much sooner than anyone could anticipate, burying itself under its own debris. The Marxist aspirants of taking the world under their wings have become part of history, like the Hellenes, Romans, Fascists and Nazis before.

In this backdrop, it is a wonder of sorts that the Islamists' aspirations to take over the world have not only remained intact but re-emerged after a gap of around three and half centuries with renewed vigour. For that is the motivating force behind the rise of Jihadi terrorism all over the world. The main reason for survival of Pan Islamism over the past 14 centuries is its inherent linkage to religious faith. And religion has the most powerful and abiding influence over human mind.

All other ideologies of world conquest were basically non-religious or mundane. Marxism was avowedly irreligious, since it regarded religion as the opium of the people. Pan Islamism on the other hand is both a political ideology and a religious faith at the same time. The utopia of a classless society vanished in the face of bitter reality of practicing communism, but Dar al Islam remains the cherished dream of muslim peoples across the world because of the sacredness attached to it. Islamism aims at translating that dream into reality. Jihad is its instrument and terrorism the weapon.

In 1979, Pir Mubarak Shah Gilani, a Pakistani then based in the U.S. formed an organization named Jamat-al-Fuqra. He subsequently shifted to Lahore and finally to Karachi, Pakistan, where he is based now as head of the organization. In 1993, Calorado police in the U.S. had arrested seven members of Al Fuqra for fraudulently claiming 355,000 dollars as workmen's compensation and sending the money to Jihadi terrorists. The remarkable fact about it is that it is not only closely linked to Al Quida but that Osama bin Laden himself pays obeisance to its Chief-Pir Mubarak Shah Gilani.

Bernard-Henri Levy, the noted French writer referred to earlier, had access to two important documents of Al Fuqra distributed to the faithfuls : (1) A map of the world entitled "The united States of Islam" outlining in green colour the Muslim universe from the Philippines to Xingiang and from West Africa to Turkey and the Middle East. And more importantly, another smaller map portraying the same `United States of Islam' encompassing the whole world in green colour within a span of 20 years (2) A propaganda pamphlet containing the exhortations of Gilani to prepare his followers for sacrifice and recalling with nostalgia the days when the "Warriors of Allah" had brought Europe to its knees. It also threw up the idea that "with the fall of the Soviet Union, a third world war had begun from which Islam would emerge victorious". (Bernard-Henri Levy in his book "Who killed Daniel Pearl published in 2003).

That leaves nothing to imagination or conjecture. It is in black and white. The 'Warriors of Allah' had done it in the past. The fight is on. The third world war has begun. It would be fought until won, ending in victory of Islam. The ultimate goal - 'United States of Islam' incorporating the entire planet – is in sight, only a couple of years away, Insha Allah. That is what the current Jihad is all about. If the rest of the world does not recognize it, or chooses to brush it aside, it would be at its own peril.

It may be noted that Pir Mubarak Shah Gilani is not only a kind of spiritual guru of Osama bin Laden, nor Al Fuqra one among many Jihadi outfits flourishing in Pakistan to export terror to India, but more. His network is world wide. His Al Fuqra is the parent organization of two fundamentalist outfits operating in the U.S. and training Jihad is in highly specialized guerilla warfare - "Muslims of America" and "Quranic Open University". And it has on its board several senior officials of Pakistan's Inter Services Intelligence - the types of ex-Lt General Hamid Gul and ex-Brigadier Mohammad Yousuf.

Reference

1 'Pan Islamic Fundamentalism' by Shekhar Gupta Rahul Pathak in *India Today*, 15 May, 1994.

4

The Gathering Storm

9/11 in Perspective

The U.S. President George W. Bush got the news of Jihadi strike at the twin towers of WTC in New York while indulging in his pet exercise – reading to elementary school children in Sarasota, Florida a little past 9 a.m. on September 11, 2001. His instant reaction was to go to war against the attackers. At 9.30 a.m ; he made a brief T.V. appearance proclaiming to the American people : "Terrorism against our nation will not stand". On reaching Washington later that evening, Bush made a short televised speech to the American people from his Oval office declaring that America was at `War' with the terrorists and those who harboured and protected them. A tall order, in the opinion of some of his advisors, but he insisted on proclaiming that. In an emotional vein, Bush said, "None of us will forget this day. Yet we go forward to defend freedom and all that is good and just in the world."

The reaction in the non-Muslim world was nearly just as strong. India, and Israel, which had been battling Islamic terrorism for long, were not only stunned by the sheer audacity of it, but also felt empathetic. If this could happen to the United States, countries like India and Israel were sitting ducks for Islamic terrorists. Russia, Japan and China also condemned the event in certain terms and Russia in particular expressed sympathy and support.

The western world was, of course, over supportive of the American war on Jihadi terrorism. Britain, Canada and Australia promptly committed their armed forces in this war. European peoples in general viewed the attack on America as attack on themselves and came out to voice their feelings loud and clear. 'Le Monde', the most influential newspaper of France, carried the headline, "We are all Americans". And the residents of Berlin, Germany, declared, "We are New Yorkers".

At the academic plane, the strongest condemnation of Jihadi terrorism in the wake of 9/11 came from Francis Fuku-Yama, Professor of International Political Economy at John Hopkins University and a well known author. Terming the Jihadi terrorists as "Islamo-Fascists", he made a plea for going after them with full force in the global war launched by America. "German fascism", he wrote, "did not collapse because of its internal moral contradictions; it died because Germany was bombed to rubble and occupied by Allied armies. Osama bin Laden gained enormous popularity throughout the Muslim world by successfully attacking the Twin Towers. If he is, metaphorically, hanged from a lamp post in the public square by U.S. forces along with his Taliban protectors, his movement will look much less appealing" (Newsweek, Special issue on Terrorism, December 2001 to February 2002).

The western perception of the rise of Islamic fundamentalism as a major threat is not altogether a new development arising out of the Jihadi strike against America on 9/11. In fact, it had been building up for around a decade before that. It found concrete expression in an imagined account of the 21st century published in "The Economist", London, in its December 1992 issue. It visualized the rise of a new Pan-Islamic Super Power stretching from part of Russia (Chechanya and Dagestan) and South East Europe (Bosnia, Kosovo and Part of Albania) to the Middle East (the Arab world) as a new 'evil empire' pitted against the western world. It went to the extent of predicting that the Islamic Super Power would emerge out of a coup in Saudi Arabia in the year 2011. (The columnists might be having Osama bin Laden or some one like him in mind).

The "Economist's" forecast about the 21st century confrontation between the Islamic world and the west found a more comprehensive, reasoned and holistic expression in the Harvard Professor Samuel P. Huntington's by now famous book "The clash of civilizations and the Remaking of world order", published in 1996. He wrote:" So long as Islam remains Islam (which it will) and the west remains the west (which is more dubious), this fundamental conflict between two great civilizations and way of life will continue to define their relations in the future even as it has defined them for the past fourteen centuries. Growing Muslim anti-westernism has been paralled by expanding western concern with the 'Islamic threat' posed particularly by Muslim extremism. If Muslims allege that the West wars on Islam and if westerners allege that Islamic groups war on the west, it seems reasonable to conclude that something very much like a war is under way".

And like "The Economist", London, in December 1992, Huntington also conceived or imagined, without actually predicting, the future global war breaking out in, say, 2010, between what he called "Confucian-Islamic" alliance on the one side and the western alliance on the other. As it happens, the global war appears to have broken out even earlier, without of course 'Confucianism' (China) being on the side of Islamism.

Huntington's thesis was evidently based on the clashes and conflicts between Muslims and non-Muslims wide across the world in Bosnia, Macedonia, Kosovo, Kashmir, the Phillippines, Sudan etc during 1990's. He particularly had in mind the Muslim attacks on Americans and American facilities, including the first attack on the World Trade Centre, beginning 1993. His reaction to the Jihadis' attack on the U.S. on 9/11 and America's declaration of a global war on terrorism was that it was not such a new development after all. According to him, "it is a confirmation and escalation of previous patterns of violence involving Muslims," And in the American and Western response to it, he sees "the makings of a general clash of civilizations" ('The Age of Muslim wars'. (News-week special Issue, December 2001 to February 2002).

What happened on 9/11, therefore, was only a high peak of Jihad started by Islamists at least a decade earlier and was seen as such by perceptive western observers before. The only caveat is that the western view of it as a clash between the Islamists and the west only, or between Islam and Christianity, is rather myopic. It is based on the western belief that modern civilization or democracy, which the Islamists are out to destroy, is exclusively of western origin or an outgrowth of Christianity. Kind of a secularized edition of the Christian precept of brotherhood of man. True, democracy in its direct form flourished in the city states of ancient Greece, of which Athens was the flagship state. But it flourished in India also around the same time, if not earlier, in the Lichhvi republic of Vaishali, Bihar. As regards the secular or religion neutral character of western states, major non-western non-Muslim countries of the world like India, Japan and China are as secular as any western country. What is under attack by the Islamists is not only the western world or civilization but the non-Muslim world as a whole. It is not simply a war between "Islam and the West" but between "Islam and the Rest", in the terminology of Huntington.

India is a telling example of how an avowedly secular and multi-cultural society, which prides in the religion-neutral character of the Indian state and its composite culture, has been under severe attack from Pan-Islamic Jihad for nearly past two decades. The Indian state has consciously rejected the "melting pot" image of imposition of the dominant culture and adopted the "salad bowl" or "glorious mosaic" concept in which every ethnic and religious constuent of the population maintains its distinctiveness. But the Jihadis have no use for a modern multi-cultural society like that. The core ideology of Lashkar-e-Toiba, the international terrorist outfit branded as such by the U.N. and linked to Al Quaida, is outlined in a pamphlet entitled "Why are we waging Jihad ?" It includes restoration of Muslim rule over all parts of India.

South East Asia is fast developing into another thrust area of Islamic Jihad. Jemmah Islamiah (JI), a Jihadi terrorist organization based in Indonesia with local roots and international linkages, is spearheading the radical Islamists in this part of the world. It was involved in deadly bomb explosion in a crowded hotel in Bali island of Indonesia killing hundreds of people, most of them foreign tourists. Jihadi terror came calling again in Bali with a repeat of the gory 2002 bombings on October 1, 2005. Severe blasts tore through restaurants packed with evening diners, mostly foreigners on a visit to enjoy the ambience of autumn in this 'island of gods', as Bali is popularly called. The jihadis chose to target Bali in particular because, for one thing, it is inhabited largely by Hindus, and, for the other, is frequented by Australian and other westerners in tourist season. The evident objective of the Jihadis is to establish an Islamic Caliphate covering Southern Thailand, Singapore, Malayasia, Southern Phillippines, Brunei and Indonesia.

Israel, of course, has been on permanent hit list of Islamists ever since its birth as a Jewish state in 1948. But the outbursts of Mahmoud Ahmdinejad, a hardline Islamic (Shia) fundamentalist newly elected as President of Iran, during the last quarter of 2005 beat all records of anti-Israeli sabre-rattling by the Muslim world. They are a part of the high tide of what Fukuyama calls 'Islamo-Fascism' which has emerged as a major threat to world peace.

Addressing a conference of students at Teheran in October 2005, the veteran of Iran's notorious Revolutionary Guards who was catapulted to the Presidency in mid-year elections, roared: "As the Imam said, Israel must be wiped off the map. The Islamic Ummah will not allow its historic enemy to live in its heartland" and then referring to the "historic war" between Islam and the west, he said:" It dates back hundreds of years. Sometimes Islam has advanced. Sometimes nobody was winning. Unfortunately over the past 300 years, the world of Islam has been in retreat. One hundred years ago, the last trench of Islam fell, when the oppressors went towards the creation of the Ziorist regime. They are using it as a fort to spread its aims in the heart of the Islamic world." (AP, `The Times of India' October 27, 2005).

In making a reference to the 'historic war' between Islam and the West, Ahmadinejad was confirming what Samuel Huntington wrote about a decade back about the 'clash of civilisations', albeit from the other side of the divide. Not even during the hardline U.S. President Reagon's first term, when the acknowledged Palestinian leader Yasser Arafat was branded as a terrorist and barred from visiting New York, had any Muslim leader so brazen-facedly called for wiping Israel off the map of the world. And this at a time when the peace process in the Arab-Israeli conflict had made considerable headway and Israeli troops and settlers were being pulled out of the Gaza strip.

It was ironic. Early in October 2005, the Israeli Prime Minister Ariel Sharon said in a newspaper interview to mark the start of the Jewish New Year: "I hope that next year there will be huge progress in the peace process and in implementing the outline established in the peace road map". He even referred to a "Pleasant phone call" he had with the Palestinian leader Mahmoud Abbas when the two exchanged greetings for the 'Rosh Hashanah' new year and Ramadan. (AFP,'The Hindustan Times', October 4, 2005).

The writing is on the wall for everyone to read. It is not Palestine or Kashmir alone. Nor exclusively America or Europe for that matter. The entire planet is in the sight of the Islamists. They are looking 350 years back with nostalgia, as Ahmadinejad implied in his speech, when the Ottoman Sultans went about conquering the western world. They are set upon taking over from where the Ottomans left and bringing the whole world to its knees. America is being targeted because it is the lone Superpower, after the collapse of the Soviet Union, which is standing in the way of Islamisation of the world. One pillar of infedility - communism- has fallen. The other solid and strong pillar - America - must be demolished too by the advancing soldiers of Islam. Once the towering pillar of "global infedility" is brought down, minor pillars like Jews, Hindus and numerous others will collapse like nine pins before the march of Islamism.When the last infidel will fall, the 'United States of Islam' extending over the entire globe will materialize. That is what the Islamists are aspiring for. A grand vision before the Jihadis well worth fighting for and laying down their lives in furtherance of the cause.

A barb doing the rounds during early 1990's went as follows; "Jews, Hindus, Serbs beware. The Islamists are coming." It might as well be recast today as: "Jews, Hindus, Americans or westerners beware. The Islamists are coming."

The Clouds of War

On the night of Jihadi bombing of the World Trade Centre, the American President Bush recorded his thought in his daily diary: "The Pearl Harbour of the 21st century took place today." (It may be recalled that it was only after the savage Japanese bombing of the American fleet at Pearl Harbour in the Pacific that the U.S. jumped in the Second World War against the Axis Powers, Germany, Italy and Japan.) Next morning, that is, on September 12, 2001, he told the media:"The deliberate and deadly attacks which were carried out yesterday against our country were more than acts of terror. They were acts of war". (Bob woodward, 'Bush at War', 2003). He was to say later that it was going to be the first world war of the 21st century.

And a world war it has come to be, but of a different kind, more about which later. First a brief account of wars or clouds of war under which the western world has lived since around the last quarter of the 19th century. The Franco-Prussian war of 1870-71 was kind of an epochal event in the recent history of wars indulged in by western nations with world wide ramifications. The defeat of France in this war brought about the unification of Germany as a viable nation state. But the humbled nationalism of the French people made them the bitterest enemy of Germany for a long time to come. Running hostity between France and Germany remained an enduring constituent of international diplomacy from 1871 to 1914 and onwards. It was in fact an outstanding factor in both the First and Second world wars. It was around this factor that a system of two rival alliances was built in Europe in late 19th century.

After 1871, the newly united Germany was haunted by the fear of French vengeance. France, on the other hand, was desperately looking for allies who could save her from friendless isolation which had brought about her downfall in 1871. In 1879, Germany entered into an alliance with Austria with provision for "reciprocal protection". In 1882, both Germany and Austria forged a similar alliance with Italy, making up the famous "Tripple Alliance". France countered it with a military alliance with Russia in 1893, which came to be known as the "Duel Alliance". After considerable wooing by France, Britain ultimately came out of its `splendid isolation' to join the "Duel Alliance" in 1907, though without specific military commitment. The counter trinity came to be called the "Tripple Entete".

Thus by 1907, it was "Tripple Entete" versus "Tripple Alliance", but the principals were France and Germany respectively. Only a provocation was wanting. When it was provided by the simmering eruptions of the unsatisfied national aspirations of the Slavic peoples of Balkan Peninsula, the First World War broke out in 1914. It set the whole of Europe and the world ablaze. When the war finally ended with the defeat of Germany and its allies in 1919, the victorious powers-France, Britain and America, sat down at Versailles (France) to dictate the terms of peace.

The Peace Treaties that were signed imposed utterly humiliating terms upon Germany, Britain and France shared Germany's overseas colonies and spheres of interest in Africa. Japan took over German Zones of influence and interest in China. And parts of pre-war German territory were ceded to Denmark, Belgium, Poland and Czechoslovakia. But it was France which walked away with the lion's share. The main Peace Treaty signed in June 1919 not only returned the territories of Alsace and Lorraine, won over by Germany in 1871, to France but also ceded the rich coal mines of German Saar Valley to France for exploitation for a period of 15 years.

The longstanding French animosity towards Germany showed in the post-Peace Treaty period also. France occupied the rich German mineral belt of Ruhr in default of payment of heavy reparations imposed upon Germany to compensate for damages during the war. It was like the proverbial last straw on the camel's back. It ignited the tinder-box of outraged German nationalism which brought about the rise of Hitler as the great avenger on behalf of the German people. The Frankestein of Nazism appeared on the scene and took charge. It was only a matter of time for the world to be plunged into the most destructive war of modern age-the Second World War – which raged from 1939 to 1945.

Although the western powers led by America and Soviet Russia came together in course of the war to fight the 'Axis' powers-Germany, Italy and Japan- the enduring adversary relationship between the western powers and communist Russia persisted. It was evident in the frantic race for occupation of Berlin between the Soviet forces on the one side and Anglo-U.S.-French troops on the other during the closing years of the war. And when the Second World War finally came to an end with the decisive defeat of Italy, Germany and Japan in 1945, the deep fissures in the relationship between the west and the Soviets started surfacing.

America and the west had to reluctantly acknowledge Soviet Russia's military authority over the countries of Eastern Europe which the Red Army had liberated from Nazi occupation. But when Russia set upon a course of quick Sovietisation of all the liberated countries of the Balkan region, the rupture between the west and the Soviets came into the open. It found an eloquent expression in war-time British Prime Minister Winston Churchill's famous observation in his address at Westminster college, Fulton, on 5th March 1946. He observed: "A shadow has fallen upon the scene so lately lighted by the Allied victory. Nobody knows what Soviet Russia and its communist international organization intend to do in the immediate future. From Steltin in the Baltic to Trieste in the Adriatic, an Iron curtain has descended across the continent." The 'Iron curtain' represented a fresh divide and a new battle line in Europe with ramifications all over the world.

That virtually signaled the onset of the protracted period of the "Cold war". Basically, what came to be known as the "Cold War" was in a broad sense continuation of the Second World War itself without, of course, actual fighting all the time in all theatres. But it came very near that on quite a few occasions. The first was over the Berlin question in June 1948 when Soviet Russia tried to drive the western powers out of its zone of Berlin. Since Berlin was 100 miles inside the Soviet Zone, it was easy for Russia to cut its rail, road and canal links with the west. When Russia began the Berlin blockade on 24th June 1948 and the western powers responded by organizing a massive airlift of essential supplies to Berlin, the Cold war came very near becoming hot.For nearly eleven months, Berlin-a city of two millions-was fed and supplied through western airlift, until Soviet Russia lifted the blockade on 11th May 1949. During all this period, the dividing line between cold and hot war remained thin. The scare over Berlin prompted the U.S. to create a powerful military alliance for the security of western Europe against Soviet onslaught. The North Atlantic Treaty was signed in April 1949, giving birth to NATO.

The victory of Mao's Chinese communists over Chiang Kai Shek's Nationalists in October 1949 took the cold war to Asia. The second major crisis of the cold war occurred in Korea resulting this time in actual fighting. After the defeat of Japan in the war, Korea was divided into a northern zone occupied by Soviet Russia and a southern one occupied by the U.S. By 1949, two separate governments dominated by the communists in the North and Americans in the south were set up, as in Germany. When in

1950 communist forces of North Korea advanced into the South, America succeeded in getting North Korea branded as aggressor by the U.N. For over two years, American troops under the garb of U.N. forces fought the North Korean and Chinese troops armed by Soviet Russia. The Korean war lasted until 1953 when Korea was formally partitioned into North and South.

The war psychosis between two heavily armed power blocks led by two nuclear heavy weights-America and Soviet Russia-continued its momentum, sweeping across the world, generating repeated crises over Berlin, Vietnam and the Middle East. To counter the NATO, Soviet Russia sponsored the Warsaw Pact tying the communist countries of Eastern Europe into a close military alliance in 1955. Until the resolution of the Cubian missile crisis of October 1962, referred to earlier, which heralded the thawing of the cold war and beginning of the détente, the world lived under the dark shadows of an impending war that, mercifully, did not happen. During all this period, war clouds hovered around, thickening here and there for a time, being swept off momentarily, appearing again over some area or another, with the threat of a nuclear holocaust always round the corner.

The Cuban missile crisis was of course the most serious, dangerous and direct point of confrontation between the two Super Powers which sent the world shuddering on the brink of a nuclear disaster. Those few momentous days loaded with the imminence of impending doom brought about an agonizing re-appraisal of Super Power relationship and nuclear logic. The uninterrupted chain of muscle-flexing and confrontation, which had characterized the American-Soviet relationship since the break-up of war-time alliance, was broken and substituted by a spirit of accommodation and avoidance of conflict. The unmistakable reversal of the hawkish trend was reflected in a series of conciliatory measures initiated by the two sides in course of the decade following Cuba.

The nuclear logic of MAD (Mutually Assured Destruction) having caught up with both the power blocks, the U.S. Soviet Russia and Britain signed the Nuclear Test Ban Treaty in July 1963. In July 1968, America, Soviet Russia and Britain signed the celebrated Treaty on Non-Proliferation of Nuclear weapons. In July 1969, the Soviet foreign minister, in his report to the Supreme Soviet, said that "in question of the maintenance of peace, the U.S.S.R. and the U.S.A. can find a common language."

The 1970's began with more promising developments in the direction of world peace. In the summer of 1972, the U.S. President Nixon paid a visit to Moscow-the first ever by an American President-in course of which he signed two strategic arms limitation agreements known as SALTI. In June 1973, the Russian President Brezhnev paid a return visit to Washington and signed the momentous Agreement on Prevention of Nuclear War. The preamble of the communiqué issued on the occasion recorded the decision of both sides to turn the development of friendship and cooperation between them into a permanent "factor for world peace". The so-called 'Cold war' was clearly on the retreat.

The on-going Vietnam war in East Asia, in which the U.S. had been sucked up in a big way by mid-1960's, had already become a mill-stone round the neck of America which it would rather shed off as quickly as possible. It had become largely a Vietnamese nationalist struggle, with their Chinese neighbours hostile and the distant Russian friends getting lukewarm under growing Soviet –American bon-homie. In the circumstances, the Vietnam war lasted for sometime and tapered off to its logical end by the end of 1970's.

Even as the end of the 'cold war' appeared to be near and lasting world peace in sight, two ominous developments took place around the same time which turned the table around. One was the Soviet occupation of Afganistan in 1979-80. It gave a fresh lease of life to the cold war which was thawing fast. There was much sabre-rattling over the issue and many started talking about the onset of the "second" or "new" cold war. It was not really so because America scrupulously avoided getting into a position where it would have to confront the Soviets directly. But it took recourse to the dubious method of instigating, aiding and abetting Islamic Jihad or holy war against the Soviets in Afganistan. As already discussed earlier, the success of Jihad in Afganistan encouraged the likes of Osama bin Laden and Mulla Umar to think that if they could vanquish the Soviet communist 'infidels' right in their backyard, they might as well do it to the global head of the infidels'-America.

It was like the Hindu mythological story of the demon 'Bhasmasur' who owed his advent into the universe to the grace of Lord Shiva, the god.

Once at the peak of his power, the demon tried to kill his creator-Lord Shiva himself. Qazi Hussain Ahmad, the Chief of Pakistan's fundamentalist Jamaat-e-Islami, almost said as much in course of an interview to "India Today" over ten years back. Describing the predicament of the U.S. after the Afgan war, he gleefully blurted out with unconcealed sarcasm in plain Urdu : "Main Ki jooti, mian ke sar" (The gentleman's own shoe to whack his own head). That said it all. ("India Today", May 15, 1994).

The second cataclysmic event in the context of Jihadi terrorism was the fundamentalist Islamic Revolution of Iran in 1979. It led to the establishment of a fanatic Islamic regime in that country, avowedly un-modern and fiercely anti-American. Almost on the morrow of their taking charge, the Islamic revolutionaries resorted to the terrorist act of taking 52 Americans as hostages. The U.S. rescue operation to free the hostages ended in fiasco in April 1980, which, incidentally, cost Jimmy Carter his possible second term as U.S. President. The Islamists' take-over of Iran towards the end of 1979, around the same time as the Soviet take-over of Afganistan and start of Islamic resistance in that country, gave a tremendous boost to the spirit of Jihad in the Muslim world.

These two monumental events reversed the trend towards a peaceful world clearly discernible in the beginning of 1970's. And set the stage for the coming up of large scale Jihadi terrorism across the world and the on-going war between fundamentalist Islam and the rest of the world.

It had come to be said, somewhat sarcastically, that the western society, which has come to be the lead society of the world in course of the last 500 years for various reasons recorded in history, had been so steeped in wars that it could not live without an enemy. May be because of its origin in the ancient Greeko-Roman civilization which almost glamorized war or its more recent history of engagement in perennial warfare, the west needed an enemy to live off. It has now got one in the shape of Islamic Jihad.

5

Makings of a World War

The Elusive Enemy

The U.S. President Bush cried war in his gut reaction to 9/11. But where was the enemy? Or who was the enemy to strike at? It was not a country like Germany or Japan in the Second World War or a recognizable political network identified with one country or another like Fascism, Nazism or Communism. There was a certain amount of confusion among the Presidential advisers in the immediate aftermath of 9/11 as to whom to go to war against.

Since terrorism flourishes on wide publicity, it is the usual practice for the terrorists to publicly boast of their terror acts and claim responsibility, But no individual or outfit had done that in this case. The American intelligence agencies, CIA in particular, had no doubt that Osama bin Laden and his Al Quida network were responsible for the 9/11 attacks. Osama bin Laden and Al Quida were clear suspects in terrorist bombings of American embassies in Kenya and Tanzania in 1998 during

Clinton Presidency. But the only action that the President authorized was firing of cruise missiles on Osama's sanctuary in Taliban controlled Kandahar region bordering Pakistan. It had proved infructuous. Incidently, a few of these missiles had fallen in Pakistan's Northern Areas bordering Kandahar, which had embarrassed Nawaz Sheriff's government in Pakistan a lot and aroused considerable interest in India.

The CIA got some indirect evidence of Al Quida's involvement in the attacks through intercepts of messages. For instance, one intercept indicated an Osama associate wrongly claiming that the White House had been destroyed, and another conveying thanks to the terrorists for causing explosion in the American Congress building, which was also not correct. Although broadly reported in the media across the world, either discreetly leaked for public consumption or scooped by the media on their own, the world at large was not quite sure if the information was enough for the U.S. to hit at Osama and his Al Quida network in an act of war. But President Bush had no doubt on that. The cumulative evidence against Osama since 1998 at least, if not earlier, was considered enough to go for him the whole hog and America decided to target him first.

In fact, evidence against Osama as the Kingpin of Jihadi terrorism world wide had been piling up since 1993. It was in that year that he took active part in a grand summit of Jihadi terrorism organized at Kartoum, the capital of Sudan by the then Sudanese strongman – Hassan-el-Turabi notorious for his tirade against the Christians. Ever since then, Laden and his network were learnt to have been involved in all major attacks against Americans and American facilities the world over. After having lived in Sudan for sometime, he had shifted to Afganistan when Taliban started gaining ascendancy in that country. And when Taliban finally took over the country in 1996, Osama established his firm base under the patronage and protective wing of the Taliban regime. It was from here that he began to train Muslim youth from Arab and other countries in the strategy and ideology of Jihad.

A Saudi-born multi-millionaire, Osama bin Laden drifted into Islamic extremism in 1980's when he got closely involved with the Jihad against the Soviets in Afganistan. He has not looked back since. Apart from an array of complaints against the U.S., the very presence of America in Saudi Arabia as an ally of the Saudi rulers offends him no end, because it is the birthplace of Prophet Muhammad and home of two holiest shrines of Islam-Mecca and Madina. For his open declaration of Jihad against the U.S., and of course Jews, and numerous acts of terrorism against them, Osama had become synonymous with Jihadi terrorism well before September 11, 2001. Once he was safely ensconced in Taliban ruled Afganistan by 1996, his angry out bursts against America and the West became louder and more frequent. Here are a few samples, which throw enough light on Jihadi mind-set.

In August 1996, he issued a Declaration of Jihad, entitled "Message from Osama bin Laden to his Muslim Brothers in the whole world and Especially in the Arabian Peninsula: Declaration of Jihad Against the Americans occupying the Land of the two Holy Mosques; Expel the Heretics from the Arabian Peninsula".

In the same month, he told the London-based al-Quidas al –Arabi newspaper: "The presence of the American crusader armed forces in the countries of the Islamic Gulf is the greatest danger and the biggest harm that threatens the world's largest oil reserves. The infidels must be thrown out of the Arabian Peninsula."

In February 1997, he threatened a holy war against the U.S. in an interview on the British documentary programme, Dispatches: "This war will not only be between the people of the two sacred mosques and the Americans, but it will be between the Islamic world and the Americans and their allies..."

And later, in an interview with CNN's Peter Arnelt, he said: "If the American government is serious about avoiding the explosions inside the U.S., then let it stop provoking the feelings of 1250 million Muslims...They would make of Ramizi Yousuf (Convicted for his role in 1993 bombing of the World Trade Centre) a symbol and a teacher. The U.S. will drive them to transfer the battle into the United States."

In February 1998, bin Laden endorsed a 'fatwa', religious decree, under the banner of the "International Islamic Front for Jihad on the Jews and Crusaders". The 'fatwa' said: "These crimes and sins committed by the Americans are a clear declaration of war on God, his messager and Muslims."

In May 1998, bin Laden issued a statement entitled "The Nuclear Bomb of Islam" under the banner of the "International Islamic Front for Fighting the Jews and Crusaders." It said that "it is the duty of Muslims to prepare as much force as possible to terrorize the enemies of God."

In a December 1998 ABC News interview, bin Laden said : "If the instigation for Jihad against the Jews and the Americans in order to liberate al-Aksa Mosque and the holy Kaaba (Islamic shrines in Jerusalem and Saudi Arabia) is considered a crime, then let history be a witness that I am a criminal. Hostility towards America is a religious duty, and we hope to be rewarded for it by God."

In January 1999, in an interview published in the U.S. magazine "News Weak", bin Laden said: "Muslim scholars have issued a `fatwa' against any American who pays taxes to his government. He is our target because he is helping the American war machine against the Muslim nation...The response from Muslim nations had been greater than we expected. We are urging all of them to start fighting, or atleast to start preparing to fight, against the enemies of Islam."

In the summer of 2001, before the 9/11 strike on America, a videotape circulated in the Middle East, features bin Laden reciting a victory poem about the U.S.S. cole bombing, and then issuing a call to arms: "To all the Mujah: Your brothers in Palestine are waiting for you; it is time to penetrate America and Israel and hit them where it hurts most." (Accessed on 19.12.05, Website....... Osama bin Laden:Profile).

The venom poured against America and the west and the savagery of the verbal assault on them surpass any hate campaign of some of the most notorious hate-mongers of history like Hitler and Mussolini. And Osama bin Laden had gone on indulging in it with impunity for a number of years before 9/11. It is a measutre of propensity of Muslim peoples all over the world to succumb to such hate campaigns and idolise fundamentalists like Osama in the name of Islam that after the attack on America on 9/11, he overnight became a hero in the Muslim world. From Algeria, Cairo and Beirut to Pakistan and India, Osama became an Islamic icon of the Muslims, both the classes and the masses. A Muslim parliamentarian of India (Bihar), often in the news for wrong reasons, proudly proclaimed that he had named his two sons as Osama and Mulla Omar. So much so that in two successive Assembly elections in Bihar in February and October-November 2005, two prominent political leaders of the state moved around with a look-alike of Osama to woo Muslim voters. In Pakistan, 'Osama' shirts and 'Osama' caps became a craze among young people of Karachi and other cities.

For America, of course, Osama bin Laden was the obvious and immediate target of attack in its declared war on global terrorism. But Osama was only an individual, however widespread his network of Jihadi terrorism might have been. At worst, he was the international terrorist number one, as Carlos the Jackal once had been. Targeting Carlos to wipe out his terrorist network could not be called a war on terror. Bush had proclaimed a war on international terrorism, but war has a much wider connotation than catching an individual terrorist, however high and mighty, and punishing him under national or international law. Hitler was also an individual criminal who had confined the Jewish people of Germany to concentration camps and perpetrated the gruesome 'holocaust'. But he was the ruler of the German state which could be made the target of attack by the Allied powers during the Second World War and vanquished. Osama bin Laden, in spite of all his terrorist acts and wide terror network, remained only an individual sponsor of terrorism with no territorial state to be identified with against which the U.S. could go to war, officially and demonstrably.

Osama had of course taken shelter in Afganistan under Taliban regime since 1996 and set up his base there to train and motivate Jihadi terrorists. He was also reported to have established matrimonial relationship with the family of the Taliban ruler-Mullah Omar. But in spite of all that, he had no more than the status of a guest of the Taliban regime living under its shelter as a fugitive from his home country of Saudi Arabia. He could not be identified with the Afgan state. How could striking at Osama be construed as a global war on terrorism which America had pledged in the wake of 9/11?

President Bush and his team had the answer. Even though they would be focused on Osama and his Al Quida as the immediate strike target, the over all war on terror would encompass those states also which sponsored and harbored Osama and his al Quida terrorists. That was a big leap in the sweep of the impending war. It could include some Islamic states, well known and not so well known, whom it was easier to locate- than to find Osama bin Laden himself. Talibani Afganistan was obviously on top of the list. There were subtle hints in the media about some others also, like Sudan and Syria. Saddam's Iraq had been a sworn enemy on the hit list of America since the Gulf war of 1990. But no evidence was forthcoming to link Saddam with Osama's latest misadventure in the U.S.

The first step before the onset of the war was to notice the Talibani leadership to hand over Osama and the whole of his Al-Quida gang to America, failing which they would have to reckon with the full might of American attack. Mullah Omar and his government were totally defiant. To them, as to Muslims generally in all parts of the world, Osama was an icon of Islam whom they would never betray, come what may. That set the stage for the American attack on Taliban and onset of the war.

The War : Afganistan and Iraq

Before going in for the kill against Osama and Taliban, the U.S. had a few things to sort out with Pakistan. For three reasons. First, Pakistan and Saudi Arabia were the only two major Muslim countries in the world which had given diplomatic recognition to the Taliban government in Afganistan. India, it may be recalled, still recognized the Northern Alliance led by the Charismatic Generals Ahmad Shah Masood and Abdur Rashid Dostum, as the legitimate rulers of Afganistan, even though they had been driven out of nearly the whole of the country, precariously holding on in the northern fringes. The Saudis, in spite of their commitment to Islamic orthodoxy, were close allies of the U.S. with no particular stake in Taliban. In fact, the Saudi rulers were internally as much antagonistic to Osama, as a possible rallying point against the ruling dynasty itself, as America. That left Pakistan only as the sole diplomatic god father of Taliban in the world.

Second, any worthwhile military offensive against Talibani Afganistan was not possible without active cooperation from Pakistan because of the geography of the region. Any effective action from the South had to be routed through the long borders which Afganistan shared with Pakistan in its south. And it was southern Afganistan, bordering Pakistan's Northern areas, with Kandahar as the epi-centre, which was the citadel of Mulla Omar and Osama bin Laden.

Finally, attacking Taliban was as good as attacking Pakistan. For the simple reason that Taliban was out and out a creation of Pakistan. Its hard core fundamentalist Islamists were the products of Pakistani Madaras in its North West Frontier Province. The area around Peshawar was once described by "The New York Times" as the "University of Jihad." And the fundamentalist Islamic movement symbolized by Taliban had tremendous appeal among the people of Pakistan.

There was another problem. Although Pakistan had been a close ally of the U.S. since the cold war days, the relationship had soured a bit after General Parvez Musharraf captured power in a military coup in 1999. A year earlier, America had clamped sanctions against Pakistan for conducting nuclear tests. But this was not the time to be hedged in by things like that. Pakistan had to be brought in line if the American assault on Taliban had to make any headway. Towards this end, Bush coined his famous message for Musharraf: "You are either with us or you are not; if not, be prepared for the consequences." And it worked magically. Parvez Musharraf's Pakistan lay prostrate before Uncle Sam. But not without some fun.

Sensing trouble, Pakistan's ISI Chief, General Mohamoud Ahmad landed in Washington almost on the morrow of 9/11. In a seemingly innocuous chat with his counterpart, George Tenet, the CIA Chief, he tried to plead for Mulla Omar, the Taliban Chief, ruling Afganistan. He told the CIA Chief that Mulla Omar was a pious religious leader pitted against Afgan war-lords and as such deserved sympathetic consideration. General Mahmoud was ushered into the U.S. foreign office, the State Department. There he met Richard Aimitage, the Deputy Secretary of State. Even as General Mahmoud was beating about the bush of Pakistan's longstanding friendship with America, Aimitage brought him back on the track of the present and the future. He conveyed the tough message from President Bush to General Musharraf: either with America or against it. That did the trick. Pakistan not only fell in line but went the hole hog to support America in its war against Taliban which was Pakistan's own creation.

But Musharraf had to do a lot of explaining to his people in Pakistan about his somersault on Taliban issue. He went public to admit that he had no option but to sacrifice Taliban in order to save Pakistan itself. The implications were grave and obvious, but Pakistan's alignment with the U.S. in the war on Taliban did not go down well with sizeable sections of Pakistanis. Hamid Gul, the ex-ISI Chief and a radical Islamist, made a highly critical comment to the effect that meek surrender was no foreign policy worth the name. Imran Khan, the Cricketer turned politician who had once said that he learnt politics from Hamid Gul, became a bitter critic of Musharraf for his abject "surrender" before Bush. Two years earlier, he had supported Musharraf for ridding the country of corrupt politicians like Nawaz Sharif and Benazir Bhutto.

There were also dark hints in the media about American experts training with Israelis to destroy Pakistan's nuclear facilities, if it came to that. It may be noted that Israelis had done that to Saddam's nuclear facilities in Iraq before. Although the news was not confirmed, the message went home to Pakistani Establishment. So much so that President Musharraf, in course of his explaining exercise, even told his people that he had to turn about and abandon Taliban in order to safeguard and preserve Pakistan's own nuclear capability.

Once Pakistan came round to supporting America in its war on Taliban, the rest was easy. The Americans got all that they wanted of Pakistan – unrestricted over flight and landing rights for their warplanes, free access to Pakistan's air and naval bases and land borders with Afganistan, sharing of information and intelligence about Osama and Al Quida network in Afgan territory, besides of course cutting of fuel supply to Taliban and stopping Pakistani Jihadis from crossing over to Afganistan and joining the Talibani ranks. What was left unsaid was an overhaul of Pakistan's intelligence agencies to shed off pro-Taliban elements, which Musharraf promised on the quiet and set about doing.

It turned out to be the "clash of civilizations", metaphorically and truly. The entire western world including Russia pledged full support to the U.S. war on Taliban. For the Russians smarting under Jihadi terrorism emanating from Chechnya, it was sweet music. And a bonus too, in as much as America and west Europeans won't be in a position to fuss about alleged violation of human rights by Russians in Chechnya. Putin even promised to use his influence with central Asian states like Uzbekistan to provide facilities like basing rights to the U.S. contingent for operating from the north. It was primarily to be in the form of providing all possible assistance to the Northern Alliance to start the offensive against Taliban from their foothold in the northern region.

Uzbekistan in particular was crucial to the northern offensive because of its location close on the northern border of Afganistan. The favourable factor here was that Uzbek President Karimov was facing serious problem from the extreme fundamentalist Islamic Movement of Uzbekistan (IMU). Once his concern regarding the threat from his internal radical Islamists were addressed, he was ready to provide necessary facilities to the U.S. forces.

The French, German, Canadians and Australians were ready to provide troops as well as any help needed in the war. The British were almost a part of the American armed mobilization. As the closest U.S. ally through thick and thin, they committed their troops to carry on the fight on the ground shoulder to shoulder with American forces. With the rest of the world fully supportive, it turned out to be not really a "clash of civilizations" but a clash between civilization and uncivilisation.

Having assembled an international coalition in the war on terror, America launched the first attack on Talibani Afganistan on 7th October 2001, exactly 27 days after the terrorist assault on the World Trade Centre and the Pentagon. It came in the shape of aerial strikes on specified targets by land -based bombers, strike aircraft from carriers and cruise missiles from U.S. and British ships and submarines. The targets evidently were Taliban military installations and Al Quida terrorist camps in Afganistan. The only action on the ground was by CIA special groups locating and pointing out the targets of aerial assault.

Ironically enough, the Arabic channel Al-Jazeera released an earlier videotape of Osama-bin-Laden gloating in the successful attack on America by Jihadis on 9/11. He was shown pontificating: "Here is America struck by God Almighty in one of its vital organs, so that its greatest buildings are destroyed....God has blessed a group of vanguard Muslims, the forefront of Islam, to destroy America."

On September 23, 2001, two weeks before the start of the American attack, Osama said: "We hope that these brothers (Muslim casualties in Pakistan) are among the first martyrs in Islam's battle in this era against the new Christian-jewish crusade led by the big crusader Bush under the flag of the cross; this battle is considered one of Islam's battles..." And further: "We ask allah to make him (Taliban leader Mullah Omer) victorious over the forces of infidels and tyranny, and to crush the new Christian-Jewish crusade on the land of Pakistan and Afganistan."

Pin-pointed and meticulously calibrated bombings of Taliban is for two weeks, avoiding collateral damages to civil population, pulverized their military and terror super structure, but Mullah Omar, Osama bin Laden and their hardcore band of Jihadis remained unstruck. They were reportedly sheltered in natural caves around Tora Bora mountainous ranges which the Jihadis had earlier successfully availed of during their fight against the Russians. Tora Bora was also targeted and bombed by U.S. war planes and missiles but no harm could come to them. On the other hand, they considerably strengthened their military build up around the capital Kabul. For the real action on the ground lay there. The American attack was confined to aerial strikes only meant to incapacitate the Taliban war machine. The actual fighting on the ground was to be done by the Afgans themselves rallied under the banner of the Northern Alliance. It was a loose conglomeration of Uzbek and Tajik forces led by veterans of the Afgan Jihad against the Soviets two decades earlier. The visible civilian face of the Alliance, which India then recognized as the legitimate government of Afganistan, was Abdullah Abdullah and the leading commanders were Mohammad Fahim, Abdur Rashid Dostum and, the most charismatic of them all, Ahmad Shah Masood. But unfortunately for the Alliance, Masood was assassinated by Talibani agents, as if by design, just two days before the September 11 strike at the U.S. That had been a set back to the Alliance which was anyhow holding on to its precarious existence on the northern fringes of Afganistan bordering Tajikistan, Uzbekistan and Iran.

The war on Taliban after 9/11 put a new life in the dormant Northern Alliance. The Americans started building them up with massive assistance in terms of arms, equipments, money and strategic support. The Alliance was the best bet to take on and vanguish the Taliban on the ground with its battle-hard generals and foot soldiers.

The strategy worked out was for the American forces to destroy the massive Taliban troop concentration around Mazar-a-Sharif and Afghan capital Kabul. Once that was done, the Northern Alliance ground forces would take on the Talibanis. The strategy started working and things started falling into place. By the middle of November, 2001, the Northern Alliance, which had controlled less than 15 per cent of Afghanistan earlier, had occupied about half of the country. The Talibanis were on the run before the advancing Alliance troops. There was no problem in capture of Kabul as the Talibans and Al-Quaida abandoned the capital and fled to the south in the Khandahar region bordering Pakistan. And before the end of the year, on 07th December, 2001, the southern Citadel of Taliban and Al-Quaida, i.e. Khandahar was captured by the Alliance and American forces. The first phase of the war on terror was over. But the most wanted Jihadi terrorist in the world Osama Bin Laden and his harbourer Mulla Omar who were the prime targets of American forces, could not be captured. They continue to be at large with a reward of 25 million dollars on the head of Osama Bin Laden.

On 26th December, 2001, the Arabic satellite channel Al-Jazeera broadcast a video tape of Osama Bin Laden in which he said :-

- "After three months passed since the blessed attacks against the global infidelity, against America, the Head of Infidelity, and after almost two months passed since the beginning of the vicious crusade campaign against Islam, we would like to talk about some of the meanings of these events. These events revealed many issues that are significant to Muslims.

- It becomes very clear that the West in general and America, Head of the Infidels in particular, bear hate and grudge against Islam and Muslims that cannot be described.

- Our terrorism is good accepted terrorism because it's against America, it's for the purpose of defeating oppression so America would stop supporting Israel, who is killing our children".

Iraq

Iraq was a different proposition. It was kind of a parenthesis in the war against Jihadi terror When Bush talked of a prolonged war which could include countries supporting terror, Iraq's name automatically cropped up along with Sudan and may be Syria. While formulating the response to 9/11, Iraq's Saddam Hussen did figure in discussions about possible targets of attack. There were vague suspicions about his possible link with the attack on the U.S. But there was no evidence to confirm that. In any case, since Osama and Taliban were unmistakable culprits, they were taken up as the immediate targets of attack.

But once the war in Afganistan was over and Taliban ousted, it was time for a close look at Saddam's Iraq. The military intervention in Afganistan was not a war against the Afgans or the country as such but action to bring about a regime change. The U.S. had succeeded in doing that with least collateral damage to the country. Could it be possible or desirable to replicate that in Iraq also? The U.S. decided it could be so. A war once started moves on its own momentum.

The first hint of Iraq being the next target came in the State of the Union address of President Bush on January 29, 2002, soon after the victory in Afganistan. The most significant part of his address, which aroused considerable interest and a certain degree of concern to the world, was his declaration that Iraq, Iran and North Korea constituted an "axis of evil." What he meant to convey was that the availability of weapons of mass destruction to terrorists or those regimes was the real threat to world peace. And he went on to add " I will not wait on events." The message was clear. All that followed, that is the U.S. effort to get a second U.N. Security Council resolution specifically authorizing war on Iraq, which did not come off, was only a formality. America had made up its mind, even if it meant going to war with only Britain and Spain on its side. At stake was security against terror, even if indirect and not direct or immediate.

All that America wanted was that Saddam Hussen should step down from power. Not because Saddam was a confirmed Islamist or Jihadi. He might often be spitting fire and venom against the Israelis or invoking the name of Islam in his running feud with Americans, but he was more secular or religion-neutral than most of the Muslims rulers of the Middle East in his approach to politics. After 9/11, he publicly denied having anything to do with it or with Osama and his Al-Quida. And yet, America decided to go to war to secure his ouster for three reasons. And here again, it was not a war against Iraq or Iraq's people but a bid to bring about a regime change.

First, the long-standing plea that Saddam was in possession of W.M.D's (Weapons of Mass Destruction), which he was not prepared to give up or disclose to U.N. Weapon Inspectors. The U.S. had succeeded in getting various kinds of sanctions clamped against Iraq by the U.N. on this score. Now that no W.M.D's or evidence of Saddam being engaged in building them up has come up, it is a moot point whether Bush-Blair duo genuinely believed in this charge or it was just trumped up to attack Saddam Hussen. The issue now boils down to ethics and ethics hardly counts in war. A more authentic ground of war on Saddam's Iraq was that Saddam was like a wounded tiger for the U.S. since the time of the Gulf War. And considering his belligerent posture and war-mongering track record

(Iran and Kuwait), he remained a constant potential threat. He might not have been linked to Al Quida then, but could do so any time to hurt the U.S. And America could not afford to leave any scope for another terror attack upon itself now that it was in war mode.

But the third and most important reason was some what paradoxical. Suddam Hussen was a tyrant resorting to ruthless repression of his opponents in the country. The Shias and Kurds who constitute a majority of the Iraqi population were not only denied a share in power but brutally suppressed. The simmering resentment and discontent of sizeable sections of his own people constituted a store-house of gun powder ready to explode. In absence of any democratic channel to come to the surface, or in absence of support from Western secular democracies, the suppressed people of Iraq might look upon Islamic fundamentalists to rescue them from Saddam's repression. As happened in Iran, for instance, in 1979. The pent up anger of the Iranians against the Shah's autocratic regime burst forth into fundamentalist Islamic Revolution throwing all liberal democratic elements in the country by the way side.

The above thesis believed to have been developed by the trio-Dick Cheney, the Vice President, Donald Rumsfield, the Secretary of Defence, and Paul Wolfowitz, Deputy Secretary of Defence, fitted in with the President's own inclinations. The central idea was to bring about a modern secular democratic state in the heart of the Middle East which could serve as a model for others in the region that was the breeding ground of. Islamic fundamentalism. It was based on a belief in the transformative power of democracy. The favourable factors in support of the view was that Iraq, with its vast oil wealth second only to Saudi Arabia, had the prospect of developing into an economically viable and flourishing capitalist democracy favourable to America.

It may be a tall order which may or may not materialize. For various reasons, the most important being the fact that it is a country sharply split among three distinct identities - Shias, Sunnis and kurds. Post - Saddam Iraq is still in a melting pot. The military intervention in Iraq has already become a hot topic of highly critical debate both inside and outside the U.S. It had been dogged with controversy even before it began and has reminded so althrough. But it must be remembered that it was not the agenda of the international coalition which launched the war against Taliban earlier. Only Britain and Spain among the western powers aligned with the U.S. in the assault on Saddam Hussen. In that sense, the action in Iraq was not strictly a part of the war on Jihadi terror. It was only a footnote in the ongoing war and as such calls for no more than a passing reference.

It may be noted that in a complex war of global dimension, side wars, not in the direct line of confrontation between the principals, are always in the realm of possibility, if not inevitability. The war in Iraq was one such. There may be others in the offing too.

As for the future of Iraq, the good news is that the Iraqi economy is picking up, the Iraqis have drawn up a constitutional framework and gone through a democratic election. And the bad news is the emergence of Shiite religious leaders as a dominant force in the unfolding political drama in Iraq. American presence in Japan and South Korea after the Second World War transformed them not only into vibrant democracies but also economic super powers. Can anything even distantly similar to that happen in Iraq? or Will it sink into interminable ethnic cum sectarian conflicts involving Shias, Sunnies and Kurds ? Only the future will tell.

6

War with a Difference

Non-State Actors

Except in very few cases where it is sponsored, aided and abetted by a Government or a State, as in the case of Taliban, the modern Jihad or Islamic holy war is carried on only by Non-State actors. In that sense, it is vitally different from the Islamic wars of conquests launched by Arabs and Turks in the past centuries. When organized states or Governments embark upon a course of conquest, they fight wars, but when not so organized groups set upon conquering the world, they take recource to terrorism. For terrorism is essentially a weapon of non-state outfits. As clarified at the outset, extra legal violence or brutality perpetrated by the state, as in the case of dictatorial regimes like those of Saddam Hussan, is another matter, which is outside the purview of this book. Terrorism is exclusively a private Sector enterprise and Jihadi terrorism is just the same.

The world has undergone a sea change since the time of the Ottoman Turks, briefly touched upon earlier, who went about conquering the world in the name of Islam. No modern state worth the name would fight a war in the name of religion, however, fanatic or religiously inclined it might be. Taliban tried to do it and had to bite the dust. In any case, Taliban was more a fundamentalist Islamic movement born out of Jihad in Afghanistan than a proper state, as evident from the fact that it was recognized as such by only three out of around 200 states in the world. And Al Quida, in spite of its world wide network, cannot by any stretch of imagination be described as a state.

That makes a war on terrorism very different in character from any other war fought between two states or countries. It makes warring both easy and difficult. Easy in the sense that the warring states don't have to face the armed might of each other, but, more importantly, it makes the war very complex and complicated. Because it is very difficult to trace, locate and pin point the enemy to take on in a direct fight. More so if the enemy is a faceless, shadowy and widely dispersed group like the Jihadi terrorists today. The fight becomes even more complicated if the enemy is not even known or knowable as in the case of enemy within. For instance, the Jihadis who struck the twin towers of World Trade Centre on 09/11 or those who caused blasts in London under ground trains on 07/7 (7th July 2005) were very much a part of the American and British society respectively when they indulged in these terrorist acts. In that sense, war against terrorism can be much more difficult.

Terrorism is also more cruel and destructive of innocent human lives because terrorists use human beings as cannon-fodder in their battle against a country or state. A telling example of sheer brutality of terrorist operations is provided by the Beslan school blood bath triggered by terrorists in Russia in early September 2004. On September 3, Islamic militants seized more than 1128 students, their parents and teachers in the southern Russian town of Beslan. For three days they were held captive in course of the stand off between the terrorists and security forces. The seize ended only after a shoot out in which 331 innocent persons, more than half of them being children, lost their lives. The innate secrecy of their operations and anonymity of the operaters make them immune to human considerations and encourage them to indulge in inhuman acts of terror like Beslan with immunity. States fight their wars in the open subject to the rules of the game. Non-state actors, that is terrorists, fight it on the sly without any ground rules. That makes it difficult to rein them in and minimize the damage caused to civil society by them or in course of countering them. To put it more bluntly, non-state warriors are in the nature of a gang of criminals indulging in ruthless killings, albeit for a cause they hold sacred.

The ongoing war against Jihadi terrorism is world wide in its scale. It has to reckon with Jihadi terrorist outfits spread from the Philippines, Malaysia, Indonesia, Bangladesh in the East through India, Pakistan and middle East to England and America in the West. These include Abu Sayyaf in the Philippines, Zimma Islamia (ZI) in Indonesia, Harkut-al-Jihad-e-Islami in Bangladesh. Students Islamic Movement of India (SIMI) in India, Hijbul Mujabedeen, Laksher-e-Thoiba, Jais-e-Mohamed,

Harkut-al-Ansar and a host of them in Pakistan, the Islamic Movement of Uzbekistan in Central Asia, 'Muslims of America' and 'Koranic Open University' in America, besides of course the doyen of them all- Al Quaida. Numerous other big and small Jihadi groups have mushroomed all over the world to carry on terrorist activities on big and small scale. They may or may not be integrated with each other but there is a fair amount of networking among them and their terrorist acts. The cementing factor is the common goal of Jihad against the non-muslim peoples. That defines the scale, dimensions and magnitude of the war against Jihadi terrorism. It is going to be a war that the world has never known before.

One of the first things that the Victorious American forces looked for in the Afgan capital Kabul after the ouster of Taliban was for suspected WMD's that Osama bin Laden was reported to be collecting for an eventual assault on the western world. Nothing of the kind was found, but that brings up the frightful possibility of Jihadis coming in possession of nuclear weapons in times to come. It is a nightmarish situation which the world has to take into consideration while dealing with Jihadi terrorism.

Some independent, free-lance writers have carried out their own investigations into the matter and come out with startling revelations. In course of personal investigation in the murder of the "Wall Street Journal" reporter Daniel Pearl, Bernard Henry Levy, referred to earlier, came to the conclusion that Pearl was kidnapped and killed because he was in hot pursuit of evidence connecting Pakistani

Nuclear Scientists to terrorist net work across the world. He discovered that the Operational Chief of a Pakistani N.G.O. named 'Ummah Tameer-e-Nau' (Reconstruction of Muslim Ummah) was a famous Pakistani Nuclear Scientist Dr. Sultan Bashiruddin Mahamood, the Head of Pakistan's Atomic Energy Commission until 1999. More importantly, Bashiruddin Mahmood was a confirmed Islamist disciple of an Ulema from Lahore who was reported to be a secret guru of Osma Bin Laden also.

And more, The Pakistani N.G.O.U. TN-which was supposed to promote development projects in Kandhar region of Talibani Afghanistan, was headed by none other than Lt. Gen. (Retd.) Hamidgul, the ex-ISI Chief referred to earlier. Bashiruddin Mahamood, the Nuclear Scientist had visited Kandhar early in August, 2001 and met Osma Bin Laden. And towards the end of August, both Hamidgul and Mahamood were huddled together in the Afghan capital Kabul in suspicious circumstances. It also came to light that Bashiruddin Mahamood, the Nuclear Physicist was no ordinary Islamist but an active member of Harkal-Ul-Mujahadeen who held the view that the Pakistani bomb was not for Pakistan only but belonged to Islamic 'Ummah' as a whole. (Bernard Henry Levy, 'who killed Daniel Pearl' 2003). The facts speak for themselves.

A much more sensational disclosure was made in a book entitled 'Osma's Revenge' authored by Paul Williams in mid 2005. The author claimed that Pakistani Nuclear Scientists led by the notorious proliferator A.Q. Khan had already armed Osma and his Al-Quaida with nuclear weapons to bring about an "American Hiroshima". Accounts from the book appeared on several web sites and internet blocks. According to the book, the plan called for detonation of seven tactical nuclear devices in seven U.S. cities simultaneously. According to Paul Williams, the matter regarding A.Q. Khan's involvement with Al-Quaida and the 'American Hiroshima' plan first came to the fore with the capture of several Al-Quaida operatives in Afghanistan during the war on Taliban and later the arrest of Khalid Sheikh Mohammad Bin Laden's Military Operations Chief, in Karachi. The `American Hiroshima' has not materialized and the author's claim may lack in authenticity, but with the Jihadis on the prowl for acquiring nuclear weapons, the dark spectre of a nuclear twilight sooner or later cannot be brushed aside altogether.

Assembling a nuclear bomb and effective detonation and delivery systems may still be a difficult preposition for the Jihadis, but with clandestine assistance of the likes of A.Q. Khan and Bashiruddin Mahmood, or unemployed Russian Scientists, it may not be beyond their reach. A panel of five former nuclear weapon designers reported to the International Task Force on the Prevention of Nuclear Terrorism that a workable nuclear bomb could be constructed by a group of persons if certain requirements are met. And even such a crude design could produce a nominal yield in the ten kilo ton range. The important point to note is that non-state actors like Al-Quaida are more dangerous in nuclear terms than nuclear armed States because they do not have to fear a nuclear response or retaliation. They are like a swarm of mosquitos which cannot be hit by a bomb. The world has lived with heavily armed nuclear states for more than half a century without their destroying each other. But if non-state entities like shadowy terrorist out-fits get hold of nuclear weapons, the planet will became very unsafe for humans to live. In that sense the war against Jihadis is as difficult as it is necessary to win.

A 'Clash of Civilisation'

War has a much wider connotation than mere clash of arms, like we talk of war on poverty, war on disease and so on. In similar parlance, the fight against terror can be construed as a war in the wider sense of the term which is going on unabated in different parts of the world.

An interesting debate developed sometime back in the U.S. administration circles about use of the term 'War' in reference to the on going fight against terror. Some senior American Government members including the Defence Secretary Donald Ramsfiled and Chairman of the Joint Chiefs of Staff General Richard Myers preferred to use the term 'Global Struggle Against Violent Extremism' (GSAVE) instead of 'Global War On Terrorism' (GWOT). They argued that the term 'War On Terror' might lead people to believe that it would end with the stoppage of actual fighting on the ground. Early in August 2005 General Myers told the National Press Club that 'if you call it a war, then you think of people in uniform as being the solution'. But once the matter reached President Bush, he brushed aside the uncalled for controversy and stood by his description of US action post 9/11 as a Global War on Terrorism.

Not withstanding the semantic debate about appropriate terminology, the war on terror has turned out to be a Virtual 'clash of Civilisations' between the Islamists and the Western world. There was already a ripple of anti-foreignism in Europe since early 1990s. This was primarily directed against the Muslims in countries like France & Germany because an overwhelming majority of foreign immigrants in these countries are Muslims. They include Turks, Arabs, Pakistanis, Bangladeshis and migrants from other Muslim countries. After 9/11, this ripple of anti-foreignism pointing to Muslim immigrants has turned into a strong current.

The five million muslims in France were already on notice that a distinctly French Islam was just about tolerable, but no more. The Muslim anger against the French establishment came to the fore some time back when immigrant youths broke into wide spread rioting in France. The French capital Paris and its suburbs witnessed large scale rioting for a number of days by the immigrants, largely Muslims, on a scale which had not been seen after the general youth uprising in Europe during late 1960s.

In other European countries, tough measures against Islamism raising its head were being taken or contemplated. The Dutch government was seriously considering a proposal that mosques of the country be forced to employ only those Imams who studied the faith in Holland. The German political leaders bluntly told the Muslims living in Germany to learn the German language. And after July 2005 London Bomb blast, the British Prime Minister started saying that Imams in British

Mosques must be able to preach in English. In all these cases, national language or culture was only a cover to convey a tough message to their Muslim immigrants to forget about Jihad and integrate with the people of the countries in which they were living.

Britain, which was considered to be more liberal than other European countries in matters of religious faith and culture, has come out very strongly to curb the raising tide of Islamism on its soil after the July 2005 bomb blast. A month after the London bombing, the Prime Minister Tony Blair declared that foreigners (read Muslims) who preached hatred or sponsored violence could be deported under strict new measures being adopted by the government. He even proposed to close down Mosques in Britain which preached violence and extremism, but the measure was dropped due to resistance by more liberal elements in the political establishment. But the extreme right wing British National Party (BNP) is already accusing both the ruling Labour and the main opposition Conservative Party of 'promoting the 'Islamification menace' in the country.

Late in December 2005, authorities in Germany banned an Islamist group after seizing materials calling upon Muslims to kill Jews and Christains and carry out suicide attacks in Iraq. The state of Bavaria said that the activities of the Muti-Kultur-Haus association threatened the coexistence of Germans and foreigners as well as security in the country. A Ministry statement cited a book in the group's library calling for Jews and Christains to be executed if they did not convert to Islam.

What western countries are concerned about is that first and even second generation Muslim immigrants in their countries who were brought up and educated in the western society have turned out to be Jihadi militants resorting to terrorism. Mohammed Atta, one of the hijackers of U.S. planes on 9/11, had lived in America and received education in that country. In the same way those who triggered the bomb blast in London in July 2005 were Muslim youth of Pakistani origin who had been brought up and educated in England. The westerners are shocked to realize that even after living in the liberal milieu of their countries, the muslim youth could turn into radical islamists. The tough measures being taken by European governments against such people indicate their determination to put a stop to it. The British Prime Minister told the press after the London bombings : "They come here and they play by our rules and our way of life. If they don't, they are going to have to go".

The western states do not perhaps know or understand fully the all pervasive concept of Islamic Umma or Quom which supersedes the concept of secular nationhood. Even though the muslim world consists of a large number of separate states, they some how consider themselves to be parts of the muslim Umma which overrides their separate statehood. The international Organization of Islamic States (OIS) is the manifestation of the concept of Islamic Umma. This is the only organization of diverse states spread all over the world which is based purely on religion. There are other groupings of nation states like Organization of American States, Organization of African states etc which are based on geographical location of the countries concerned. There is no such grouping like organization of Christian states or Buddhist states or any other. That only goes to show the importance attached to the idea of Islamic Umma by muslim peoples all over the world. And to radical islamists, loyalty to the Islamic Umma supersedes their loyalty to the country in which they were born and brought up. The muslim immigrants living in Western countries are constantly tossed about by this dual loyalty. Most of them abide by the rules of the game, ie, live as loyal citizens of their host countries. But there are many who come under the spell of Islamic fundamentalism sweeping across the world to reject their loyalty to the host countries in favor of the Umma. It is such people who turn into Islamic militants or terrorists.

In a broader sense, what the world is witnessing today in the form of war on Jihadi terror boils down to a 'clash of civilizatios' of a kind different from what Samuel Huntington has been talking about. To see it as a clash between Islam and Christianity only or between Islamism and western society is too narrow a viewpoint to correctly understand what exactly is happening. The civilisational conflict that is shaking the world is between two time blocks or stages in the evolution of human civilization. In other words, it is a conflict between medieval and modern civilizations.

The Jihadis represent the medieval milieu of religious orthodoxy and intolerance common to both Islam and Christianity during the Middle Ages. It was in Christian Europe that the Italian astronomer Galileo was hauled up by the Ecclesiastical Court of the Inquisition for supporting the Copernican thesis that the Earth is not the center of the Universe but only a planet revolving around the sun. In the year 1616, the Christian religious Court held this purely scientific finding as 'heretical' being contrary to the Holy Scripture. In 1632, Galileo was pronounced guilty for espousing the 'heretical' thesis. But the western society, or the Christian west, fast emerged out of the stifling morass of the Middle Ages, also dubbed as the "Dark Age", into the modern era of religious tolerance, secular polity, path-breaking scientific advances and socio-economic development. The Muslim world, on the other hand, remained stuck up in the morass of religious bigotry and clerical polity which was the hall mark of the Middle Ages.

A conflict situation is inherent in the hiatus between medievalism and modernism that separates the Muslim world from the rest. An Islamic revivalism consequent upon the rise of Muslim power and oil-generated prosperity during the later half of the 20th century has greatly sharpened the conflict. That is what really is the clash of civilizations all about, and not strictly a clash between Islam and Christianity only. Jihadi terrorism and the war on it are its tragic manifestations.

7

The Muslim World

The Left-overs of History

The most distinguishing trade mark of the Muslim world in general, with the solitary exception of Turkey, is its professedly religious character and espousal of Islamism in varying degrees. It ranges from the hard Wahabi Islam of Saudi Arabia to the soft and mild one of the South East Asian countries like Malayasia and Indonesia, with Bangladesh and Pakistan some where in the middle. These countries have no compunction in officially proclaiming to be Islamic States, even though Malayasia and Bangladesh have sizeable non-Muslim populations.

In Saudi Arabia, school children are taught not only to be loyal to their Muslim brethren but also to consider infidels (non-believers) as their enemies. In the Muslim holy month of Ramadan, all eating-houses in Riyad and other cities and towns are compulsorily closed from dawn to dusk during fasting hours of the Muslims. The religious police keep patrolling the streets to haul up the defaulters. At the airport, the baggages of Indians (Hindus) are thoroughly checked to ensure that they don't carry the images of gods because Islam strictly prohibits image or idol worship. And Shariat law which prescribes the punishment of eye for an eye and tooth for a tooth is strictly enforced. Lierally. When an Indian immigrant caused damage to an eye of a local in course of a brawl, it was ordered that one of his eyes be gorged out under the Islamic system of criminal justice.

The case of Saudi Arabia is just illustrative. The excesses of the Islamic Revolutionary guards in Iran after the overthrow of the Shah are well known. After the election of a fundamentalist like Ahmadinejad as President of Iran in 2005, the religious police appear to have become active again. According to media reports, they are out on the streets stopping people from listening to Western music and seizing audio cassettes. Between Saudi Arabia, the custodian of the two holiest Islamic shrines at Mecca and Madina and apostle of rigid Sunni Islam, and Ayatollah Khomeni's Iran, the hub of Shiete Islam, the picture of the Muslim world is complete. It is a picture of Muslim peoples ceasing to grow in civilisational terms beyond the Middle Ages. It is a picture of a whole chunk of humanity numbering over a billion remaining stand still in a period of history when religion superceded everything else in man's collective endeavour.

It was a period when religion had overriding influence over the lives of the people in the western world also, as mentioned before. In the 16th century and earlier, the western society was also under the grip of the tradition-bound-supra-national institution of the Christian church. Those who lived in Central and Western Europe were members of the Roman Catholic church while those living in Russia and majority of those in the Balkan Peninsula belonged to the Greek Orthodox church. But beginning 16th century, the European society took a giant stride in the pursuit of knowledge and intellectual enlightenment which started thoroughly eroding the hold of religion over the minds of the people. When the Polish priest Copernicus set the records straight about the place of earth in the solar system, the Italian astronomer Galileo confirmed it by perfecting the telescope and also laid the foundation for development of mechanics and dynamics, the Scotman John Napier invented logarithms and first used the decimal point and the Englishman William Gilbert experimented with magnetic bodies and named a certain phenomenon as 'electric', the European society moved closer to the modern age.

Such foundational developments in natural sciences were matched by significant advances in the mental horizon of people above and beyond the crippling stranglehold of religion. An Italian preacher Bruno became an ardent exponent of 'modern' philosophy as distinguished from religious orthodoxy. Francis Bacon of England held that the 'new philosophy' must be inductive, experimental and utilitarian. Truth, according to him, could not be accepted on authority or verdict of past thinkers or deduced from some given axioms but derived from experience and experiments. Humanitarian scholars like Erasmus and Thomas More satirized and exposed the evils that had set in the lives of Christian clergymen.

All these modernizing influences resulted in the great religious upheaval of 16th century Europe going by the name of the 'Reformation'. It shook the very foundation of religion in the European society. Broadly, three main reformist groupings labeled as Lutherans, Calvinists and Anglicans, with a number of splinter groups, rose up to challenge the established church. To begin with, the radical 'Protestants' as the reformist groups were broadly referred to, were as intolerant of the Catholics as the latter had been to the reformists earlier. But in course of time as the dust of the upheaval settled down and the turmoil ended, the Europeans realized the value of tolerance of religious differences and accepted it as a way of life. The ultimate and most important impact of the Reformation' was the dethroning of institutionalized religion from the dominant position it occupied earlier in the sphere of human activities. It paved the way for the eclipse of theocratic polity in Europe and ushering in of religion-neutral or secular polity which is an essential attribute of the modern age.

All this while, the Muslim world remained blissfully immune from all that was going on in the most active part of the world. The Muslim peoples, by and large, are still immune to the seminal change that has taken place in the rest of the world discarding religion as the prime mover of social and political development. They have remained static, still stuck up in their stagnant moorings of religious orthodoxy. The result is that although inhabiting the earth at the same point of time, they are still living mentally in the pre-16th century world when religion reigned supreme over all other institutions of social and political life. To put it candidly, they are the left-overs of history.

It is not necessarily true of the ruling elites of Muslim countries. They are products of the modern age and are going about their business of governance with all the institutions of a modern state. But with all the frills of modernity, only a counted few states like Turkey and to a certain degree Malayasia, Indonesia and Bangladesh can claim to be modern political democracies today. The rest of the Muslim countries are under absolutist rulers of one kind or another, dynastic Kings, dubiously installed Presidents, military dictators etc. May be the Quoranic model of Caliphate suits them better to rule over their people.

But it is not the Muslim rulers, unlike their Arab and Turk ancestors, who are in the vanguard of the Islamist push. Far from that. They are political leaders of modern age, too wise and practical to think in terms of Islamisation of the world. On the other hand, most of the Muslim governments condemned the terrorists' attack on the U.S. on 9/11. Some of the leading Muslim countries of the Middle East like Saudi Arabia, Jordan and Egypt are close allies of the U.S. It is the radical Islamists having strong foot hold in these countries capable of swaying public opinion who are out to conquer the world for Islam.

In fact, the rulers of most of these countries are themselves facing the threat posed by Islamic extremism to their own regimes. Osama bin Laden is up in arms against the Saudi ruling establishment for its ties with America allowing U.S. troops on Arab soil. Calling upon Muslims to revolt against the Saudi regime in 1996, he declared: "The regime betrayed the 'Ummah' (Community of believers) and joined the 'Kufr' (unbelievers)". The fundamentalist 'Muslim Brotherhood" in Egypt has similarly been bitterly opposed to the ruling dispensation since the time of Nasser on the ground that it was un-Islamic. President Karimov of the Central Asian republic of Uzbekistan is being seriously challenged by the fundamentalist Islamic Movement of Uzbekistan. Same is the story about Algeria, Tunisia, Morocco and other Muslim countries which are not ruled by radical Islamic leaders themselves. In fact the Muslim world is in the throes of a war within, between moderate Muslim rulers and radical Islamists who have great popular appeal.

It is commonplace to attribute the rise of radical Islamism in Muslim world to the absence of political democracy in Muslim countries. With no secular political platform available for dissenters to protest against the regime, mosque becomes the only rallying point and hardcore Islam the only solution. It is a facile plea which has long been touted by well-meaning apologists to explain the rise of fundamentalism in Muslim countries. But they fail to explain why should Islamic fundamentalism be the only alternative to despotic rule in these countries. Despotism is a political problem and is supposed to arouse political opposition. Why should a despotic political dispensation give rise to fundamentalist religious opposition? Why is there no political opposition to an oppressive religious regime like that of Khameni's or Ahmadinejad's Iran?

The answer lies in the fact that the Muslim world is still sunk in the medieval milieu of over-riding supremacy of religion in polity. The autocratic rulers of Egypt, Algeria, Tunisia etc. are targets of fundamentalists not because they are despotic but because they are dubbed un-Islamic. That is the crux of the problem of the Muslim world. The moderate rulers of Muslim countries are faced with the war within not because they are authoritarian but because of the medievalist or anachronic mind-set of their people.

A few facts will illustrate. When the Emir of Kuwait proposed to give the women the right to vote, the duly elected Kuwaity Parliament totally rejected the proposal. Similarly, when the Saudi crown Prince Abdullah (now King) proposed to allow women in his country to drive, stiff popular opposition forced him to drop the move. Even in Palestine, the moderate PLO leader Mahmoud Abbas, successor to the legendary Yasser Araft, is being seriously challenged by Islamic militant groups like Hamas and Islamic Jihad. "A similar dynamic" writes Fareed Zakaria, "is evident elsewhere in the Arab world. In Oman, Qatar, Bahrain, Jordan and Morocco, on virtually every political issue, the monarchs are more liberal than the societies over which they reign". ("The Future of Freedom" by Fareed Zakaria, published in 2003).

The upshot of it all is that the Muslim peoples, by and large, are still mentally living in the Middle Ages when religion reigned supreme. They are the left-overs of history who have not yet arrived in the modern age. Yet these are the people with anachronistic mind-set who are calling the shots and setting the tone in Muslim countries.

Turkey is the solitary exception, but that is a different story. Here modernism was thrust upon the people by an absolutist secular ruler like Mustafa Kemal Attaturk. He not only kept religion totally out of the public sphere but also outlawed the Dervish sects, purged Arabic and Persian words from Turkish language, introduced the Latin alphabet and abolished the caliphate in 1922 to snap all links with Arab Islamism. He succeeded largely because he emerged as the redeemer of Turkey after its defeat in the First World War which had robbed it of the glory of the vast Ottoman Empire. As a result, Turkey has since grown into a vibrant democracy with a flourishing economy nearly at par with the developed world.

Another absolutist ruler, The Shah of Iran, tried to foist modernism on his left-over people in course of the second half of the 20th century but he came a cropper. He was not only overthrown himself but Iran plunged into the dark age of Shiite theocracy which has continued to this day. More of it in the next chapter.

Head count democracies are not necessarily the panacea for a people who are still captive to medieval moorings. Algeria in North Africa which wrested freedom from French imperialism in date 1960's had a taste of it in 1989. In the election held that year, radical Islamists emerged victorious over the moderates who ruled the country. The ruling party had to reject the electoral verdict to keep the fundamentalist Islamists at bay. If a head count is taken in the Muslim world today, it would be fundamentalist Islamists who will capture power in most of the countries and then destroy the very liberal democratic character of the state as Hitler and Mussolini did in Germany and Italy. That is the predicament of the Muslim world today and not necessarily the absence of formal head count democracy. For democracy is both an attribute and product of the modern age. As such, it is no remedy for the mind-set of left-over peoples without other modernising influences coming into play.

The Regression Syndrome

When the Muslim world from Malaysia in South East Asia to Egypt in the Middle East became free from the shackles of western imperialism around mid 1950's, religion or Islam was nowhere the center of attention for the rulers or people of these countries. Malaya, which later expanded into Malaysia, was concerned with polishing off the last vestiges of communist guerrilla's battling it out in remote areas on the birth of the independent republic. Indonesia after attaining independence from Dutch imperialism was the home of the largest Muslim population in the world, but promoting Islam was nowhere in its national agenda. On the other hand, it had the dubious distinction of having the biggest Communist Party in the world after the erstwhile Soviet Union and China. It emerged as a leading light of the Non-Aligned Movement in a bi-poler world by organizing the famous Bandung meet.

In the Middle East, rise of Nasser to power in Egypt in late 1950's lightened the scene in the Arab world long under the grip of imperial powers and decadent rulers. He emerged as the messiah of Arab unity and socio-economic development on modern lines. He made his mark in the international arena as one of the pillars of Non-Alignment alongwith Nehru and Tito. With his metropolitan education and Army background, much like Kamal Attaturk, he was a tailor-made modern leader who could do to Egypt and the Arab world what Kemal Attaturk did to Turkey. Even if he could not do that, he was clear in his mind not to mix religion with politics.

Nasser's vision of a united, modern and progressive Arab world was shared by most of the rulers of the region. The Baathists in Iraq and generals in Syria who ruled these countries were modern men with secular approach to politics. The capitals of Arab countries like Cairo, Baghdad, Damascus and Beirut appeared as modern and progressive as those of the western world. So much so that in 1956 an Arab intellectual wrote in a survey for the 'Atlantic Monthly': "Today Islam is moving toward a position more lijke that of western religion, with separation of Church and state". (Quoted in "Future of Freedom" by Fareed Zakaria, 2003).

The other major Muslim country outside the Arab region – Iran – was going through its own phase of modernization under the strong arm of the Shah. Moulded every bit in the western way of life, he prided in being a link in the chain of a dynastic monarchy which was 2500 years old, thus harking back to the pre-Islamic glory of the old Persian Empire. It was like the 16th and 17th century Europeans recalling their pre-christian past with nostalgia about the virtues of the pagan civilization of ancient Greece. And just as it helped the west to herald the modern era, the Shah hoped to hustle his country through to the modern age in quick time.

With proddings and financial and technological assistance from America, with which he was closely aligned in the bi-polar world, the Shah launched upon the modernization of Iran with unusual alacrity. The country was put on the road to socio-economic development with growing economy and emergence of a prosperous middle class. Women were prodded to come out of seclusion, receive education and join the men-folk in different walks of life. Emulating the Shah and the ruling elite, men and women were increasingly taking to modern western style in their dress and demeanor. All this, particularly women's education and discarding the 'chador' was anathema to the Iranian clergy.

The tragedy of the Shah was that in his drive to modernize, he reckoned without his hosts-the Muslim people of Iran steeped in medieval orthodoxy. You can not transform a whole people overnight by the fiat of the state. As opposition to his modernizing drive grew, the Shah tried to suppress it despotically. This offended the liberal democratic opinion in the country. As the opposition to his rule grew, repression increased alienating large segments of the population including left inclined intellectuals, middle-class intelligentsia, liberal democrat opponents of the regime and of course the Shiite Muslim clergy having large following. The doyen of them was Ayatolla Rudollah Khomeni.

What is not so well known about the Shah's reformist zeal is the progressive land reform measures he adopted during his rule. He curbed the power of certain ancient landed elite groups by expropriating large and middle-sized estates for the benefit of about four million small farmers. His policies led to strong economic growth in Iran during 1960's and 70's. One of his major modernization measures was the extension of suffrage to the women of Iran which enabled them to come out and participate in the political process. In 1963, women loyal to the Shah were admitted into the Parliament. Above all, the Shah implemented the policy of compulsory unveiling which was taboo for Muslim women. Under it, women of all ages were ordered to forgo the Islamic dress code and enjoy the western and eastern fashion prevailant in the world. These measures in particular made the Muslim clergy furious against the regime.

Ayatollah Komeni came out in the open as a bitter critic of the Shah and his American backers. He was exiled to Turkey in 1963-64 from where he later shifted to France and built up an opposition movement based at Paris. Meanwhile, opposition to the Shah was mounting in the country. The leftists and nationalists were angry against his palpably pro-American stance. The liberal democratic elements were annoyed with his repressive measures against political dissent. And the fundamentalist Islamic groups were up in arms against his secular reformist policies, particularly in respect of women's rights. The combined opposition to the regime burst forth on the streets of Teheran in September 1978 when thousands of protesters were brutally suppressed by armed forces. As violent protests ceased to stop, the Prime Minister, Dr Shapour Bakhtiar, a liberal democrat and a long time opposition leader himself, asked the Shah to abdicate and leave Iran. On January 16, 1979, the Shah made an inglorious exit from Iran with no one to shed any tears for a man who had done so much to modernize and develop the country.

The remarkable outcome of the developments was not the ouster of the Shah, which was perhaps the inevitable denouement of his absolutist regime, but the process of regression of Iranian society that followed. Dr Shapour Bakhtiar, the liberal democrat Prime Minister who headed the government after the departure of the Shah, took a number of steps to calm down the situation and herald a new democratic dispensation in the country. He dissolved the SAVAK (national Organisation for information and security) which had become infamous for its ruthless prosecution of political dissenters and freed all political prisoners. To cap it all, he allowed Ayatollah Khomeni to return to Iran asking him to create a Vatican-like state in "Qom", his religious headquarters. He called upon the other opposition groups to cooperate in preserving the democratic constitution and promised free elections.

But Ayatollah Komeni and his fundamentalist Islamic revolutionaries had no interest in liberal democracy. They would settle for nothing short of a hard Islamic rule under the Ayatollah. Komeni fiercely rejected Dr Bakhtiar's proposals and appointed an interim Islamic government on his own. His Islamic militia, the Revolutionary guards did the rest. Liberal democrats, nationalists who did not coalesce with the Islamists, and leftists – who had all joined in demanding the ouster of the Shah

– were now themselves at the receiving end of the Islamic regime.

The overthrow of Shah's despotism did not usher in a democratic dispensation but a worst kind of dictatorship of the Mullahs. The liberal and progressive elements fell by the wayside. In the immediate aftermath of the Revolution, the Islamic Revolutionary Guards dictated terms to all other segments of society. Women were the worst sufferers at the hands of the fundamentalists. There were numerous cases of brutal torture of women for violation of strict Islamic laws.

According to Ghazoll Motiagh, an Iranian woman living in the US, a quote from an online book on the subject says: "According to a `religious' decree, virgin women prisoners must as a rule be raped before their execution, lest they go to paradise". Therefore, the night before execution, a guard rapes the condemned woman. After her execution, the religious judge at the prison writes out a marriage certificate and sends it to the victim's family, alongwith a box of sweets. In a written confession in January 1990, Sarmast Akhlaq Tabandeh, a senior Guards corps interrogator, recounted one such case in Shiraz prison. ('Robbed of simple pleasures' by Ghazoll Motiagh, 2004).

In the follow up of the Islamic Revolution in Iran, the Mullahs spilled more blood through gallows and torture chambers than the previous regime. As Ayatollah Khomeni gradually drained power from the civilian government, opposition began to grow. The Islamic Republic then entered the usual cycle of repression, dragging the country into a virtual civil war. At the end of it, Khomeni's theology prevailed. They rammed through a new constitution making Ayatollah Khomeni the supreme head of the Islamic regime. Thus in one giant leap backwards, Iran regressed into 1400 years old theocracy. Like Caliphs Abu Bakra and Omar, he became 'King and Pope in one', exercising supreme authority over the Iranian state from his religious headquarters at 'Qom'.

After Ayatolla Khomeni's death in 1989, a more moderate leader Hasemi Rafsanjani headed the government. In 1997, he was succeeded by Khatami, another moderate politician, as President and head of the government. But the supreme authority in matters of state vested in Ayatollah Ali Khameni, Ayatolla Khomeni's successor, firmly ensconced at 'Qom'. And with the election of Ahmadinejad, a hardcore Islamist with Revolutionary Guard antecedents, as the President of Iran in August 2005, Iran is back to square one as far as the hard Islamic character of the republic is concerned.

The remarkable fact about the Iranian Revolution is that the Shah was overthrown not because his regime was despotic or repressive (there were other equally despotic regimes in the Muslim world) nor because the country's economy was in doldrums as during the communist regimes in Eastern Europe before their downfall (Iran was industrializing and Iranian economy was growing under the Shah), nor again because the Shah was closely aligned with America (there were and are many other Muslim countries closely aligned with the U.S), but because the Shah was modernizing

Iran socially and politically which was considered Unislamic.

Iran is an archetypal case of regression into the dark ages at its worst or most glaring. But other Muslim countries have not been immune from the regression syndrome that set in the Muslim world after its emergence from the shackles of western imperialism in the latter half of the 20th century. As long as the first generation political leaders of immediate post-independence years like Nasser, Sukarno and Bourguiba were around, the societies over which they presided appeared to be forward looking. For they were metropolitan educated men with thoroughly secular outlook and approach in matters of national and international politics. They were deeply involved with socio-economic development of their peoples and steering their states through a troubled world sharply split between two power blocks. Israel was a chronic irritant in the Arab world, but they handled it on a state to state basis rather than going berserk with Islamic fundamentalism.

But with the departure of those leaders from the scene, the Muslim society somewhere along the line got caught up in the whirl-wind of a regression syndrome. It was not a result of economic decline or poverty or anything like that. On the other hand, the Arab world in particular got unusually rich on account of its oil wealth during the period in question. The non-Arab countries like Indonesia and Malaysia were also doing fairly well in terms of economic development. It was the anachronic mind-set of Muslim societies across the board that got afflicted with regression syndrome. The process has continued unabated. As a result, modernist leaders like the charismatic Nasser of yester years or Jordan's liberal king Abdullah or even secular nationalists like the late Yaser Arafat and his successor Mahmoud Abbas are no longer hailed in the Muslim world. The heroes of today are Osama bin Laden, Ayman-al-Zawahiri, Mullah Omar and the likes of them. It is the octopus like grip of this malady of regression over the Muslim world that has turned it into a fertile breeding ground of Jihadi terrorists.

Another area of darkness is Pakistan which has steadily marched backwards in time since its inception. More of it in the next chapter.

8

The Pakistan Connection

A Failed State Turned Jihadi

Pakistan was the child of the dubious two-nation principle which postulated that the Muslims of the Indian sub-continent constituted a separate nation. (The two-nation theory is palpably fallacious for the simple reason that India today is home to a bigger Muslim population than Pakistan). The apparent mid-wife that delivered it was the Muslim Leaque party of pre-partition India headed by its charismatic leader-Mohammad Ali Jinnah. A prectising barrister in India and England, having received his law degree from London, starting his political career as a young freedom-fighter in the Indian National Congress, M.A.Jinnah was a most unlikely leader of fanatical separatist Muslims of India. In their best-selling book on the advent of freedom in the sub-continent, Larry Collins and Dominque Lappierre write : "A more improbable leader of India's Muslim masses could hardly be imagined. The only thing Moslem about Mohammad Ali Jinnah was his parent's religion. He drank, ate pork, religiously shaved his beard every morning and just as religiously avoided the mosque each Friday." ("Freedom at Midnight", Lorry Collins and Dominque Happierre, 1976).

It was natural for a thoroughly modern and westernized leader like that to come to his own once his goal of a separate Muslim state was achieved. He made it very clear what his concept of Pakistan was at its very birth. His authentic definition of the state he founded single-handed was contained in his first address to the Constuent Assembly of Pakistan on 11 August 1947. He said : "You are free to go to your temples, you are free to go to your mosques, to any other places of worship in this state of Pakistan. We are starting in the days when there is no discrimination between one community and another, one caste or creed and another." And then referring to the Roman Catholics in England, he went on to say: "Today you might say with justice that Roman Catholics and Protestants do not exist; What exists now is that everyman is a citizen, an equal citizen of great Britain and they are all members of the nation. Now, I think, we should keep that in front of us as our ideal and you will find that in course of time Hindus would cease to be Hindus and Muslim would cease to be Muslims, not in the religious sense, because that is the personal faith of each individual, but in the political sense as citizens of the state."

That was the clarion call of a modern nationalist leader steeped in British secular democratic traditions. It was another matter that prior to independence, he had vigorously preached for a separate homeland for India's Muslims. Once he succeeded in achieving his goal, he availed of every opportunity to proclaim that Pakistan was not going to be an exclusive or obscurantist Muslim state but a modern nation state for all its inhabitants irrespective of their religion. He thought it necessary to put it across to his people time and again to correct the aberration of the virulent separatist political movement which had brought about the creation of Pakistan.

Addressing a public rally at Dacca, the capital of erstwhile East Pakistan on 21 March 1948, Jinnah said: "You belong to a nation now. Make no mistake, Pakistan is not a theocracy or anything like that." Earlier in a broadest to the people of Australia on 9 February 1948, he clearly stated that Pakistan was not going to be a theocratic Muslim state. He repeated that in his broadcast to America also. Jinnah had good reasons to lay stress on the religion-neutral character of the nation-state he had carved out of united India of pre-independence days. For he visualized Pakistan as a modern multi-religious state with a sizeable population of Hindus and Sikhs. And if there had been no large-scale massacres and migrations of Hindus and Sikhs from Pakistan, they would have accounted for about 30 percent of the population of that country. Muhammad Munir, a retired Chief Justice of Pakistan, writes: "The Quido-e-Azam had not even imagined that there would be communal carnage and cross-migration on such a large scale as actually took place. He was confident that the non-Muslims would willingly accept the citizenship of the new state, as it was to be founded on principles which nobody, whether a Muslim or non-Muslim, could deny." ('From Jinnah To Zia',1981).

But Jinnah did not live long enough after the birth of Pakistan to cast it into the mould of modernity he had designed for it. He died of a terminal illness quietly in Karachi, unsung and unwept, on September 11, 1948. And, what is not so well known, he died a disappointed and disillusioned man because he could see signs of Pakistan sliding back into religious orthodoxy even before he passed away. Strong pressure had started building up to bring in Islam as the core ideology in the constitution of Pakistan which Jinnah was not prepared to accept. As his physical condition started declining, the Islamic-minded political leaders having the reins of government in their hands started brushing him aside in matters of the state (As the Governor General, Jinnah was only the constitutional head of the state and not of the government which was headed by Prime Minister Liaquat Ali Khan). So much so that according to some reports, he told his doctor as a dying man that creation of Pakistan was his greatest mistake in life.

The undoing of Jinnah and Islamisation of Pakistan began soon after he was out of the scene. In March 1949, six months after his passing away, the Pak Constuent Assembly passed the "Objective Resolution" containing unmistakable reference to religion and Islam in the following terms: "Whereas sovereignty over the Entire Universe belongs to Allah Almighty alone, and the authority which he has delegated to the state of Pakistan through its people for being exercised within the limits prescribed by Him is a sacred trust.....

"Where in the Muslims of Pakistan should be enabled individually and collectively to order their lives in accordance with the teachings and requirements of Islam as set out in the Holy Quran and Sunnah." Needless to say, the "Resolution" was passed by Muslim members only because the few Hindu members of the Constituent Assembly boycotted the session.

In the light of what followed, the "Objective Resolution" was only a modest beginning of Pakistan's backwards march to Islamism. Liaquat Ali Khan, who took credit for hammering out the "Objective Resolution", was not actually an Islamist. He had to bring in Islam in the constitutional document to satisfy the growing Islamism of his constituents. As long as he was around as the only towering leader after Jinnah, Pakistan's slide back into religious fanaticism was somehow kept in check. But even before the state of Pakistan could draw up an outline of its constitution, the Prime Minister Liaquat Ali Khan was assassinated on 16 October 1951. That was the beginning of the end of Pakistan as a modern secular democratic nation state.

With Mullas and Moulvis calling the shots and no Hindus and Sikhs to target at, their number having shrunk to negligible level in Pakistan, they started hunting for Ahmadi community – a Muslim sect which was anathema to the orthodox Muslim clergy.

Large-scale anti-Ahmadi rioting and violence broke out in all the major towns of Pakistan (then West Pakistan) in February-March 1953 in which about a hundred Ahmadies were reported to have lost their lives. These disturbances were the first over manifestations of the Pakistani society in regression.

A commission of enquiry headed by justice Mohammad Munir (who later rose to be the Chief Justice of Pakistan) enquired into the events and submitted an exhaustive report in April 1954. The report is a store house of materials pointing to the backwards march of Pakistan into the quagmire of Islamic fundamentalism. On going through the report, an enlightened Pakistan's intellectual wrote to justice Munir: "Being very close to the Quaid-e-Azam since 1936 until his demise, I have learnt at his feet lessons which I shall never forget. I swear he did not at any time envisage the creation of a backward theocratic state. He did not create Pakistan to put on the map a state which should live in the clouds of pre-medievalism sliding backward instead of marching forward and in indecent haste to slide in the nether depths of degradation and theocracy."

That might have appeared to be an over-reaction at the time the letter was written, but it proved to be remarkably prophetic in more senses than one. The political structure of the Pakistani state started collapsing and democratic frame work decaying fast after that. Between 1954 and 1956, there was change of Prime Ministers from Khwaja Nazimuddin to Mohammad Ali Bogra to Chaudhri Mohammed Ali to H.S. Suhratoardy. While Pakistan anyhow managed to adopt its first constitution in 1956, it was unceremoniously abrogated in 1958 with the establishment of Ayub Khan's military rule. Since then Pakistan has alternated between military dictatorship and dubious democratic regimes with ominous regularity.

While anti-Ahmadi frenzy remained in check during the long period of Ayub's and his successor Yahya Khan's military dictatorships, the backslide to Islamism was not so. Ayub Khan gave to Pakistan his own constitution introducing the Presidential system in order to consolidate and legitimise his rule. And by his first amendment of 1963, he formally declared Pakistan as an 'Islamic Republic'. From Ayub Khan's ouster in March 1969 to the adoption of a new constitution in August 1973 re-establishing the Parliamentary system, was a period of unprecedented turmoil in Pakistan. During this period, the country went through the trauma of defeat in the short war with India, separation of East Pakistan as independent state of Bangladesh, ouster of Yahya Khan and assumption of power by Zulfiquar Ali Bhutto. These traumatic events precluded any sectarian polemics, but Pakistan's regression into Islamic theocracy continued unabated

Z.A. Bhutto who emerged as the redeemer of Pakistan after the separation of Bangladesh took another big stride towards theocracy in Pakistan. Ayub Khan had declared Pakistan as an 'Islamic Republic' and left it at that. Z.A. Bhutto officially declared Islam as the official religion of Pakistan. Not content with that, he adopted the Principles of Policy which talked of compulsory teaching of the Holy Quran and giving encouragement to Islamiat, Islamic way of life, Islamic morals etc. That set the tone for further Islamisation of the country.

Once he uncorked the genii of religion, anti-Ahmadi fanaticism, lying dormant for nearly two decades of extra-ordinary political developments, erupted with full force. There were numerous cases of violence against members of the Ahmadi community in Pakistan causing considerable damage to life and property. According to Ahmadi sources, about 75 Ahmadis lost their lives in the process. And, instead of reversing the trend as any modern ruler would have done, Z.A. Bhutto succumbed to the orthodox Muslim clergy and did what the earlier rulers had shrunk from doing. On 7 September 1974, Bhutto's government declared Ahmadis as a non-Muslim minority in Pakistan. Jinnah had been Zulfi Bhutto's idol in his younger days, and yet when in power, he undid Jinnah as no one else had done before.

But it was left to General Zia-Ul-Haque, who upset Z.A. Bhutto and captured power in July 1977, to take the process of regression to its logical end. By his provisional constitutional order of 1981, he made a legal distinction between Muslims and non-Muslims, putting the Ahmadis in the latter category and thus reducing them to the status of second class citizens in their own country. To top it all, General Zia promulgated his Ordinance number 20 in April 1984 putting severe restrictions on the religious freedom of Ahmadis. That opened the gateway to the persecution of this highly talented community by the state in Pakistan. This resulted in the flight of the religious head of the community Mirza Tahir Ahmad - from Pakistan to London towards the end of April 1984. Since then, the head of this religious sect having followers in both

Pakistan and India has been living, preaching and practicing his faith in exile in England.

Incidentally, Ahmadis were among the more qualified and successful professionals in Pakistan when the new state came into being. Apart from a sizeable chunk of officer cadre in the Armed forces, the first foreign minister of Pakistan - Sir Mohammad Zafrullah Khan - belonged to the Ahmadi community. And the most notable of them all was the distinguished scientist Dr.Abdus Salam based in America, the only Muslim scientist born in Pakistan to be awarded the Nobel Prize. For a highly qualified community like that to become alien in their own country on account of their religious faith, is a measure of Pakistan's regression into the dark ages of religious intolerance.

For his part, General Zia did everything during his long regime to take Pakistan backwards to the 'Nizam-e-Mustafa' of 1300 years ago. The first instalment of 'Nizam-e-Mustafa' was introduced when the General promulgated five Ordinances on Islamisation of criminal laws in 1979. These related to offences like drinking alcohol, adultery and offences against property for which barbarous punishments reminiscent of medieval times were provided.

Scenes of medieval savagery were witnessed when there were public whippings of offenders under the Islamic law in General Zia's Pakistan. The punishments were publicized in advance and large numbers gathered to watch the outrageous scenes. It was given out that those who witnessed the horror would be deterred from committing those crimes. A patently facile presumption disputed by modern criminologists and penologists. But General Zia and the Muslim clergy had no use for advances made in criminological sciences in modern times.

Not quite satisfied by what he had done, General Zia declared that all laws would be replaced by 'Shariat' and "there will be nothing in Pakistan which is repugnant to Islam." The suffocating situation in Zia's Pakistan was summed up by Saleem Qureshi in an article in "International Political Science Review", 1981: "In Pakistan, an extremely repressive and brutal regime has entrenched itself by championing Islamic reforms and by imposing fiscal and penal laws which, to the rest of the world, look barbaric and medieval, but which have aroused hardly any opposition within the country because they have been implemented in the name of Islam." (Quoted in "Pakistan: The Garrison State", Dr. K.L. Kamal, 1982)

From a thorough Islamisation of Pakistan for which his predecessors had prepared the ground, it was but a short step to Jihad in the neighborhood. With the chronic Kashmir dispute coming in handy, India was a readymade target for General Zia to launch a virulent jihad. But by a combination of international circumstances, gateway to a more promising playing field for Jihad was opened to Pakistan in neighboring Afganistan. It was around the time General Zia was hurtling Pakistan through to medieval Islamic rule, Soviet occupation of Afganistan and American resolve to fight it out through Mujahideen came as a windfall to Pakistan. America was looking for a surrogate to take on the Russians with any amount of support in terms of funds, arms and equipments. It was General Zia's opportunity of a life time to step out and set upon a course of jihad in international arena. He grabbed it with both hands.

Then onwards, Pakistan became a conduit for transfer of enormous amount of money, arms and ammunitions to the odd assortment of Jihadis comprising hardcore Islamists from different Muslim countries, besides the Afgan tribal warlords, for fighting the Russians. Incidentally, Osama bin Laden was one of them. The agency which handled the Afgan Jihad was Pakistan's Inter Service Intelligence (ISI) which had already earned notoriety for sponsoring and directing Jihadi terrorism in Kashmir and Punjab (India). General Zia took full advantage of American profligacy in the jihad against the Russians in Afganistan to equip Pakistan for its eternal war against India. One of the major side benefits that Pakistan reaped out of its role in the Afgan Jihad was crossing the line in its clandestine nuclear programme with the help of China while the U.S. kept looking the other way. More about it later.

General Zia was at the peak of his glory as a leading Jihadi in this part of the world when his career was abruptly cut short by Providence. He died in a mysterious plane crash inside Pakistan in August 1988, even as the Afgan Jihad was nearing its successful conclusion. The V.V.I.P. aircraft which took off from Bahawalpur with President Zia and some top Army officials on board crashed soon after being air borne, leaving no survivors. The crash was reportedly attributed to some mechanical fault in the aircraft, which was highly surprising considering the extraordinary nature of the passengers it was carrying. His son who later became some one in Pakistani politics went public with the charge that the crash was man-made, but no more. It still remains a mystery. It is another matter that not many tears were shed in Pakistan, or outside for that matter, for him.

It would be wrong to assume that Pakistan's tryst with Jihad ended with Zia-ul-Haq. Far from that. May be Zia was a fundamentalist Islamist by conviction. May be not. May be his successors as heads of government - Benazir Bhutto and Nawaz Sharrif were liberal Muslims by faith. Benazir Bhutto actually touted her western education to claim that under her leadership, Pakistan had emerged as a moderate liberal Muslim state in the backdrop of growing fundamentalism in the Muslim world. But when it came to the crunch, particularly in regard to the intensifying Jihad against India, she did not flinch from asserting that Pakistan was a part of the Muslim "Ummah". Nawaz Sharrif had no such pretensions. The Pakistan Muslim Leage faction which catapulted him to power after Benazeer Bhutto had actually the blessing and support of General Zia during his life time. In any case, the emergence of Taliban as a potent fundamentalist Islamic force and its eventual capture of power in post-Soviet Afganistan happened during post-Zia regimes of Benazeer Bhutto and Nawaz Sharrif with their full support.

With the benign support of Pak government and its ISI, Peshawar was the hub of international Islamic Jihad during the Afgan campaign. It continued to be so well after the end of the campaign with Soviet withdrawal from Afganistan in 1989. Pakistani Madarsas in and around Peshawar continued to train and motivate Jihadis from diverse Muslim countries. One of the well known training center was 'Maktabai-Khidmiat' which served as the nucleus of jihad across the world. It is reported that most of the terrorists involved in the first World Trader Centre bomb blast in 1993 had been at the 'Maktaba' some time or the other.

Among the notorious Arab fundamentalists sheltered in Peshawar at that time were Mohammad Showkial Islambouli, a borther of the Egyptian President Anwar Sadat's assassin and a ring leader of Egyptian Jihadi outfit 'Ikhwanul Muslimeen'. And also Colonel Mohammad Ibrahim al Makkawai sentenced to death in absentia by the government of Egypt.

After the ouster of the Russians from Afganistan, the U.S. virtually abandoned the country leaving it to its ally Pakistan to handle it, put some order so that a pro-American regime could take over. It was another God sent opportunity for Pakistan to establish its own hegemony over Afganistan. The Pakistanis first set their bet on the Pushtoon warlord Gulbuddin Hekmatyar who was already involved with Jihadi terrotrism against India in Kashmir. But he was an Afgan warlord in his own right, having given a tough fight to the Russians, with a strong base among the majority Pushtoon community. Apart from the fact that he was not able to end the intensive conflicts among the diverse warlords let loose after Russian withdrawal, Hekmatyar could not be trusted to play second fiddle to Pakistanis if he somehow succeeded in consolidating his position.

Pakistan would settle for nothing short of complete control and supremacy over Afganistan as a part of a bigger Islamic Republic of Pakistan. That would give it a tremendous boost in its Jihad against its eternal adversary-India.

In view of the above, Pakistan discarded Hekmatyar in favour of a more subservient and dependable customer of its own creation. Mullah Omar and his Taliban were the obvious choice. For Taliban consisted almost entirely of young men from the Pushtoon tribal belt of Southern Afganistan and Pakistan's Northern Areas well indoctrinated by Madarsas in and around Peshwar. The Madarsas in Pakistan are well known for catching them young and turning their pupils into hard-core Islamists. These highly motivated youngmen were trained, armed and equipped by Pakistan Army under the over all supervision of the ISI and launched into Taliban's fight for control over Afganistan. The Pak Army not only trained, armed and equipped them but also fought alongside with them in course of the campaign. Senior Pak Army officials guided them in strategy and tactics of the operations.

All this went on in the open, without America or any other international body raising a little finger. With the U.S. gloating over the demise of the Soviet Union and relaxing at the end of the cold war, Afganistan was left at the mercy of Pakistan to do as it liked. America did of course expect that Pakistan would bring about a semblance of order in Afganistan. As the Taliban, comprehensively aided and guided by Pakistan Army, kept on advancing, the U.S. kept expressing its concern to Pakistan about the religious character and composition of

Taliban. Pakistan kept assuring the U.S. that Mullah Omer was a pious religious leader pitted against tribal warlords and that Afganistan would be stable and pro-American under the Taliban. Under the circumstances, Taliban established its rule over 85 percent of the Afgan territory barring the northern fringe bordering Central Asia and Iran by 1996. Pakistan promptly recognized the Taliban regime headed by Mullah Omar as the legitimate government of Afganistan.

Meanwhile, international Jihadis drawn from different Muslim countries continued to be sheltered in and around Peshawar. If the U.S. pressurized Pakistan to expel some of the most notorious among them, like the two Egyptian fugitives mentioned above, the Pakistanis carried on the formality by just pushing them out of the border into close-by Jalalabad of South Afganistan well under the control of the Taliban. It did not matter to Pakistan that the Islamic brigade based in Pak-Afgan territory under its control bombed the World Trade Centre in U.S. and India's commercial hub in Bombay in 1993 and was threatening American interests in Egypt, Algeria, Morocco etc.

It did not matter to Pakistan even when Osama bin Laden quietly moved into Afganistan and set up his Al Quida base under the patronage of Mullah Omar in 1996 when Taliban took control of the country. Osama kept fine-tuning his terror network, targeting American interests worldwide, planning and executing attacks on American embassies in Kenya and Tanzania, receiving medical treatment in Pakistani military hospitals. As long as the Clinton administration kept over-looking these ominous developments, except for a little squeezing here and there and questioning about the fundamentalist character of the Taliban, Pakistan couldn't care less.

On the other hand, a Jihadi regime in place in Afganistan was kind of a bonanza for Pakistan in its ongoing Jihad against India. It was not a mere chance that the success of Taliban in Afganistan coincided with the peak of Jihadi terrorism in Kashmir. As the Talibanis went on scoring victories after victories in Afganistan, the Pak sponsored Jiahdis went on intensifying their terror campaign in Kashmir and India. Both went on hand in hand as there was a close causal relation between the two. It was not a mere coincidence that the Indian Airlines plane that was hijacked from Kathmandu in December 1999 was taken to Kandahar or that the Taliban authorities played a prominent role in securing the release of hard-core Jihadis like Moulana Masood Azhar and Omar Sheikh. The ring master behind all these feats of Taliban's conquest of Afganistan and devastating terror in Kashmir and India was none other than the super Jihadi state of Pakistan.

Created by the British to maintain their foothold in South Asia after the end of the empire, sustained by America as a client state during the cold war and ruled by military dictators for over 31 years out of 58 from its birth in 1947 to 2005, with lucid intervals of tottering democratic regimes, Pakistan has turned out to be an eminently failed state. No wonder that it has taken to Jihad against India to keep itself afloat. That is its only raison deter in the eyes of its people. And yet it claims to be, and has been accepted as such, a part of the international coalition in the war against Jihadi terrorism. That is one of the crowing ironies of international diplomacy in the opening years of the 21st century.

Benazeer Bhutto once said that Pakistan can be ruled only by those who are blessed by the three A's, that is, the Army, America and Allah. It has come to be literally true. For Pakistan is ruled today not by those who are blessed by the Army but by Army itself. The rulers are evidently blessed by America which has hailed them as coalition partners in the war against terror. And as 'warriors of Allah' in the ongoing Jihad against India, they obviously have His blessings too.

Pakistan's Multiple Face

It surprised even the Americans, Pakistan's instant acceptance of all demands made on it in the war against Taliban provoked by 9/11. In the run up to the war, Collin Powell, the U.S. Secretary of State, and his Deputy Richard Armitage jotted down seven hard points that needed to be clinched with Pakistan, even if it meant talking tough. The list contained stiff demands as follows: -

(1) Stoppage of transportation of arms and all logistical support to Osama bin Laden and his Al Quida based in Taliban territory.

(2) Full over flight and landing rights for air strikes against Taliban.

(3) Access to Pakistan's naval and air bases and borders.

(4) Sharing of intelligence and information about immigration.

(5) Pakistan to condemn 9/11 strike against America and curb all internal expression of support for terrorism against the U.S. and its' coalition partners.

(6) Stoppage of all transportation of fuel to Taliban and preventing Pakistani Jihadis from joining the Taliban.

(7) If Osama bin Laden and his Al Quida network was found involved in 9/11 and Taliban continued to harbor them, Pakistan should end support to Taliban and help the U.S. to demolish Osama and Al Quida.

It would be a hard call. If Pakistan accepted the above demands, it would mean the end of all that Pakistan had so assiduously built up for around a decade since the end of Russian occupation. The Americans could not be so sure about Pakistan's response. Their last card was: "either with us or against us". It worked, right on target as it hit the bull's eye. So when Collin Powell called Parvez Musharraf to convey what the U.S required of Pakistan in the war on terror, the Pak President immediately yielded on each of the seven counts in one breath, without even taking a breather. There were no ifs and buts in Musharraf's response. The American Secretary of State and his colleagues in the State Department not only felt relieved but also agreeably surprised.

But there was nothing so surprising about it after all. Pakistan knew that if it dithered this time, initiative in the war against Taliban and Al Quida in this part of the world would pass on to its arch rival India, long smarting under the onslaught of Jihadi terror. Pakistan would never allow that to happen, even it meant eating its own humble pie. In fact Pakistan's vulnerability to U.S pressure goes back to its very inception as an independent state.

Thanks to its inborn anti-Indianism, Pakistan has been a state on offer for any world power to take it under its wings right from the beginning. It proclaimed its antagonism to India by attacking Kashmir on the morrow of its inauguration and offered itself for adoption by a godfather to score over India. It was a time cold war had begun and the two Super Powers were on the lockout for satellite states across the world. The Americans were particularly keen to spot out their targets among newly independent states to contain communism in Asia. Pakistan ideally suited the U.S strategic interest in this regard. Here was a new state waiting to be fitted in the U.S Scheme of things in the on-going cold war for a pittance in terms of arms and military hardware. The Americans made no mistake and picked up Pakistan as one of their satellites in Asia. They knew or must have known that Pakistan's real interest lay not in fighting communism but building up its armed muscles to settle scores with India. But they didn't care as long as it served their overall cold war strategy.

The U.S tried to rope in India also in its scheme of alliances against communism. The American Secretary of State, John Foster Dulles visited India in May'1953 in pursuit of this mission. On the eve of his visit, an idea was floated that India should have its own Zone of influence in South East Asia covering Burma and Thailand as a protective ring against communist expansion. But India under Nehru opted for non-alignment instead, in keeping with his oft-repeated observation: "India is too big a country to align herself with either of the Super Powers".

Following on the heels of Dulles, Richard Nixon, who later became the U.S President, visited the sub-continent in December 1953. Veteran Journalist Durga Das who met Nixon during his visit was to write later: "The American attitude to Pakistan, I gathered from Nixon, was: 'Here is a little chap who is prepared to stand up and fight the Moscow bully. Shall we not applaud him and give him all the help and encouragement we can?".

With the U.S thus ready to embrace with open arms, Pakistan entered into a defence pact with it in 1954. It provided for helping Pakistan with around 2-3 billion dollars worth of free arms ranging from modern aircraft and latest American tanks to sophisticated Armour. In return, Pakistan joined the SEATO (South East Asia Treaty Organization) in September 1954. It also joined the Baghdad Pact (Which was later re-named as Central Treaty Organization after withdrawal of Iraq from it) in June 1955. The treaties were parts of Dulles plan of encircling Soviet Union and communist China with anti-communist military alliances.

As a *quid pro quo,* the U.S. and its allies propped up Pakistan by adopting a Pakistan friendly approach to the Kashmir issue in the U.N Security Council. For Pakistan's sole motive and interest in joining the American band wagon in the cold war was India-baiting, particularly over Kashmir, and the U.S was, prepared to go along with that as long as it served its foreign policy objectives. At times, India had to depend on the Russian Veto to safeguard its position on the Kashmir issue in the U.N Security Council.

But to Pakistan's predicament, the cold war itself started progressively thawing after the Cuban missile crisis of 1962, as described earlier. As the détente stabilized and the two Super Powers started engaging with each other across the board by late 1960's, the U.S started losing interest in Pakistan's brief over Ksahmir issue. Pakistan was still an ally of the U.S' but no longer as necessary or useful as during the Dulles era. Pakistan got another opportunity to establish its usefulness to the U.S with the Russian occupation of Afganistan in early 1980's. The U.S used Pakistan as a channel to pump the Afgan resistance groups with funds and arms, allowing General Zia to strengthen Pak military machine also in the process. But no more. And eventually, when Russia was driven out of Afganistan, Soviet Union disintegrated and cold ended, America almost gave up Pakistan to sort out its problems with India bilaterally.

An American official in senior Bush administration clarified the position in clear terms. Peter Galbraith, the Chief South Asia Policy Advisor to the U.S senate foreign relations committee, told media persons in 1990 that "the basic fact is that the cold war is over, particularly in regard to South

Asia". He went on to elaborate that Pakistan and India could no longer play America and Russia against each other for their own benefit. He summed up by saying that the U.S and Soviet Russia "are not in the business of trying to solicit clients in that part of the world anymore".

With the end of bipolarity and America emerging as the lone Super Power during 1990's, Pakistan was no longer of much use to the U.S except as a past ally to be used occasionally in case of need. And not at the cost of India anyway, which was a much better bet for America as a strategic partner in Asia. This was amply demonstrated in the closing years of 1990's when the Pak Army under the command of General Musharraf crossed the line of control in Kashmir and indulged in the Kargil misadventure against India. Even as the Indian Army was giving a bloody nose to the Pakis in the rugged high mountainous region, the incumbent U.S President Clinton pressurized the Pak Premier Nawaz Sherif to withdraw from Kargil and respect the Line of Control. Incidentally, the hawks in Pakistan Army led by General Musharraf himself did not forgive Nawaz Sherif for his back tracking in Kargil and ultimately ousted him in a coup.

In this background, America's call to Pakistan to fall in line in the run upto the war on Taliban and Al Quida was not based on any warmth in the relationship but for logistical and tactical reasons. Pakistan's geographical location covering almost the entire southern flank of Afganistan made it the most suitable launching pad for the American offensive against Taliban. But for Pakistan, the situation was quite different from the cold war period for two reasons. First, it was required to provide full logistical support to the U.S in actual fighting right on its borders and not merely be a passive participant in a diplomatic war between two Super Powers, which was cold war all about. Second and more important, this time round, the enemy was not a distant Super Power or ideology of communism but Pakistan's own beloved progeny born and brought up in its own backyard.

In the circumstances, to be party to the destruction of its own creation was a bitter pill for Pakistan to swallow. General Musharraf jumped into the American bandwagon in the war against terror with a very heavy heart. And it was not a joy ride either with nothing to lose and everything to gain as during the halcyon days of the cold war (for Pakistan). Parvez Musharraf has since been doing a lot of tight rope walking to keep up his mask as a warrior against terror and keep the terror structure intact in his country at the same time.

His first task on joining the international coalition was to salvage his Army and ISI personnel deeply involved with Taliban and Al Quida in Afganistan. During the short interval between 9/11 and 10/7 (When America first struck the Taliban), large contingents of officers and men of Pakistan Army and ISI on duty with the Taliban were hastily evacuated back home. The exercise was both clandestine and open. It was aimed at covering up Pakistan connection in Osama's terror network on the one hand and rescuing Pakistani soldiers from being killed in the impending American strike. It served the U.S policy of demolishing the Taliban and Al Quida with minimal blood spilling.

Musharraf also heeded the U.S advise of shifting pro-Taliban elements from the top echelons of Pak Army and the I.S.I. But the cosmetic changes that he made were more in the nature of preventing any challenge to his own authority than purging the fundamentalist elements strongly entrenched in the set up. Pakistan also broke off diplomatic relations and de-recognized the Taliban regime as dictated by the U.S. It quietly acquiesced in the use of its air space and bases for lethal aerial attack on Taliban and its territory for landing of U.S Special Forces for intelligence and mopping up operations. It also made a pretence of sharing intelligence about Osama and Al Quida with the Americans, even though they did not trust the ISI in this regard.

During the thick of the war on November 10, 2001, the U.S President Bush met the Pak President in New York on the side lines of the U.N General Assembly meeting. The Talibanis were already on the retreat both in the north and the south. Mazar-e-Sharrif had fallen to the advancing Northern Alliance Forces the previous day. During the brief meeting, Musharraf affirmed his solidarity with America in 'the war against terror' only mildly expressing his concern about the Northern Alliance taking over Afganistan. By the time Kandahar fell to coalition forces and Taliban was decimated on December 7, 2001, Pakistan was touting itself as an active partner in the war against terror.

But facts tell a different story. During the closing days of the regime, Osma Bin Laden and Taliban leaders were holed up in the caved shelters of Tora Bora white Mountains. For four consecutive days, their suspected hiding places, as pin-pointed by the U.S Special operations and C.I.A men, were heavily bombarded by Amercan strike air-craft to flush them out. But Osama and Mullah Omar-the prime targets-could neither be hit nor captured. By all accounts, both of them along with a group of hard core terrorists escaped into the bordering Pakistani territory jutting into Afganisthan. And this inspite of Pakistani troops being posted all along the border to intercept and capture all fleeing terrorists. They remain still at large inspite of world-wide effort to catch them, with Osma issuing threats from time to time to strike at America from his safe haven some where in Pakistan's Northern Areas bordering Afganisthan.

That reveals the other, more grotesque face of Pakistan, showcased as a 'frontline state' in the international war on terror. Here are some facts, which speak for themselves. In the high profile Islamic Seminary or Madarsa at Binori in the center of Karachi (Pakistan), referred to earlier, a large portrait of Osama is prominently displayed. He is learnt to have stayed here at Binori on several occasions before and after 9/11. After a serious wound in course of America bombing in Tora Bora, he was treated by Pakistani military doctors at Binori during 2002.

And more. Osama used his stay at Binori to send his message of Jihadi terror across the world. The famous audio-cassette of November 12, 2002, in which he spoke of terrorist attacks in Yemen, Kuwait, Bali and Moscow and called for fresh action against Americans, Europeans, Canadians and Australians, originated at his safe sanctuary of Binori. It was from here that the audio-cassette was sent through Bangladesh to the Qatar TV Channel Al Jazeera.

And Binori was no exception. That is, it is not only the Madarsa at Binori, which provided safe shelter to Osama. In fact, the whole of Pakistan was equally safe for him. It is learnt that just before 9/11, he had been treated for a kidney problem in a Pakistani military hospital at Peshawar or Rawalpindi.

How is it that Pakistani military and intelligence officials who had been in intimate contact with Osama before 9/11 and after could not locate him when the war on terror was launched by America in October 2001? What kind of intelligence assistance was Pakistan offering to the American forces in targeting Osama and his hard core terrorists in terms of its commitment to join in the war on terror? How is it that inspite of Pakistan's professed allegiance to the international coalition in the war, and its ill concealed proximity to Osama and Mullah Omar, they could not be captured in course of the war or after? It would be obvious to the meanest intelligence that Pakistan was not only not assisting the U.S in catching Osama and his core group but actually helping them to flee away to safety, probably within its own territorial jurisdiction.

It was a bizarre case of a so-called 'frontline state' in the war against terror itself sheltering on the sly the prime target of the war. The world would have been aghast if either the Russians or the western powers capturing Berlin towards the close of the Second World War had spirited away Hitler to safety. Pakistan has performed similar feat in respect of Osama and his Al Quida, without anyone raising a little finger at it. It must rank as the most sensational international double cross of the 21st century. It is difficult to believe that the Americans do not know it, or, for that matter, that the Pakistanis do not know that they know. But the rest of the world does not know who is fooling whom. In any case, the world's most wanted terrorist with a reward of 25 million dollars on his head, is safely sheltered within the territorial jurisdiction of a 'front line' state in the war against terrorism.

This was confirmed by the American Predator strike on a building in the Bajour tribal region of Pakistan's Northern Areas on January 13, 2006. The aerial assault was targeted at top Al Quida leadership believed to be hiding there. The incident in which 18 locals were killed led to a national outrage provoking condemnation of the U.S action by the Pakistan government. Sections of the Pakistani establishment and the opposition led by Jamat-e-Islami raised an uproar against America. But the uproar was muffed when it was found that the attack was right on target in respect of at least three top Al Quida functionaries. One of those killed in the U.S air strike was an Egyptian named Abu Khabab-al-Said Umar who is on America's most wanted list with a five million dollars reward on his head. He was an expert in explosives and poisons according to the U.S government web site rewards-forjustice.net. The other two were Abu Ubyada al Misri, the Chief of insurgent operations in the Southern Afganisthan province of Kunar adjoining Bajaur, and the most important of them all, Abdul Rahman al Maghrebi, the Moroccan son-in-law of

Osama's second in command Ayaman-al-Zawahiri. He was incharge of AL Quida propaganda campaign in the region.

According to one report, the air strike nearly got Osma's Deputy Aayman al Zawahiri himself who just escaped because he skipped a dinner invitation at the place. The list of Al Quida operatives hit in the American action took the bite out of Pakistan's protests. The Pak Prime Minister Shaukat Aziz on a visit to the U.S toned down his criticism by simply describing the incident as "regrettable" arising out of "a communication gap" between the CIA and Pakistani intelligence agency. And President Parvez Musharraf, after keeping mum for nearly a week, made a mild protest to the visiting U.S under Secretary of State Nicolas Burns on January 21, 2006 to the effect that such incidents could affect co-operation with the U.S against terrorism.

What Parvez Musharraf can't hide is that Pakistan's Northern tribal area has become the hub of Al Quida and Taliban hard-core terrorists after their rout in the U.S led war in Afganistan. And that they are being nourished and sustained by covert support from Pakistan. Here is what a report by Lee Hamilton, Vice-Chairman of the 9/11 Public Disclosure Project which examined action taken by U.S Administration on the recommendations of the 9/11 Probe Commission, said in November 2005: "Pakistan remains a sanctuary and training ground for terrorists." Regretting that the Pakistan President had not lived upto his promises to regulate the Madarsas or religious seminaries, he said, "Taliban forces still pass freely across Pakistan-Afganistan border and operate in Pakistan tribal areas. Terrorists from Pakistan carry out operations in Kashmir".

It is no longer a secret. It is so well known, out in the open for anyone to see. The remnants of Taliban, funded and supported by Pakistan, in conjunction with Al Quida are creating chronic instability in Afganistan with sporadic terrorist acts like ambushes and blasts. After keeping a low profile for some time in the wake of the U.S war against Taliban, Pakistan's I.S.I is back at its old game of propping up Taliban. Pakistan wants the Talibanis back in action to promote the extremist brand of Islam bred inside Pakistani Madarsas and thereby destabilize the moderate Afganistan regime.

At the 57th Session of the U.N sub-Commission on the promotion and Protection of Human Rights held at Geneva in August 2005, several speakers described the Madrasas run by religio-political parties in Pakistan as " nurseries of death and destruction". It was pointed out that the Madarsas run by the Jamat-e-Islam have been the "Production Units" of Jihadis for over three decades. In this regard it was observed that most of the Taliban cadres were trained in Madarsas run by Jamat-e-Islami and other religio-political parties of Pakistan. In fact Mullah Omar himself, as pointed out by one speaker, was the product of one such Madarsa in Pakistan. The speakers at the U.N session stressed that "unless these are dismantled and sustained international pressure brought upon the state, which sustains and nurtures this evil, the world would continue to suffer the threats of global terrorism".

Significantly enough, many of the speakers who roundly condemned the Pakistani polico-religious establishment on this score were liberal Muslim scholars from different parts of the world. For instance, a paper presented by a Muslim participant Arif Aajakia said: " Even the perpetrators of the London blasts, though British citizens, fell prey to the indoctrination imparted by these Pakistani Madarsas".

Here is another sever indictment of Pakistan's double role as a partner in the war against terror on the one hand and sponsor of Jihadi terrorism all over the world on the other, by one who ought to know. On the occasion of launch of a book entitled "Pakistan Between Mosque and Military" authored by Hussain Hakkani, an ex Pakistani diplomat, Robert Oakley, a former U.S ambassador to Pakistan, observed in July 2005 that Pakistan was the "most dangerous country" in the world. And Robert Oakley was no ordinary run-of-the mill American diplomat. As the U.S ambassador to Pakistan in the crucial period of Afgan resistance against Soviet occupation, he enjoyed tremendous power and prestige. So much so that some in the Pak media started describing him as the 'Viceroy of Pakistan'. He went on to assert that the national leadership itself had been fanning the flame of fundamentalism in Pakistan.

Steven Cole, managing editor of the "Washington Post" daily, supported Robert Oakley's observation about Pakistan being the most dangerous country of the world. And went on to accuse Pakistan of duplicity in regard to terrorism because it was being promoted in Pakistan's own tribal belt. Hussain Hakkani, the author of the book, dubbed Pakistan as the center of anti-American activities and Islamic fundamentalism. He asserted in clear terms that while Pakistan posed to be supporting the U.S campaign against terrorism, it was secretly inciting anti-American feelings among the people. He asserted that fundamentalism was the official policy of Pakistan and went to the extent of saying that stability eluded Pakistan because its very creation was a hasty step.

The circumstances in which Pakistan was born and the midwife that delivered it shall be dealt with in the next chapter. Meanwhile, it must be said that there cannot be a more forthright and appropriate description of the swamp that the Pakistani state has come to be. And that also by one of Pakistan's own ex diplomats.

There is an ominous ring to Oakley's dubbing of Pakistan as the "most dangerous" country in the world. There is more to it than mere rhetoric. It relates to the nuclear weapons dimensions of Pakistan's involvement with Jihadi terrorists. The hobnobbing of top Pakistani nuclear scientist Dr. Sultan Bashiruddin Mahmud with Osama bin Laden prior to and on the eve of 9/11 has been briefly referred to earlier. His fundamentalist Islamic antecedent has also been touched upon. It may now be added that Mahmud was in charge of the plutonium factory built at Khusab in Pakistan with Chinese assistance and also headed the Pakistan Atomic Energy Commission till 1999. Even at that stage, he indulged in vehement public protest against Pakistan joining the nuclear non-proliferation regime, which embarrassed the Nawaz Sherif government. He was then relieved of his post and retired, but continued to engage with Osama& Co as the operational chief of Pakistani NGO ' *Unmah Tameer-e-Nav'*. The UTN headed by the ex ISI Chief Hamid Gul was in reality a cover organization engaged in boosting up Taliban and Al Quida in various ways, including providing them with nuclear know how.

The bean was spilled around March 2005 by a well known Pakistani weekly *'The Friday' Times'* whose editor Nazam Sethi has been in and out of jail for his liberal views and anti-establishment stance. According to the weekly, on a search of Dr.Mahmud's UTN's office in Kabul, the U.S intelligence agencies came across lots of information about making of a nuclear weapon brought from Pakistan's Kahuta atomic research center. They also stumbled upon evidence of correspondence between the U.T.N and Islamic terrorist organizations like Laskhare-e-Toiba and others. Dr. Mahmud and other nuclear scientists were also reported to be taking part in the functions of Lashkar-e-Toiba and Dr.Mahmud particularly was visible in its rallies.

Under American pressure after the start of the war on terror, Dr. Mamud was arrested in the U.T.N. office on October 23, 2001. According to *'The Friday Times'*, he admitted after considerable grilling that he had met Osama bin Laden and passed on the know-how about making of a nuclear bomb. And then the usual drill, which has become Musharraf's trade mark way of dealing with dangerous Jihadis in his country, was gone through. Mahmud was interrogated, kept in prison for some time, then under house arrest a little longer and finally set free.

But Mahmud's flirting with Jihadis, both as a nuclear scientist and a hard boiled Islamic fundamentalist, pale into insignificance before the exploits of the doyen of them all – Abdul Qudir Khan, the father of the Pakistani bomb. When the bubble of Dr. Khan's network spreading know how about nuclear weapons to so-called 'rogue states' burst, Pakistan came right in the center of the world's worst nuclear proliferation scandal. It brought to the fore Pakistan's role in running one of the world's deadliest black markets in nuclear weapons materials. The world was stunned at the impunity with which the Pakistani nuclear icon Dr. Abdul Qadir Khan created and ran a virtual nuclear *'Wal-Mart'*.

It was known "*off the record*" for a long time. But it came into the surface when, in the wake of America's proclaimed policy of pursuing its war on terror to the logical end, Libya opened the lid in 2003. Libya, it may be noted, was one of the recipients of nuclear weapons technology from Khan. In October 2003, a German ship carrying 5 giant containers with 1000 centrifuges headed for Libya was seized in the Suez Canal. Nuclear bomb designs wrapped in plastic bags sent by an Islamabad dry cleaner were also seized. That led to the unearthing of Khan's elaborate proliferation network.

It was revealed in the follow up probe that bomb designs and equipments were sent to Iran, North Korea and Libya through a transportation chain spanning East Asia and Africa. The parts were made in Malaysia and shipped through the Middle East. It also came to light that Khan had been sending hardware, designs and nuclear technology to various Muslim countries from around the year 1980 to 2001.

Consequent upon the revelations, the U.S squeezed the Pak President to roll up the Khan network and lock him up. After selective leaks in American media, in early 2004, President Musharraf had to arrest Dr. Khan and make a show of interrogating him, ensuring at the same time that the U.S or any international agency did not interrogate him. What was more interesting, Khan was made to confess publicly on Pak TV that he had actually proliferated nuclear know how to Iran, North Korea and Libya for personal monetary gain only. His unsolicited admission that he did it for money was a real gem. The sole purpose behind this palpably stage-managed show of a confession was to absolve the entire Pakistani establishment of any complicity in his unconcealed proliferating activities carried on for years. There was no explanation for the use of Pakistani military air crafts by Khan in his travels to and from North Korea, Libya etc which for all practical purposes were treated as official. There was no explanation either of the supreme head of Pakistani's nuclear establishment making frequent visits to Saudi Arabia, Algeria, Syria, Malaysia, Indonesia and Egypt-all Muslim countries-over the years. It was utterly naïve for the Pak President to think that the world was going to be fooled by Khan's meticulously tailored confession.

No one was fooled, certainly not the United States. The U.S administration, which has ever been over indulgent to Pakistan, woke up at last and took note. It put its concern across to Pakistan in no uncertain terms. For the first time, attention was focused not only on Dr. Khan personally, but on his sinister network with close linkages to the highest and darkest corners of Pakistani military establishment. Here again, President Musharraf used his trade-mark method of dealing with Pakistani Jihadis in the eye of an international storm. Dr. Abdul Quadir Khan was deprived of his official status and frills, arrested, interrogated by a friendly Pakistani agency, made to confess and kept safe under ' house arrest'. But no more. Musharraf stubbornly refused to allow the U.S or any other international agency to interrogate him.

He has good reason to shield Khan from any American or international investigation. For that would squarely expose Dr. Khan's patrons in the Pakistani military and political establishment. The U.S of course knows it and is evidently using it to extort clinching evidence against Iran's none too secret exercise to make the bomb. But Pakistan has a more important reason domestically to protect Khan from being disgraced any further. For Dr. Abdul Qadir Khan is no ordinary nuclear scientist. TO the people of Pakistan, he is a national hero next only to M.A. Jinnah who is credited with having brought Pakistan into being. He is an Islamic icon whose birth is celebrated in the mosques of Karachi and other cities.

What is not so well known about Dr. Abdul Qadir Khan, father of the Pakistani bomb and a national celebrity after whom Pakistan's biggest nuclear laboratory is named, is that he is not only a nuclear scientist but also a confirmed Jihadi. He is officially a member of Lashkar-e-Toiba, an international terrorist organization dubbed as such by the U.N. What is more, the Lashkar is not only in the inner most circle of Al Qaida but has emerged as its surrogate in carrying out deadly terrorist acts in India and other parts of the world. As a committed Islamist, Dr. Khan and his associate Bashiruddin Mahmood, according to *'The Friday Times'*, report referred to earlier, had held meetings with Osama bin Laden during the Taliban regime before 9/11 and handed over data on the construction and maintenance of nuclear weapons from Khan's Kahuta laboratories.

It is inconceivable that Dr. Khan would have performed all these feats-nuclearsing North Korea, providing centrifuges and nuclear hardware to Iran and Lybya and handing over bomb designs and nuclear data to Osma bin Laden-without active support of successive governments of Pakistan. The daring American reporter, Daniel Pearl of "*The Wall Street Journal*", tried to probe it and just as he was getting close to proving the direct link between Pakistan's ISI and Osamas' efforts to assemble a dirty bomb, he was abducted and brutally done to death. The French writer Bernard-Henry Levy who investigated the killing concludes: " This crime was not petty, a murder for nothing, an uncontrolled act of fundamentalist fanatics-it is a crime of State, intended and authorized, whether we like it or not, by the State of Pakistan". (*who killed Daniel Pearl", 2003).*

That brings out the true face of Pakistani state- a 'frontline' ally of America in the war on terror, saviour and harbourer of top Al Qaida learship Osama bin Laden, Mullah Omar, Ayman-al-Zawahiri, protector of notorious Islamic nuclear proliferatiors Abdul Qadir Khan and Bashiruddin Mahmud, and sponsor of deadly Jihadi terrorism against India – all at the same time. It is a face distorted not only by duplicity but a degree of multiplicity rare in the recent history of the world. Like a German juggler playing with four balls at a time, General Parvez Mushraff is playing a ball game simultaneously with America, Al Qaida, nuclear proliferators and India. This is a Mackiavellian feat which Mackiavelli himself would have been proud of.

In regard to India, Pakistan is the only major state in the world to have developed the mechanism of terror into a fine art and indulged in it in the open as a matter of state policy, even though terrorism basically is a private sector enterprise indulged in mainly by non-state actors. In comparison to what Pakistan has done to India in course of the last two decades on the front of Jihadi terrorism, the sporadic pyrotechniques of states like Iran and Syria in their perennial conflict with Israel pale into insignificance. More about it in the next chapter

9

India's Brush with Islamism

Through the History

India had a bitter taste of its first direct encounter with Islamism, if not Islam, in Sindh within a hundred years of the birth of the religion. As already discussed, Islam became politicized immediately after the departure of the Prophet from the scene in the year 632. The Caliphs who followed lost no time in setting upon a course of conquering their known world to expand their empire as well as to spread Islam. The primary motivating force behind their drive and dazzling successes both in Asia and Europe was spread of Islam. At that stage, the whole of Middle East, North Africa and Southern Europe were in their direct line of attack. India was only on the fringe of their targets, but not altogether out of sight.

Even as the Arabian Islamists were marching from success to success in their prime target areas, the Caliphs kept sending expeditious to conquer the coastal areas of India along the Arabian sea without much success to start with. It was in course of this campaign that a large force under Mohammad-bin-Qasim was sent in the year 712 to conquer Sindh. That he conquered Sindh with ease was not big deal. The Islamists were conquering other parts of the world at that time anyway. The notable aspect of the conquest was that it was motivated primarily by the idea of spreading Islam and eliminating the infidels. The Hindus and Buddhists were given the choice of embracing Islam or facing death. A great massacre went on for three days in which all adults who refused to become Muslims were put to death. All young women, including the widow and daughters of the defeated Hindu King Dahir, were captured as prized booty for the conquerors, and hold your breath, the Caliph. (Women, it may be noted, were treated as no more than 'consumable' commodities in the Arab world at that time. In fact, the Prophet had ordained considerable reforms in the position of women, but his followers continued with their old attitude through much of the Middle Ages.)

At the end of the successful campaign, the Victorious Mohammad-bin-Qasim wrote to Hajjaj, the Viceroy of the Eastern Provinces of the Caliph,: "The nephew of Raja Dahir, his warriors and principal officers have been slain and the infidels converted to Islam. Instead of idol-temples, mosques and other places of worship have been created. Khutbah (Fri day prayer) is read, the call to prayer is raised, so that devotions are performed at stated hours. The Takbir and praise to the Almighty God are offered every morning and evening". That was an articulation of Islamism loud and clear.

From Sindh, Mohammad-bin-Qasim marched to Multan, the chief city of upper Indus. He faced tough resistance on the way but bin Qasim succeeded in capturing Multan through treachery, common in those times. Even as he was planning to conquer the other parts of northern India, he was himself put to death under orders of none other than the Caliph himself for reasons shrouded in mystery.

After the gory introduction of Islam on the fringes, its further advance into the heart land of India was on hold for three hundred years, not on account of any fight back by Indians, or Hindus to be precise, but for other reasons. For one thing, an internal power struggle for capture of the Caliphate between two branches of Prophet Mohammad's family kept the forces of Islamism under check for some time. For the other, the Abbaside Caliphs who replaced the Ommeyades, the other branch of the Prophet's family, started enjoying the fruits of the large Arab Islamic Empire. They shifted the capital of the Caliphate, that is, the head-ship of the Muslim world, to Baghdad in Iraq and began living in great luxury. Meanwhile Muslim Arabs kept visiting coastal India, building their mosques, preaching their religion, sometimes even converting people. In keeping with the Indian ethos, more about which later, there was no opposition or concern to that kind of Islamic intrusion.

The next stage in the Islamic penetration of India came three and a half centuries later, and not exactly as a part of the mainstream Islamic push in other parts of the world but as an offshoot of it. Islamism as a polico-religious force was primarily involved in a fight against the Christian West, holding on to its foot hold in Spain and threatening

Constantinople. This time round, minor actors or foot-soldiers of Islam took up the cudgel for the faith as far as India was conquered.

A Turkish slave of the Caliph namded Subuktagin carved out his own state around Ghazni in Afganistan towards the end of the 10th century. It was his son Mahmud who came to India, "sword in hand" with the twin objective of spreading Islam and plundering the country. He had the blessings of the Caliph Al-Qadir-Billarh who conferred on him the title of *Amin-ul-Millat (Custodian of the Faith)* and asked him to lead expeditions against India year after year. Accordingly, Mahmud of Ghazni, the rapacious Islamic conqueror, raided India with "fire and slaughter" 17 times beginning the year 1000 until his death in 1030.

Among the more brutal battles that he fought and won were at Peshawar in which 15,000 Hindus were killed, at Mahawan in Mathura district were 50,000 Hindus were massacred and drowned in the river Jamuna, Mathura and Brindaban, the holy places of Hindus where all the temples and idols of Lord Krishna were destroyed and Kannauj where 10,000 Hindu temples were demolished. But the most savage dance of death and destruction took place at Somnath in Gujarat where he destroyed the most venerated idol of Lord Somnath and butchered around 50,000 devotees who had gathered in the famous temple. He walked away with huge wealth accumulated through centuries of offerings made by worshippers at the temple.

He was a ruthless plunderer all right, as all conquerors are, but the moving spirit behind his raids and devastations in India was the cause of

Islam. The messianic zeal with which he went about breaking idols of gods worshipped by Hindus and demolishing their places of worship and piligrimage in Mathura, Brindaban, Kannauj and Somnath bear ample testimony to his fanaticism. His Hindu opponents were forced to embrace Islam or get killed. Wherever they agreed to accept Islam, their lives were spared. For instance, when Mahmud Ghazni reached Bulandshahar, its ruler Hardatha converted to Islam along with 10,000 men to save his live and principality.

He did not even spare Abdul Fateh Daud, the Muslim ruler of Multan, because he belonged to another sect considered heretical by orthodox Islamists. The Qarmatian sect to which Daud belonged had contempt for the rituals of Islam and had no objection to eating forbidden meat. Mahmud Ghazni considered Daud as bad a Kafir (Infidel) as a Rajput, for which he invaded Multan and captured it after seven days of bitter fighting. That would go to show that he was not only a crusader for Islam but also a fundamentalist Islamist.

Many conventional historians, with the vintage of the 20th century, have sought to downplay his crusading Islamism by highlighting his penchant for plunder and loot of the venues of his conquests. But facts recorded in history with human blood cannot be obliterated by any amount of doctoring to fit in with the historians' own predilections. Even Dr Ishwari Prasad who sings praises of Mahmud Ghazni as a "great leader" and "gifted soldier" writes on his victory at Somnath: "To him and his followers it was the triumph of the cause to which they were so intensely devoted. The Khalifa (Caliph) who rejoiced in the success of the Muslim arms in an infidel land, sent letters and robes of honor for him and his sons. The Muslim world rang with the praises of Mahmud and he appeared to many as a great hero who had appeared upon the earth to extirpate infidelity and establish the true faith".

The state historians of that time have set the records straight about the nature of his campaigns of conquests in India. Ibnul Athir observed in his obituary reference on Mahmud's death in the year 1030 that, besides being greedy by wealth, which accounted for his repeated Indian campaigns, he was "fanatical, cruel to Muslim heretics as well as to Hindoos (of whom he slew an incalculable number.....)" Mahmud's own court historian Utbi was more forthright. He viewed Ghaznavi expeditions to India as Jihad or holy war for the destruction of Hindus and spread of Islam.

But neither the Arab conquests of Sindh and Multan early in the 8th century nor the invasions and ravages of Mahmud Ghazni in the first half of the 11th century marked the beginning of Muslim rule in India. These intrusions of Islam in India were mere unhappy episodes in the history of India, but they paved the way for the ultimate establishment of stable Muslim rule in the country. It was another Afgan Chief - Shahabuddin Muhammad Ghori or Muhammad of Ghur, who can be regarded as the real founder of Muslim Empire in India towards the end of the 12th century. He was the brother of Ghiasuddin who had conquered Ghazni and put an end to the Ghaznavite Empire in Afganistan. He was an ambitious empire builder fond of conquest and power and a competent warrior.

Taking a cue form the Sultans of Ghazni whom he had superceded in his homeland, he launched his campaign to conquer India in the last quarter of the 12th century.

Starting with the conquest of Multan and Sindh, Muhammad Ghori captured Peshawar and Lahore and came right on to the doorsteps of Delhi. Prithvi Raj Chouhan, the legendry Rajput king of Delhi and Ajmer, marched forward to check his advance with a large force near Thaneshwar supported by other Rajput princes except for the Raja Jaichandra of Kaunauaj. The reason was personal hostility. Prithvi Raj was in love with Jaichandra's daughter Sanjukta and had carried her away to marry much against her father's wishes. Raja Jaichandra never forgave him for that.

Prithvi Raj with his large army encountered Mohammad Ghori at Tarain near Thaneshwar in the year 1191 and defeated him roundly. Legends say that Muhammad Ghori was actually captured by Prithvi Raj who could have killed him, as was the usual practice in those days, but showed magnanimity in allowing him to return back to Afganistan. Historians do not authenticate this legend though.

What the recorded history says is that Muhammad Ghori returned to Ghazni, assembled a huge force, planned out his strategy well and came back to attack Delhi the next year with all his might. In the battle that followed at Tarain, Prithvi Raj and his Hindu coalition was defeated by Muhammad Ghori as comprehensively as Ghori had been defeated in the previous year. He was captured by

Ghori and put to death in a manner shrouded in mystery. Chandra Bardai, his court poet, says that the great Rajput warrior was taken to Gazhni and tortured to death. This version again is supported by legend but not by other record-keepers or historians.

Sultan Ghori's victory in this battle sealed the fate of India for centuries to come. The noted historian V.A Smith writes: "The second battle of Tarain in 1192 may be regarded as the decisive contest which ensured the ultimate success of the Mohammadan attack on Hindustan. All the numerous subsequent attacks were merely consequences of the overwhelming defeat of the Hindu league on the historic plain to the north of Delhi".

In an ironic turn of events, Raja Jai Chandra of Kannuaj who had rejoiced at the destruction of Prithvi Raj, and according to legend again had actually helped Sultan Ghori clandestinely in that process, was himself the next target of attack. In 1194, Ghori attacked Kannauj and handed down a stunning defeat to the Raja of Kannauj in the battle of Chandwara. A Muslim record-keeper writes: "when the two armies met, there was great carnage; the infidels sustained by their number and the Muslims by their courage; but in the end, infidels fled and the faithful were victorious. The slaughter of the Hindus was immense". After routing Jai Chandra in the battle and plundering his treasures, Muhammad Ghori marched to Banaras (Varanasi), destroyed hundreds of Hindu temples and raised mosques on those sights.

Muhammad Ghori may not have been as fanatic an Islamist as Mahmud Ghazni, as many favourable historians of the 20th century have tried to make out, but from what he did in India, his ardent Islamism cannot be over looked. In fact, he was a more determined and pragmatic Islamist than Mahmud Ghazni who broke idols, plundered and left India to its fate. On the other hand, Muhammad Ghori had made up his mind to establish Muslim rule in India on a lasting basis and succeeded in doing so.

There was nothing exceptional about the planting of the banner of the crescent (Islam) on India at this point of time. It was part of a bigger war going on between the crescent and the cross, Islam and Christianity, in west Asia and Europe. This was the period of the Christian crusades and Islamic Jihad, which was rocking the Christian and Muslim world. In fact, it was a period of Islamic wars. While the Seljuq Turks, who had taken over the banner of Islam from the Arabs, were shaking the Christendom in Europe, their junior partners like Muhammad Ghori and his successors were engaged in Islamising India. Right through the 12th to 16th centuries, with over a century's interval during the Mongal's tornado of terror in the 13th, the Big Brothers of Islam were fighting to conquer the more important parts of the world in Europe and Central Asia, while their junior siblings went about conquering the softer peoples of the Indian sub-continent with comparative ease. In Europe, they were breaking churches and Cathedrals, in India temples and idols. It was part of a pattern.

Rulers changed, dynasties changed from Afgans to Turkish slaves to indigenous Musalmans, but chaotic Islamic rule continued in India. Based at Delhi, it kept expanding to Bihar and Bengal in the east, Gujarat in the West and Devagiri and Telengana in the South. One of the more ruthless and rapacious among the Muslim rulers was Alauddin Khalji who ruled from 1296 to 1316. And one of the more destructive of his military coampaigns was that against the legendry Rajput king of Mewar. He laid siege of Chittorgarh, the capital of Rana Ratan Singh of Mewar, for five months. The Rajputs resisted and fought with great bravery but failed to beat back the invaders. And such was the fear of Muslim conquerors ravishing and enslaving their women folk that before they perished fighting, their wives and daughters numbering in thousands performed the horrific rite of '*Jauhar*' by immolating themselves. Chittorgarh was devastated and captured in August 1303.

But the worst part of Alauddin Khalji's rule was his contempt for the Hindus on religious grounds and he did every thing to reduce them to poverty and misery. In this, he was guided by the dictates of the Qazi of Bayana who explained the state policy towards Hindus thus: "If the Muhassil (state official) chooses to spit into the mouth of a Hindu, he must open his mouth without hesitation..... The meaning of doing such a thing is that the Hindu by acting in this way shows his meekness and humility and obedience and respect. The glorification of Islam is a duty.... God himself has commanded their subjection, in as much as the Hindus are the deadliest foes of the Prohpet. The Prophet has said that they should either embrace Islam or they should be slain or enslaved and their property should be confiscated to the State". That was unadulterated Islamism guiding Alauddin's Hindu policy and that of other Muslim rulers more or less, depending upon their personal predelictions.

One of the measures adopted by all Muslim rulers all over the world was the levy of Jizya or Jazia tax on non-Muslims. It was avowedly an Islamic levy against Hindus in case of India and Christians and Jews in case of Europe in lieu of the protection of life and property of the Zimmies (infidels).

A major fall-out of the continuation of Muslim rule was the slow but steady Islamisation of India. Not by sword, as the Islamic dispensation stabilized in the country, but for other reasons. Many converted to Islam out of fear or under pressure or to be on the winning side. Among the upper classes, desire to gain high office or to curry favour with the ruling elite acted as a motive to conversion. But for the poorer classes, the Jizya tax on non-Muslims, that is Hindus, was the principal reason for acceptance of Islam. It was a great burden for a majority of the people who became Muslims just to escape the economic burden, more so because the Jizya tax was exacted very rigidly by Muslim rulers.

Somewhere along the course in the Islamic surge, the famed Mughals came over to establish a more organized Muslim rule over India in the first half of the 16th century. How they came to be called Mughals is not quite clear except for the fact that Babar, the founder of the Moghal dynasty, was a distant descendant of the Mongols of central Asia-

Chenghiz and Timur. Babar became the ruler of India by defeating Ibrahim Lodi, the Sultan of Delhi, at Panipat in 1526 and laid the foundation of the Mughal Empire. By the time the Mughals took up its mantles, Muslim rule was over three centuries old in India. They have stolen the limelight in the history of Muslim rule in India because they consolidated and extended it and made it more stable than their fickle and wayward predecessors. After his victory at Panipat, Babar had to reckon with a more formidable adversary in Rana Sanga, the gallant Rajput ruler of Mewar. The Rana who aspired to oust the Mughal intruder from the throne of Delhi advanced with a large army to confront him. Babar charged back and the two armies met and fought a bitter battle at Kanah in 1527. In the end, Babar won and that confirmed him as the emperor of India. During the remaining three years of his life (He died in 1530), Babar went on to conquer large parts of northern India from the Punjab to Bihar in the east and to Ranthambhor in central India.

Though not a fanatic, Babar was not immune from Islamism. He was an orthodox Sunni and wrote with contempt about Hindus. What was more, he recognized Jihad against Hindus as a sacred duty.

His son Humayun had a charmed existence as the Mughal emperor because he was overthrown by his own Afgan general-Sher Sah Suri, after 10 years of rule. Humayun escaped to Persia where he was given shelter by the ruler. He returned to India after 16 years with a large army and succeeded in recapturing the the throne of Delhi from Sher Shah's successors in June 1555. But he was on the throne hardly for six months when he fell down a stair case and died. Thereby goes the saying; "Humayun tumbled through life and tumbled out of it".

His son Akbar ascended the throne at the tender age of 14 years early in 1556 and ruled India for nearly half a century till the end of 1605. Akbar's numerous achievements in diverse spheres like empire building, conquests in wars, building of the fort at Agra and the city of Fatehpur Sirki, patronage of art and culture etc are staple diet of historians right from his courtier Abul-Fazl and court historian Badauni down to those of modern times. As a warrior, Akbar triumphed across the board and added Kashmir in the north and Sindh, Gujarat, Bengal and Orissa to his empire. He was successful in subjugating central and parts of south India also. Chittorgarh which had been recovered by the Rajputs after its capture by Alauddin Khalji was also attacked and besieged by Akbar's army. After a gallant fight by the Rajputs, Chittorgarh fell to Mughal army, but not before the Rajput women performed the terrible 'Jauhar' ceremony by immolating themselves.

But Akbar is 'great', as the epithet attached to his name by historians proclaims, not because of those achievements. He is truly great because he was the only Muslim ruler of India who was not bitten by the bug of Islamism. And not because he married a Hindu lady, the sister of Raja Man Singh. Many other Muslim rulers had done that before him. That was also a part of Islamisation or symbol of subjugation of Hindus because women were regarded by them as booty of war or property. It is said that the immediate cause of Alauddin Khalji's attack on Chittorgarh was his desire to marry Padmini, the wife of Rana Ratan Singh of Chittor. And before Chittor was captured by him, Padmini burnt herself to death. In fact, the gory practice of 'Jauhar' by Rajput women before their men folk were defeated by Muslim conquerors was a bi product of the conquerors' attitude towards Hindu women.

Akbar was cut above the rest in his extra-ordinary liberal attitude towards the Hindus on other counts. He abolished the Jizya Tax on Hindus at a time when even in Europe the ottoman Turk Sultans were imposing poll tax on Christians and Jews in the countries they conquered. He appointed Hindu officials (Rajput nobles) to the highest posts in his empire. Many of his ministers and governors were Hindus. Even Kabul in Afganistan was placed under Raja Man Singh for some time. Another able Hindu administrator Todar Mal was his finance or revenue Minister. Raja Birbal and Tan Sen, the famous musician, were respected members of Akbar's court. And this at a time when Christians and Jews were excluded from public offices in the Ottoman Turkish empire in other parts of the world. As a further gesture of good-will towards his Hindu subjects, he abolished the tax on Hindu pilgrims coming on for a long time.

That was not all. He removed all restrictions on construction of buildings as places of worship for Hindus as a result of which a large number of temples were built across the country. This was a slap on the face of Muslim rulers before him who went about breaking idols and temples. He set up a translation department to translate Hindu religious books into Persian. In deference to the sanctity attached to cows by Hindu masses, Akbar prohibited the killing of cows and use of beef. He freely participated in the Hindu festivals Raksha-bandhan, Diwali and Shivratri. As a true well-wisher of the Hindus, he went to the extent of initiating measures to remove some of the evils corroding the Hindu society itself. Towards this end, he encouraged widow remarriage among Hindus and prohibited the practice of '*Sati*', that is, burning of Hindu widows on the funeral pyre of their husbands. In all this, he acted not as a Muslim ruler but true Indian ruler of India embodying the essence of Indianism. In that sense, Akbar can be treated as the real founder of modern Indian nationalism.

Historians generally regard all these conciliatory steps towards Hindu countrymen as a political move to consolidate his hold over the country. He was clever enough, it is believed, to realize that he could not bring stability to his autocratic regime by alienating the largest segment of the country's population through religious persecution or discrimination. Even if his motive in reaching out to the Hindus was purely political, it was not only a wise move but also well ahead of his time.

For although Europe had already been thoroughly shaken by the turbulent religious Reformation at the time Akbar ruled India, religion still weighed heavily with the emerging national monarchies. The Catholic and Calvinist Protestant Kings were still indulging in persecution of their people on religious grounds, resulting in large scale exodus of minorities to the newly discovered world of America. It was only about a century later at the end of the Thirty years' war between the Austrian Hapsburgs and French Bourbons in mid 17th century that the concept of nationalism, shorn of any religious veneer, came to its own in Europe. The emerging national monarchs of Europe in the 17th and 18th centuries realized that religious toleration was the best option to foster and strengthen the feeling of nationalism among their subjects. It was only through religious toleration that they could secure their own hold over power.

In as much as Akbar recognized this basic attribute of nationalism and implemented religious toleration in practice, he was ahead of his European counterparts and head and shoulders above his predecessors as well as successors. But political motivation apart, Akbar was by conviction ecclectical or liberal in matters of faith. He used to invite leading exponents of Hinduism, Jainism, Zoroastrianism and even Christian Fathers to acquaint him with tenets of their faith. He began to find some good in every religion and told them as well as the Mullahs of Islam that his object was to ascertain the truth and principles of true religion. His search for truth as well as national cohesion led him to the foundation of some kind of a religious order which could be acceptable to both Muslims and Hindus. Known as 'Din-I-Iahi', it contained some good points from all religions which could serve as a national religion. Irrespective of its merits or demerits as a religious faith, it was a monumental outgrowth of his instinctive Indian nationalism as against Muslim imperialism.

His 'Din-I-Ilahi' had few takers though among Hindus and Muslims. The Mullahs and Ulemas were quite opposed to the new religious order because Islam has never been open to any change whatsoever, unlike Christianity or other religions. Badauni, an orthodox Muslim historian of his reign, thoroughly disapproved of Akbar's liberalizing endeavors and minced no words in castigating him on that score. He has recorded that after the promulgation of Din-I-Ilahi, Akbar issued many ordinances against Islam. Much reliance cannot be placed on Badauni's observations because of his well known bias against Akbar for personal as well as religious reasons. In keeping with his liberal spirit and rational attitude towards religious faith, Akbar did not pressurize or goad people to join the new faith. It did not have a large following even in his life time. It faded out after his death.

If Akbar's successors had followed in his footsteps, perhaps the history of India would have been different. But that was not to be. Both Jahangir and Shahjahan were generally affable and considerate rulers well disposed towards their subjects and great patrons of art and culture. But they not only lacked Akbar's liberalism in respect of religion, but started reversing the process of religious toleration taken so much forward by Akbar. Though not on a wide scale, religious persecution was restarted in the reign of Akbar's son and immediate successor Jahangir himself. He took strong exception to the conversion of people, particularly Muslims to Sikhism. Accordingly, he got the 5th Sikh guru Arjan Das tortured to death soon after taking over the reins of the Empire. It was also under Jahangir's order that the Hindu temples near Pushkar in Ajmer were desecrated and destroyed.

Although Jahangir's successor Shahjahan continued his political alliance with Rajputs and had a good number of Hindu officers in the service of the empire, his Islamic zeal led him on to the path of religious intolerance. It was Shahjahan who got the Hindu shrines at Banaras and other places destroyed in pursuance of his zealous Islamism.

But in the light of what followed during the reign of his successor Aurangzeb, traces of religious intolerance noticed in the policies of Jahangir and Shah Jahan pale into nothingnesses. It would be an understatement to say that Aurangzeb completed the process of reversal of Aknar's liberal policy of religious toleration. What Aurangazeb did to Hindus, Sikhs, Jains etc., was unprecedented in the history of Muslim rule in India. Mahmud Ghazni, one of the more ruthless Muslim conquerors, was an inveterate Islamist. But he was also a greedy plunderer. Aurangzeb, a puritan in personal life, was a pure, unadulterated Islamist and Hindu-baiter.

He started by barring Hindus from official positions in his administration right from the clerical to higher levels. A general order was passed prohibiting employment of Hindus. Those Hindus already in employment could secure their jobs by embracing Islam. He set upon a systematic course of destruction of Hindu temples and prevention of construction of new ones. As governor of Gujarat earlier, Aurangazeb had got a number of temples including that of Somnath desecrated or destroyed. IN 1665, he sent an order to his officials in Gujarat that all temples which had since been repaired and restored byHindus be destroyed. He sent an order to his officers in Orissa to demolish every temple built during the previous ten or 12 years and prevent the infidels from repairing their old temples. In 1669, the most revered temple of gods Vishwanath and Gopinath at Banaras were demolished. When he marched from Amber in Jaipur to Deccan, he ordered for destruction of all temples on the way.

To hit the Hindus hard where it pinched most, he reimposed the pilgrimage tax and Jizya Tax on Hindus which had been abolished by Akbar. In order to humiliate them, every Hindu was ordered to pay the Jizya tax in person. It was aimed at not only harassing the Hindus but also inducing them to embrace Islam. Any Hindu who became a Muslim could escape the levy of Jizya tax. A large number of Hindus converted to Islam in order just to avoid the Jizya. In course of his drive to purge the administration of Hindu employees, they were given the option of converting to Islam if they wished to retain their jobs. Most of them succumbed to the bait to earn their bread. It was Islamization of India par excellence.

Aurangazeb's anti-Hinduism knew no bounds. The historian Khafi Khan, narrates a chilling incident related to his rigid stance on Jizya. Thousands of Hindus gathered together to protest the re-imposition of this poll tax. He warned them to dispense in an hour's time. When they did not disperse, he ordered that elephants should run over them. As a result, a large number of the Hindu protestors were trampled to death.

In Delhi's Chandni Chowk, there is a place now called "Bhai Mati Das Chowk' opposite to the famous Sikh Gurudwara Shisganj. During Mugal times, Delhi Kotwali (Police station) was located there. Three associates of the 9th Sikh Guru Teg Bahadur-Bhai Mati Das, Bhai Sati Das and Bhai Dayala were arrested at Ropad by Mughal police, brought to Delhi and kept in the Kotwali during Aurangzeb's time. The Muslim Qazi asked them either to convert to Islam or face death. All the three refused to be converted. Then under royal orders, they were put to death one by one, the first being cut into pieces by saw, the second being thrown into a tub of boiling water and the third being wrapped with cotton and burnt. On 11 November 1675, the Sikh Guru Teg Bahadur himself was ordered by Aurangzeb to embrace Islam. On his refusal, he was made to sit under a tree in the Kotwali premises and beheaded.

Aurangzeb ruled India for about 49 years from 1658 to 1707, almost as long as Akbar. In regard to empire building, he excelled Akbar, and in fact any other emperor of India before him. Under him, the Mughal Empire extended from Ghazni in the West to Chittagong in the east and from Kashmir in the north to Karnatak in the south. And his provinces were governed not by sub-kings but directly by the Emperor or through his appointees. But it was an internally hollow and empty empire built at the cost of sufferings of vast majority of its people, thanks to Aurangzeb's consuming zeal for Islamism. During his long rule, he did every thing to demolish the edifice of Indian nationalism, which Akbar had so assiduously built up. And this eventually brought about the end of the Mughal Empire sooner than anyone, much less Aurangzeb himself, would have visualized during his life time. Just in around 50 years after Aurangzeb's death in 1707, the grand empire collapsed and was superceded by an alien polico-economic empire beginning the victory of the British over the Nawab of Bengal at the Battle of Plassey in 1757.

Aurangzeb's Islamist extremism and religious intolerance completely corroded the fabric of the Mughal empire in course of his long rule. His torrid religious persecution of large segments of the people was building up a volcano of discontent simmering underneath. It started erupting during the latter years of his rule in the form of rebellions by Rajputs, Jats, Satnamis, Sikhs and, most important of them all, Marathas. The last Sikh guru, Govind Singh, and Maratha warrior hero Shivaji, apart from the Rajputs of Mewar, gave a tough time to the Mughal empire during the closing years of Aurangzeb's reign. He died after raising against him the Marathas in the south, Sikhs in the north and Rajputs in the mid west. They ultimately succeeded in polishing off the empire in course of around half a century after his death, when the British stepped in to fill up the vaccum, Jawahar Lal Nehru summed up; "The Mughal Empire was not overthrown by the British, but by these religious-nationalist movements, and specially by the Marathas. These movements naturally gained strength by Aurangzeb's policy of intolerance"[1]. It is true that Aurangzeb unified India as no other ruler had done before, but it was "not the unity of a national state as Akbar had foreseen, but of an Islamic State-the rule of a conquering minority over India".[2]

It was not surprising that Aurangzeb did what he did to Islamise India in course of his long rule.

Almost all Muslim rulers of India, with the solitary exception of Akbar, did their bit to promote the politico-religious ideology of Islamism, as distinguished from Islam as a pure religious faith, more or less, depending upon their capacity. The distinguishing fact about Aurangzeb was that he removed all stops and did it more vigorously, ruthlessly, and loudly. And yet India could not be comprehensively Islamised inspite of over 500 years of Muslim rule. That is the more surprising part of the story of Muslim rule in India. In that respect, India stands alone and apart from other parts of the non-western world which came under Muslim rule.

In West Asia itself, Egypt, Mesopoamia and Persia had been seats of thousands of years old civilizations in ancient times. Of these, the Persian civilization was the most lasting as a parallel to the Hellenic or Greek civilization of ancient times. For around a hundred years or so, the empire-builders of Persia were in constant conflict with the Hellens or Greeks. In 538 B.C., the Persian emperor Cyrus fought and conquered the Babylonian Empire. In 547 B.C., he also conqered Lydia, a part of the Hellenic world. In 525 B.C., the next Persian Emperor conquered Egypt. And the next Persian Emperor Darivs I set on a course of conquering the whole of the Hellenic world. He sent an expeditionary force by sea in 490 B.C., but the Persians were repulsed at the beaches of Marathon by Greek Ahtenians. Ten years later, his successor Xerxes attacked the Greeks after great preparation and had considerable initial success. But ultimately, the Hellenic allied forces won a crushing naval victory off the island of Salamis which finally ended the Persian challenge.

Persia continued to prosper as a great empire under Xerxes and his successors for nearly a century and a half. The Emperor of Persia came to be hailed as the "Kind of Kings". But it was during the reign of Emperor Darius III that the scourge of the Mecedonian - Greek Alexander descended upon Persia and comprehensively defeated it. For the next 300 years, Alexander's general Seleucus and his discendents ruled over Persia. They were driven away by another central Asian tribe known as Parthians who ruled for another 50 years. But after around five and half centuries of alien rule, the Persians rose in revolt and succeeded in overthrowing the alien rulers. A native Persian, Ardeshir I, took over as the Emperor of Persia whose dynasty ruled for nearly four centuries. Ardeshir was an ardent Zoroastrian himself and Zoroastrianism was the official religion of Persia during the rule of his dynasty known as the Sassanid dynasty. During this period, in the early Christian era, the Greeks had been superceded by the Romans as the leaders of the Hellenic or Western world. And just as the Persians under Darius Emperors had harassed the Greeks no end earlier, the Sassanid Persians gave a torrid time to the Romans through perennial warfare.

But in the first flush of the poltico-religious ideology of Islamism, the Arab pioneers of the ideology conquered Persia in the 7th century A.D. And that was the end of not only the Persian Empire and Zoroastrian religion in that country, but also the great ancient Persian civilization which had co-existed with and rivalled the Hellenic civilization of the West. With the aggressive and all pervasive Islamism of the Muslim Arab conquerors, the followers of Zorastiran religion became aliens in their own country. They had to embrace Islam or flee to other countries to escape severe persecution. A good number of them took refuge in India. The Parsies of India are the descendents of those very Zoroastrian refugees who fled their homeland after its complete Islamisation.

In 1921, Reza Khan, an army officer, organized a coup d'eta to become the Shah or ruler of the country and founder of the Pahalvi dynasty. In his bid to modernize the country, the Shah changed the country's name from Persia to Iran, the Persian synonym for Aryan, in the year 1935. His son and successor Reza Shah Pahalvi tried to ram Iran through a stiff doze of modernity which rubbed, among others, the Islamists hard. It resulted in the overthrow of the Shah and establishment of the Islamic Republic of Iran in 1979. The Country was back to square one of Shia Islamic Orthodoxy. And like the Zoroastrians earlier, the Bahais, followers of another reformist faith originating in Iran, were ruthlessly persecuted and hounded out of the country. A venerated religious preacher, Baha-ullah, the founder of the faith, taught universal brotherhood of man and other eternal verities which attracted a good number of disciples in Iran and out side that country. But any preaching other than what is prescribed in the holy book is anathema to the Ayatullahs in supreme command of Iran today.

Iran today is a ghost of the great ancient Persian Empire. The country has no use for its glorious pre-Islamic past. It would like to bury it deep down the memory hole. For the people of Iran, the ancient Persian civilization did not exist.

The same more or less is true of other countries of Asia and Africa that came under Muslim rule. Egypt was another center of a great ancient civilization that flourished in the Nile Valley. It was around two and a half thousand years before Christ that the great Egyptian pyramids were built during the Memphite Empire lasting from 2800 to 2300 B.C. Alexander 'the great' conquered Egypt in the year 332 B.C but before he could himself rule over it, he died. After Alexander's death, Egypt came to be ruled by one of his generals Ptolemy who founded a dynasty that ruled over Egypt for long. Under Ptolemy and his successors, Alexandria was the capital of Egypt, deriving its name from Alexander. After the reign of the celebrated Cleopatra, the last Ptolemy ruler, Egypt came under Roman over-lordship. But Alexandria continued to prosper and became a great center of knowledge and learning.

But when the Arab Islamists conquered Egypt in the 7th century AD, one of the first things that they did was to burn the famous library of Alexandria which was a store house of centuries of collected knowledge in science and philosophy. They proclaimed, it is said, that 'if the books were in agreement with the Quran, they were redundant', if not, they were repugnant and pernicious'. In either case, they deserved to be burnt.

Incidentally, book-burning was a favourite pastime of Muslim rulers elsewhere in the world also. One of the commanders of Muhammad Ghori named Ikhtiaruddin bin Bakhtiar Khalji, attacked Bihar in the year 1197. He captured its capital, then known as Odantapuri, and stormed a fortress occupied by a large number of 'Brahmins' with shaven heads ('evidently Buddhist monks) and big stock of books. The fortress was not only ransacked and destroyed and large numbers of Buddhist monks slain, but all the books stored there were put to flames. The reasoning was the same as put forward by the arsonists of the Egyptian library at Alexandria around four and a half century elarier. The fortress that was destroyed was the famous Nalanda 'Vihar', that is Buddhist Semnary, renowned throughout the Buddhist world as a center of learning. The ruins of Nalanda are now maintained by the Archaeological Survey of India as a great tourist center. In fact, the state of Bihar owes its name to this Buddhist 'Vihar' which was destroyed by Bakhtiar Khalji.

Egypt today, like Iran, has been so thoroughly Islamised that it has almost forgotten its great ancient civilization. It lies buried in the sands of the Nile remembered only for the magnificent pyramids built in those times, which attract mainly foreign tourists.

Like Iran and Egypt, other important Muslim states like Afganistan, Indonesia and Malayasia had a different past which they have totally blanked off. Afganistan was predominantly Buddhist since the time of Ashoka and remained so for nearly a thousand years before it was conquered by Arab Islamists. But it was so thoroughly Islamised that the largest Buddha image of pre-Islamic vintage at Bamiyan was demolished by the Taliban regime as being unislamic. Indonesia and Malaya also shared Hinduism and Buddhism as their predominant religion before they were superceded by Islam. And they also have written off their past as of no consequence. It is a wonder of history that Islam so completely washed off the religious and civilizational past, good, bad or indifferent, of countries and peoples in Asia and Africa once they came under its wings.

In this background, it is a greater wonder that inspite of over 500 years of unadulterated Islamic rule, India did not turn into an Islamic state like Iran, Egypt, Afganistan, Indonesia etc. That is a puzzle which calls for adequate explanation. India is the only country outside Europe which was under Muslim rule for so many centuries and yet did not become a Muslim Nation. How Come? But before that, what about Europe? How did it cope with persistent incursion of Islamism for centuries in course of which parts of it came under Muslim rule, one time or the other?

It was Southern Europe, co-terminus with the present day states of Spain and Portugal, which was the first to be conquered by the Arab Islamists early in the 8th century. Like the Muslim Afgans in India a few centuries later, the Muslim Arabs settled down in Spain, prospered and imposed their own culture and religion on the people of Spain. Known as Moors, the Arab Muslims were constantly under attack from the Christian peoples of northern Europe, but they continued to rule over nearly the whole of Spain for about 500 years and over a small Kingdom of Granada in Southern Spain for another 200 years. It was only in the year 1492 that the Spanish threw out the Arabs, or Moors as they were called, from Granada and the whole of Spain was freed from Muslim rule.

That was the beginning of the end of Islam in Spain. Millions of Arab Muslims were driven out of Spain by force. Those who remained had to face the fury of religious persecution. The Roman Christian Institution of the "Inquisition" was set in motion to force them to change their religion or face severe persecution including death by burning. Under the 'Reconquesta' campaign, the Christian Spanish took care to obliterate every vestige of Islamic culture from their land. The Arab Muslims or Moors were ordered to renounce not only their religion but also their language, customs, even their names, and adopt Spanish dress, language and names. Far from becoming a Muslim State inspite of 500 to 700 years of Muslim rule, Spain has hardly any trace of Muslim culture today.

In a replication of what happened in Spain, the Osmanli or Ottoman Turks conquered Romania and Bulgaria in course of the later Islamic push into Europe during the 14th century. They ruled over them for nearly 400 years and, as common to Muslim conquerors in other parts of the world, converted a good number of the conquered people to Islam. But once the Bulgarians were freed from Muslim rule, they did what the Spanish did under the 'Reconquesta' campaign. The Bulgarians totally repudiated the Islamic culture, forbidding their people even to use Muslim names.

Europeans, thus, coped with repeated Islamic onslaught in the only way they knew, and have always known since the times of their Greeko-Roman ancestors, by warring on the Islamists. As a result, modern Europe, inspite of its professed liberalism and secularism, remains a Christian land. There are around five million Muslims in France and sizeable numbers in other European countries. But they are only in the status of insignificant minorities on the periphery of the European society. Bosnia, Kosovo and Chechnya are tiny remnants of a vanished past, existing as islands of Islam in an ocean of Christianity. For, the defining culture of Europe, and in fact of the entire Western world, is, Christianity and Christianity alone. Since Islam as a politico-religious identity is exclusive and incompatible with any other culture, the Muslims in general have not really been assimilated in the mainstream of the social and political life of the western world. They are in fact in latent conflictual relationship with the western society which has now come to the surface. It shows in recurrent irritations and occasional eruptions of conflicts between the immigrant Muslims and their European hosts, especially after 9/11, on one pretext or another.

In sharp contrast, India coped with the Islamic onslaught in its stride in its historical perspective. North India had become used to intrusions by diverse central Asian tribes since long before the entry of west Asian Islamists and knew how to handle them. There was more than one such invasion in course of 200 years before Chrrist, the more notable ones being those of Sakas, Seythians and Kushans. The Sakas were a tribe of Turki nomads who came in large numbers to northern and western India. The Sakas in turn were overpowered by Kushans, another central Asian tribe, who invaded India during the first century before Christ. They established an extensive empire spread across India's north western borders. The Kushan empire extended from Banaras in the east to the borders of

Persia (modern Iran) in the West and Kashmir in the north to Vindhya mountains in the South. Since the Kushans had taken to Buddhism in the hey-day of the faith during Ashokan period, they were easily absorbed in the Indo-Aryan culture of India which had given birth to the Buddhist religion. As a result, the Kushans ruled India for nearly 300 years. Kanishka was one of the famous Kushan rulers and Takshashila near Peshawar had developed as a great center of Buddhist learning during the Kushan period.

Then came the dreaded Huns, a nomadic tribe from central Asia, the likes of whom had terrorized Europe around the same time. They first descended upon India from the North West during the reign of the fifth Gupta King Skand-Gupta and were beaten back. But they came in waves after waves and established a kingdom under their Chief Toroman. They ruled over northern and a part of central India for a short time, around half a century or so, in course of which they perpetrated atrocities upon the Buddhists. But they soon faded away as a ruling power and their descendents eventually got absorbed in the Indo-Aryan culture of the country.

Thus, ever since the chariotee-ring and horse-riding pagan tribes from Central Asia known as Aryans came to India in distant past and made it their home, the overriding cultural milieu of India has been one of absorption and not rejection. Any number of tribes, races, religions and cultures have been coming into India through ages and getting absorbed into the great Indo-Aryan civilization of the country. They have come, conquered, influenced and have themselves been so comprehensively influenced as to become a part of the Indian indentity. Rooted in the core value of letting a hundred flowers blossom in the realm of thought, philosophy and faith, the Indian identity has remained intact through the vicissitudes of time and ravages of history. It was in this foundational background that India faced the onslaught of Islamism for centuries and got over it without being overwhelmed and becoming a part of the exclusive Muslim Ummah, as in the case of other parts of the non-western world.

India's placid over confidence in its core value of extreme tolerance of diverse religions and cultures, has been a source of weakness also. It has been a weakness in the sense that Indians never fought persistent attacks on their basic beliefs, culture and way of life by outsiders with the same passion as European Christians did when confronted with Islamic assaults. The Islamists came to India as crusaders for their religion, but the Indians never fought them as defenders of Hinduism, which has been the predominant faith of India as Christianity of the West. They were lulled into complacency by the earlier experience of foreign invaders like the Sakas, Kushans and Huns who came, conquered, and ruled over large parts of the country but eventually themselves got absorbed into the religious and cultural milieu of India. Islamism, as an ideology of Islamisation of the world, was a different proposition altogether which the Indians were not familiar with. They were floored by it for a while, but not effaced or obliterated like other parts of the non-European world.

India's pervasive culture of inclusion and absorption and innate strength of Indianism cushioned it against the determined assault of Islamism. India did not have to fight back the Islamists as the Europeans did. Its innate strength as an epitome of freedom of faith and toleration of diverse modes of worship saw it through the worst phase of Islamism symbolized by the likes of Mahmud Ghazni, Allauddin Khalji and Aurangazeb. At the end of it all, India emerged intact as a fortress of Indianism, encompassing not only the Hindus constituting an overwhelming majority of its people but also a large Muslim population finely woven into the fabric of Indian nationalism. It met the challenge of aggressive Islamism not by rejecting Islam but by accommodating it in its pantheon of diverse faiths like Jainism, Buddhism, Zoroastrianism etc, without compromising on its core value of Indianism.

And it was in conformity with the basic tenets of Hinduism which broadly defines Indian culture in the same sense that Christianity defines western culture. This is borne out by the brief first address of Swami Vivekanand, than whom there can be no greater mouthpiece of modern Hinduism, to the inaugural session of the Parliament of Religions at Chicago. He said; "I am proud to belong to a religion which has taught the world both tolerance and universal acceptance. I am proud to belong to a nation which has sheltered the persecuted and the refugees of all religions and all nations of the world. I am proud to belong to the religion which has sheltered and is still fostering the remnants of the grand Zoroastrian nation".

The same concept of the dominant religion of India was put across by Sri Aurobindo, another great exponent of enlightened Hinduism, in 1909 when he observed that "it is in the first place a non-dogmatic inclusive religion and would have taken even Islam and Christianity into itself, if they had tolerated the process". He elaborated it further in August 1919: 'The religious culture which now goes by the name of Hinduism .... gave itself no names because it set itself no sectarian limits; it claimed no universal adhesion, asserted no sole infalliable dogma, set up no single narrow path or gate of salvation; it was less a creed or cult than a continuously enlarging tradition of the Godward endeavor of the human spirit. An immense many-sided and many staged provision for a spiritual self-building, it has some right to speak of itself by the only name it knew, *eternal religion*, 'Sanatan dharma.....".

It was this eternal religion or 'Sanatan darma' which was under attack by the ideology of Islamism during the long period of Muslim rule. It successfully repulsed the attack because eternal religion, which Indianism is all about, is indestructible. It resisted and repudiated the ideology of Islamism which considers the entire non-Muslim world as Dar-l-Herb (Home of war), but did not reject Islam as a pure religious faith or mode of worship.

Indianism, which is the embodiment of 'Sanatan darma', or eternal religion, permits complete freedom regarding mode of worship. Under it, one is free to worship a formless God and call him Allah, as Muslims do, or 'Nirakara' as many Hinsdus do. One is free to offer prayers facing west, regard Fridays as special days for obeisance, or fast during day for a month. One is free to regard Christ as the Prophet and messenger of God on earth and celebrate his birth and resurrection. Even an atheist or agnostic is considered a part of the wide fraternity of Hinduism or 'Sanatan Dharma' in India.

It is this culture of eternal religion or Hinduism which acted as a shock-absorber during the long period of Islamic rule and enabled India to remain quintessentially Indian. That is the best part of the story of Indianism through the ravages of history. It has not only stood the test of times but also the test of modernity. For the modern concept of secular, religion-neutral polity is inherent in Indianism which is an outgrowh of the Hindu ethos.

But the triumph of Indianism over the exclusive ideology of Islamisation was limited. It accommodated and gave space to Islam in its pervasive universalism, but could not succeed in curbing Islamist separatism altogether. Commenting on the overall impact of Muslim rule in India, the famous historian, Sir Jadunath Sarkar writes; ' The Indian Muslims, through out the succeeding centuries turned towards a spot in Mecca, had their own law code, their own administrative system, their own language, literature, shrines and saints, They never restricted to India as is the case with the Hindus. They always looked to the countries outside India and sought models from Arabia, Syria, Iran and Egypt"[3]. The spirit of India or Indianism made every effort to absorb them in its ethos. Some Muslism rulers and their descendents were absorbed in the Indian milieu, Akbar being the most illustrious example. And Hindus almost idolized Akbar, raising him to the level of an Avatar in Allopanishad. But there were far more Aurangzebs than Akbars in India during the period of Muslim rule. As a result, the Muslims who settled in India, by and large, were *"in the land but not of it"*.

But this Muslim separation cannot really be regarded as a failure of Indianism to absorb them. It is a universal phenomenon flowing out of the ideology of Islamism which has sway over Muslim peoples all over the world even today. If the Muslim settlers in England and America could not be fully integrated into Englishness and Americanism even today, it is little wonder that segments of Muslim population could not be thoroughly absorbed by Indianism. It was this latent Muslim separatism, which eventually led to the creation of Pakistan, which has turned out to be the prime agent of Jihadi terrorism in India. More about it in the next two sub-chapters.

Birth of Pakisatan and After

It is a paradox of history that while India emerged in one piece with its basic Indianism intact out of over five centuries of Islamic rule, it lost a part of it to Muslim separatism exactly when the country finally became independent in 1947. What the Islamists could not do, that is carve out of an exclusive Islamic state, in over 500 years, the British imperialists did in less than 200 years of their rule. The Muslim rulers did everything to spread Islam by force, patronage and inducements and indulged in religious persecutions, destruction of places of worship etc, but they left India united as one big country. The British, on the other hand, played upon the latent separatism of the Muslim psyche, initially to 'divide and rule' and finally to divide and quit. The "Vivisection" of India, as Gandhiji called it, was the final parting kick of British imperialism to India which the country is still reeling under.

It all started with the first major challenge to British rule posed by the big Army Revolt of 1857. The British called it the 'Sepoy Mutiny'; the Indian nationalists regard it as a war of independence that failed. It was a bit of both. The Hindu and Muslim soldiers of the East India Company's army had their own grievances against their British superiors. Apart from other grievances, rumours about the alien government's secret designs to convert the soldiers to Christianity by foul means made them desperate. There were whispers about mixing of animal bone dust with wheat flour. The mercenary army personnel were drawn from the Indian peasantry who were groaning under economic misery brought about by the East India Company's rule. The simmering discontent of the Indian soldiers came to a head with the introduction of the Enfield rifles in the army. The new rifle had to be bitten off before loading and the grease was believed to contain beef and pig fat which were taboo to Hindus and Muslims respectively. The Soldiers, both Hindus and Muslims, unitedly, crossed the line and rose in open revolt in May 1857.

What lent legitimacy and national character to the soldiers revolt was their proclamation of Bahadur Shah II, the last Mughal Emperor, as "Shehanshah"-e-Hindustan', the Emperor of India. That was enough to prompt other disgruntled Indian princes and nobles, dispossessed by the British, to jump in the fray. At Kanpur it was Nana Saheb, the adopted son of the last Maratha Chieften, banished from Poona, at Jhansi it was Rani Lakshmibai and at Arrah Babu Kunwar Singh, the Zamindar of Jagdishpur. A sizeable section of civil population, particularly in Oudh and north western provinces joined the rebel soldiers. At its peak, the revolt encompassed most parts of North India, except Punjab, as well as central and western India and fringes of Bengal in the east. Only South India remained unaffected, but south had traditionally been out of the orbit of empire builders of India.

The Revolt of 1857 failed, as it was doomed to fail from the start. It was an unplanned, almost spontaneous outburst of accumulated discontent and anger, largely leaderless and disorganized. Such an amorphous and heterogeneous combination, however motivated, was no match for the organized might of the British who had succeeded in subjugating the whole of the country in the first place. But it did put the British on notice. It was kind of a wake-up call for them which they took note of. The East India Company was made to fold up and India came directly under the rule of the British crown.

What would not have escaped their attention was that for the first time since their advent into India, Hindu and Muslim soldiers as well as nobility had raised the banner of revolt against the British so unitedly across the board. That was a pointer to the rise of nascent Indian nationalism which they could ill afford to ignore. So when the Indian National congress was founded in 1885 by about 70 leading political activists from Bomaby, Bengal and Madras to create a common political platform for political workers across the country, the British rulers felt concerned, but not too much. Apart from the fact that a retired English I.C.S. officer A.O. Hume had played a leading role in its formation, the objectives of the Congress in its beginning years were fairly modest. Its first President, W.C. Bannerji, summed up the aims and objects as "growth of national feeling and unity of Indians" based on "common sympathies and common ends". The British were suspicious of the Congress though as a possible rallying point against the Raj.

But when nationalist activities started gaining momentum and Bengal developing as their epicentre, the British got seriously concerned. Bengal then was not only the seat of the British viceroy of India but also the largest province comprising both east and west Bengal, Bihar and Orissa. They decided to cut it to size and brought about the partition of Bengal in 1905. The ostensible purpose was to make it administratively more manageable, but the real objective of partition of Bengal was highly sinister. By doing so, the British started the process of driving a wedge between the Hindus and Muslims of India, who had shown signs of evolving into a strong Indian national identity, as a potential threat to the colonial regime.

The viceroy Lord Curzon; the unabashed imperialist, mooted the idea of partition of Bengal with the prime motive of sawing through the heart of Indian nationalism and minced no words about it. In a speech at Dacca, he declared that through the partition, Dacca would become the capital of a new Muslim majority Province "which would invest the Mahammedans in Eastern Bengal with a unity which they have not enjoyed since the days of the old Mussalman Viceroys and Kings". (Amlesh Tripathy, "The Extremist challenge", 1967). The partition of Bengal was the first overt act of the British to foster and nourish the latent Muslim separatism, which culminated in the partition of India. It was 'divided and rule' in the making.

The British never looked back and the Indians kept falling in their trap. As the Swadeshi movement kept on gathering momentum not only in Bengal but in other parts of the country also, the imperialists kept sharpening their weapon of 'Divide and Rule'. They announced the decision to partition Bengal on 19 July 1905. There was instant reaction in nationalist circles in Bengal. There were spontaneous protest meetings in all major and minor towns including Dacca. All national leaders held a meeting at Calcutta on 7 August 1905 and passed a resolution to boycott British goods. The day partition of Bengal was put into effect - 16 October 1905 - Calcutta observed general 'hartal' and huge mass meetings were held, addressed by nationalist leaders. Leaders like B.G. Tilak, Lala Lajpat Rai,. Bipin Chandra Pal etc. took the protest movement to other parts of the country and boycott of British goods became a rage among political activists.

The Indian National Congress supported the Swadeshi movement and call for boycott of British goods at its Benares session in 1905 presided over by G.K. Gokhale. And at its Calcutta session in 1906, the Congress presided over by Dadabhai Naoroji took a momentous step to expand the scope of the movement. The Congress President declared that the goal of the Congress was 'self-government or Swaraj'. The partition of Bengal thus galvanized the rising nationalist aspirations of the people and gave a tremendous boost to the struggle for freedom.

But the British rulers were not sitting idle either. They had fired the first shot and responded to the rising tide of Indian nationalism in a cool and calculated manner. They had already started wooing Muslim community leaders like Sir Sayyed Ahmad Khan, the founder of Aligarh Muslim University, to try and keep the Muslims away from the emerging nationalist upsurge spearheaded by the Indian National Congress. With the spread of the Swadeshi movement in the wake of the Bengal partition, the British sharpened their weapon of communal divide and gave a more concrete shape to it. In October 1906, a so-called 'All India Muslim Delegation' was made to wait on the Viceroy Lord Minto holidaying at Simla with a charter of demands. The composition of the delegation was interesting. It comprised of the Aga Khan, Nawab Samiullah of Dacca and Nawab Mohsin-ul-Mulk as its leaders. While the miniscule representative character of the two Nawabs was self-evident, the Aga Khan, it may be noted, was the head of a relatively small sect of Khoja Muslims confined mainly in Kutch area of Gujarat. And after India's independence, he gave up his Indian citizenship.

By all accounts, the whole show of the Muslim delegation meeting the Viceroy was stage-managed. Regarding its representative character, the 'Amrit Bazar Patrika', a leading Calcutta daily, dubbed it as neither all India, nor Muslim so-called nor a delegation at all, because its members did not represent anyone except themselves and were hand-picked by the colonial government. Their charter demands was no more than a charter of Muslim separatism, the most important being the demand for reservation and patronage to Muslims in government jobs and other spheres. The response of the Viceroy was more interesting. He went out of his way to express his gratitude to the so-called 'delegation' for affording an opportunity to associate the Mohammedan community with the benevolent rule of the British.

It was no mere coincidence that soon after that the All India Muslim League was founded by a group of Muslim nobility led by Nawab Samiullah of Dacca and Nawab Mohsin-ul-Mulk. No wonder that one of the first pronouncements of the Muslim league was in support of the partition of Bengal, then being so fiercely opposed by the nationalists. The basic ideology of the League was that the interests of Muslims were not only different but also opposed to Hindu interests. And its demands included separate electorates and reservations for Muslims in government services. To suit the interests of its British patrons, the League sought to dissuade and prevent Muslims in general, particularly the emerging Muslim intelligentsia, from joining the National Congress which was fast emerging as a powerful platform of opposition to colonial rule.

Earlier, Sir Sayyed Ahmad had already queered the pitch for the rise of Muslim separatism, with his base at Aligarh Muslim University. When the Indian National Congress was founded in 1885, he advised Muslims not to join it. He told them that if the British withdrew, Hindus would dominate over

Muslims and continuation of British rule was their only safeguard against Hindu over lordship. He had emerged as a leading light not only of Muslim separatism but also of a counter movement swearing loyalty to the British Empire. Since the newly founded Muslim League adopted Sir Sayyed's separatist and communal agenda in toto, all his followers hailed it whole-heartedly after his death. And Aligarh Muslim University continued to be the grand Madarsa of Muslim separatism right upto the partition of the country.

The Aga Khan delegation to the Viceroy Lord Minto in October 1906 was not an isolated event. It was a well calibrated precursor to what was to follow in the shape of the much vaunted Minto-Morley constitutional Reforms introduced in India in 1909. The so called Reforms provided for enlargement of Provincial Legislative councils to include elected non-official members so that they could constitute a majority over official members. An element of election was also introduced in the central Legislative council, though the official majority over non-official members was maintained at the center. But the most significant part of the Reforms was reservation of seats in the Legislative Councils and separate electorate for the Muslim community. Under this system, Muslim candidates could be elected only by Muslim voters put in separate constituencies. Since the voters belonged exclusively to the Muslim community, the candidates making the most blatant appeal on communal lines were sure to defeat the moderates and liberals. It was like the Gresham's Law of Economics which says that bad penny drives the good one out of circulation. And the British rulers meant it to be so. It was for the first time that the seed of Muslim separatism was firmly planted in the very foundation of India's constitutional system.

The Aga Khan representation to Lord Minto, formation of the Muslim League by the same set of self-appointed leaders and introduction of separate electorates for Muslims were all parts of one and the same sinister plot of 'Divide and Rule' hatched by the British. In fact, all the three events happening in a sequence within a span of three years constituted the three angles of the triangle of Muslim separatism consciously and calculatedly drawn on the map of India by the imperialists. And yet, the nationalist leaders remained blissfully ignorant about it or chose to ignore it as evident from what followed.

The nationalists were lulled into over-confidence by a healthy development on the Muslim front. A number of Muslim leaders were opting for the nationalist mainstream discarding the pro-British and separatist wand bagon of the upper crust leadership of the Muslim League. Notable among them were Hakim Ajmel Khan, Hasan Imam, Mazhar-ul-Haque and Moulana Abul Kalam Azad, a great Muslim scholar educated at the famous Al Azhar University of Cairo, Egypt. And the most notable among them was the young Muslim barrister of Bombay-Mohammad Ali Jinah. In 1912, the Muslim League itself looked like shedding off its pro-British complexion and adopted self-government as one of its objectives.

Buoyed by such promising developments on the Hindu-Muslim front, the nationalists wanted to move an extra step forward to accommodate the Muslim League with a view to putting up a united front before the British at a time when Britain was involved in a deadly war against Germany. (The First World War of 1914-1918). And ironically, the nationalist leader who took the initiative in this regard was none other than Lokmanya Tilak, an orthodox Hindu who had raised the Ganesh festival in Bombay Province to the level of a mass movement for self-rule. In his extra eagerness to forge complete Hindu-Muslim unity in the struggle for freedom, Tilak as the leader of the Indian National Congress signed a pact with the Muslim League at Lucknow in 1916 accepting all its separatist demands. Defending the pact at the Lucknow session of the Congress in 1916, Tilak said: "When we have to fight against a third party - it is a very important thing that we stand on this platform united, united in race, united in religion, united as regards all different shades of political creed." (Tilak's `Writings and Speeches' quoted in 'India's Struggle for Independence', Bipin Chandra and others, 1990). By agreeing to the ill-famed Lucknow-pact, the Congress committed itself to separate electorates, weightage and reservation of seats in legislative bodies for Muslims which amounted to sanctifying communal and separatist politics.

The British had already been rooting for it since 1906 and had made a beginning in the Minto-Morley Reforms of 1909. Now the most important nationalist organization-the Indian National Congress –had also put its seal of approval on this most divisive step initiated by the imperialists to keep India permanently divided. Adopting separate electorates for Muslims to put an end to Muslim separatism was a remedy worse than the disease. It was like administering a dose of purgative to a patient of diorrhea.

And sure enough, the Montagu-Chelmsford Reforms that were introduced by the British at the end of the war in 1919, further reinforced the system of reservation of seats and separate electorates for Muslims in the enlarged Central and Provincial legislatures. This time round, they had the sanction of the main nationalist party spearheading the movement for self-government. They had so nicely fine-tuned their strategy of keeping India divided on religious-communal lines that the nationalists were easily playing into their hands without being even conscous of it. Thinking in retrospect, it would appear that the entire show of the Muslim League coming up with a moderate agenda and opting for unity with the Congress in the run up to the Lucknow Pact was stage-managed by the British to lure the nationalists to succumb to Muslim separatism. It was a long-term strategy drawn up by the British imperialists, the fall-out of which is still hovering around and troubling the country no end. It is a sad commentary on the credulity of the nationalists that they fell into the trap so readily.

The Lucknow pact was not the end of the nationalist leaders quest for unity with Muslim separatists through wrong means which were sure to produce the opposite result. After Tilak, it was the turn of the tallest of the nationalist leaders - Mahatma Gandhi-to yield to the temptation of seeking unity by catering to the patently Islamic agenda of fundamentalist Muslim leaders.

The Muslims of India regarded the Caliph or Khalifa of Turkey as the spiritual head of the Muslim world. It may be noted that historically the Caliphate had not really been as centralized and sacred an institution in the Muslim world as Papacy in the Christian world. Special sanctity was attached to the original Caliphs Abu Bakra and Omar who were Arabs coming from the Prophet's family. But in course of time, another branch of the Prophet's family descending from his uncle Abbas captured the Caliphate. The Abbaside Caliphs, as they were called, ruled over the Muslim world from Baghdad and lived in great luxury. The most famous of the Abbaside Calips was Harum-al-Rashid whose reign lasted from the year 786 to 809. But after his death, the succeeding Caliphs kept declining until a time when a Caliph ruled over Baghdad and its neighborhood only. In fact, one of the Caliphs was pulled out of his palace and killed by his own soldiers. And in later years, Mahmud Ghazni, the notorious conqueror of India, had threatened the reigning Caliph or Khalifa at Baghdad with death if he refused to give him Samarkand. As such, Caliphate or Khilafat was not such a sacred religious institution for which Muslims of India should have been so passionately concerned. But they did come to be very much concerned in 1919.

It so happened that the Caliphate had been taken over by the Ottoman Turks during their heyday when they had assumed the mantle of Islam to conquer the world. But by a quirk of destiny, Turkey sided with Germany in the First World War in which Britain and France roundly defeated them. As a result, the larger Turkish Empire built up by the conquering Ottoman Turks during 15th and 16th centuries was completely dismembered at the end of the war. The victorious powers cut Turkey to size which automatically meant diminution in the stature and sway of the Sultan of Turkey who was also the reining Caliph or Khalifa. The Indian Muslims, propped up as a separate entity by the British themselves and incited by orthodox Moulanas dabbling in politics, felt incenced at the downfall of the Turkish Sultan. And Gandhiji, having recently taken over the leadership of the freedom movement and in search of allies among the Muslim community, unhesitatingly joined the Khilifat agitation led by the Moulana brothers-Muhammad Ali and Shaukat Ali. He justified his move by making a significant observation to the effect that he would not get such an opportunity to befriend the Muslims of India "in a hundred years". For once, he could not be more wrong. You can set a thief to catch a thief but you cannot convert a religious fanatic into a nationalist by pampering to his fanaticism. In so far as Gandhiji was doing just that, he was attempting the impossible.

There was immediate gain of course in terms of enlisting Muslim support for freedom struggle being launched by Gandhiji. In November 1919, the Khilafat conference invited Gandhji as a special invitee when he proclaimed his whole-hearted support to their cause. As a quid pro quo, he solicited the Khilafat committee's support for non-cooperation movement against the British rule being launched by him. In June 1920, the Khilafat committee at its Allahabad meeting accepted the suggestion of joining the non-cooperation movement under Gandhiji's leadership.

The entire exercise, however, proved to be infructuous when the new charismatic Turkish leader Mustafa Kemal Attaturk abolished the institution of Turkish Caliphate or Khilafat itself in 1922 in course of his bold bid to secularise the country's polity. It was a slap on the face of the Indian Moulanas who were mobilizing the faithfuls in India in the name of a phantom which just vanished into thin air. For Gandhiji who was hoping to bring in the separatist Muslims into the nationalist fold, it was disastrous. For it gave a phillip to the notion of Muslim solidarity at the expense of national solidarity and reinforced the tendency among the Muslims to look at political issues from a narrow religious angle. In as much as the Khilafat fiasco further consolidated Muslim separateness from the national mainstream, it gladdened the heart of the imperialists who had fostered and assiduously nourished it since 1906. At the end of the whole flop show of contrived Hindu Muslim unity, the British had the last laugh. There is a lesson in this for the latterday 'secularist' politicions of India today who are reviving the ghost of Muslim separatism by raking up the issue of reservations and weightages for Muslims in various fields. But that is part of another story.

The non-cooperation movement started by the Mahatma in August 1920 failed to remain non-violent. On 5 February 1922, a mob of congress processionists attacked chauri chaura police station in Gorakhpur district of eastern U.P. and killed 22 policemen. True to his conscience, Gandhiji promptly called off the movement. His brief affair with the Maulanas of khilafat agitation ended with the end of the caliphate itself at the hands of Kemal Attaturk.

At the end of it, the Maulanas went back to their old groove of Islamic orthiodoxy. So much so that Moulana Muhammad. Ali at one point went to the extent of observing that if he had to choose between a saintly Gandhi and a sinful Muslim, he would opt for the latter as a member of the Islamic Ummah. So much about the failed attempt to woo the Muslims by pampering to their separatist religious fanaticism.

M.A. Jinnah was still in the congress when Gandhi took the center stage in the freedom movement and the congress party. It is not so well known that Jinnah did not approve of Gandhiji's hobnobbing with the Khilafat leaders when the issue cropped up in 1919 and was opposed to the Congress joining the Khilafat agitation. By this time, Jinnah was feeling sidetracked and marginalized by Gandhiji in the Congress Party and national politics. And for him, the Nagpur session of the congress in December 1920 proved to be the last straw on the camel's back. In course of the proceedings when Jinnah got up to make a point and addressed Gandhiji as Mr. Gandhi; the congressmen shouted him down and asked him to address him as 'Mahatma'. That was a final turning point in the life of Jinnah and a fateful moment in the history of the country. He not only parted company with the nationalist party he had been associated with since he entered politics, he treaded along a path which ended in the partition of India.

It would be no exaggeration to say that if creation of Pakistan could be attributed to any one person, though it was not exactly so as to be elaborated a little later, it would be M.A. Jinnah. Addressing the Royal Empire Society London in 1949, a British MP, David Gammans observed : "The creation of Pakistan is one of the most fantastic happenings of this age, and shows how individuals can still determine history, for Pakistan was the creation of one man-Mr. Jinnah."

As for Jinnah turning his back on the Congress, the Nagpur Congress session episode was only a catalyst. It was building up right from the moment Gandhiji started emerging as the top leader of the national movement. Dr. Sachchidanand Sinha, a liberal nationalist closely associated with T.B. Sapru and M.R. Jaykar of yester years, attributed it to Jinnah's basic personality trait of trying to be "the first and foremost in every walk and sphere of life" that he strode. In the journal "Hindustan Review" of September 1949, which he himself edited, Dr. Sinha wrote: "Jinnah grasped it immediately that the predominance of Gandhiji over the Congress was to be wholly exclusive and no one could successfully compete with a leader like the new one, who was a conglomeration of asceticism, mysticism, non-cooperation, non-violence, charkha spinning, renunciation of the world, coupled with the intensely patriotic demand for the independence of India."

That aptly sums up the basic reason for Jinnah's abandoning the nationalist platform with the advent of Gandhiji on the scene, though Nehru accounts for it slightly differently. In his book "Discovery of India' published in November 1947, Nehru wrote : "Jinnah left the Congress not because of any difference of opinion on the Hindu-Muslim question, but because he could not adapt himself to the new and more advanced ideology, and even more so because he disliked the crowds of ill-dressed people talking in Hindustani who filled the congress". Commenting on Jinnha's personality in a similar vein though in a different context, Larry Collins and Dominique Lappierre observe: "Jinnah despised India's masses. He detested the dirt, the h eat, the crowds of India". ("Freedom At Midnighyt". 1976).

All that boils down to one conclusion. Jinnah's change of track from the nationalist to a separatist path which changed the course of history was a fallout of ego clash with the Mahatma. And once Jinnah took to the separatist course, he never looked back. But his transition from nationalism to separatism was not abrupt. Even while being in the congress, he had also been associated with the Muslim League. In fact, he had played a role along with Tilak in making the Congress and the League sign the Luckhnow Pact in 1916 in the hope of uniting the Hindus and Muslims in the struggle for freedom. After leaving the Congress, he s aw his political future with the Muslim League and started reviving it from 1924 onwards, but had not yet been transformed into a full-fledged separatist of the later days. In 1925, he rebutted a Muslim youth who said that he was a Muslim first in these words: "My boy,no,you are an Indian first and then a Muslim." (Quoted in "India's Struggle For Independence" by Bepin Chandra and others, 1990.) And when the nationalists led by the Congress decided to boycott the visit of Simon Commission to India, Jinnah supported the boycott call.

In fact, Jinnah was torn by kind of a conflict between nationalism and separatism during this period. He could not think of returning back to the

National Congress which had organized a mass movement against the British in 1930 under Gandhiji's leadership. And he had not yet reached the point of complete break with his nationalist past, so he decided to stay mostly in England and carry on with his practice of law. It was in this period that Rahmat Ali of the Muslim League met him in London and mooted the idea of Pakistan to him. Evidently, it was the idea of upper class pro-British Muslim leaders like the Aga Khan and Allama Iqbal. Jinnah rejected the idea straightaway as not practicable.

But a highly talented, energetic and ambitious political person like Jinnah could not remain in political hibernation for long. May be under suitable prodding by the British, Jinnah returned to India in 1936 to revive the Muslim League with a new vigor. Meanwhile the political situation in India had undergone a sea change. The British rulers had announced the notorious 'Communal Award' in 1932 which conceded all demands of Muslim communal leaders formulated earlier during 1927-28 around the time of the Simon Commission's visit. These included separation of Sindh from Bombay to make it a Muslim majority Province, the North West Frontier, another Muslim majority area, to be treated at par with other provinces, 33 1/3 per cent representation for Muslims in the Central legislature, continuation of separate electorates and reservation of seats for Muslims in government services and self-governing bodies. More importantly, elections to the Provincial Assemblies were going to be held early in 1937 under the scheme of Provincial Autonomy envisaged in the Government of India. Act 1935, which the Congress had accepted. Jinnah wanted to test the waters by leading the Muslim League in the Elections.

He started by assuming the posture of a liberal Muslim leader, asking the Muslims to show their strength as a separate religious community but at the same time swearing loyalty to the country. The mixed sort of message emanating from him did not cut much ice with the Muslim electorate. The election results disappointed him. The Muslim League won only 109 out of 482 seats reserved for Muslims under the scheme of separate electorates. A large number of reserved seats were won by those who came to be called nationalist Muslims. Jinnah had not bargained for this. He had returned back to active politics in India with the objective of becoming the sole leader of Muslims of India. Having burnt his boat with nationalist leadership of the Congress, the only option before Jinnah, if he wanted to play a leading role in the politics of the country, was to try and become the undisputed and exclusive leader of Indian Muslims. And the only way he could do that was to shed off the façade of a liberal Muslim and assume the role of saviour of Indian Muslims from the impending disaster of Hindu rule. Once he assumed that role, he went the whole hog with no holds barred.

From 1938 onwards, he started talking of Hindu over-lordship over Muslims if Congress wrested freedom from the British. He told his co-religionists that if the Congress succeeded the British as the rulers of India, Muslims would be enslaved and Islam wiped out from the country. The slogan of Islam in danger had an instant appeal among the Muslim masses and Jinnah started emerging as a mass leader which he had never been in life. It was a heady experience. He overnight became a mass leader of Muslims without having to sweat it out in "the dirt, the heat, the crowds of India" which he hated. He created the utopia of Pakistan which far over-shadowed the image of Azad Bharat or Independent India in the psyche of India's Muslims.

To legitimize his case for creation of Pakistan, Jinnah propounded the preposterous two-nation theory and raised it to the level of a dogmna. He elaborated it at some length in an interview to Beverly Nichols, a British conservative journalist who visited India in 1943. He told him: "You must remember that Islam is not merely a religious doctrine but a realistic and practical code of conduct. I am thinking in terms of life, of everything important in life. I am thinking in terms of our history, our heroes, our art, our architecture, our music, our laws, our jurisprudence... In all these things our outlook is not only fundamentally different, but often radically antagonistic to the Hindus. We are different beings. There is nothing in life which links us together. Our names, our clothes, our foods-they are all different; our economic life, our educational ideas, our treatment of women, our attitude to animals.... We challenge each other at every point of the compass. Take one example, the eternal question of the cow. We eat the cow, the Hindus worship it." ('Verdict on India' by Beverly Nichols, 1944).

That was an amazing outburst of a Muslim leader who was the descendent of a Hindu. Here was M.A. Jinnah, once an ardent nationalist, a follower of Dadabhai Naoroji, "Ambassador of Hindu-Muslim unity" in the words of Sarojini Naidu, in his new avatar as an arch separatist pontificating upon the 'Mantra' of separatism before a British journalist in 1943. How come he was so radically transformed during the last chapter of his eventful political career? But first, who was this British journalist who came to explore India at a time when all nationalist political leaders and activists were behind the bars in the wake of the 'Quit India' movement and Britain itself was engaged in a grim world war? The book he authored on his return gives out the nature and purpose of his visit. The very title of the book "Verdict on India" reflected the judgmental and patronizing, if not outright condemnatory, fare that it was serving before the readers. He showered praises on Jinnah as the most articulate political leader in India, thought rather poorly of Gandhiji and more poorly of India. His verdict then in his own words: After all, Indian history, until the arrival of the British, was a record of unbridled despotism. India had always been a land of glittering palaces, surrounded by masses of human ant heaps; there was never any middle class, and no breath of democracy had ever stirred the Indian dust until we came. We were changing all that, and the change was gathering momentum everyday. In the meantime, nobody but the most purblind nationalist could claim that India, as a whole, was a modern country. Some of it was still in a period corresponding to that of Peter the Great; some of it was Elizabethan, some of it was unashamedly medieval; it was, in fact, a whole bunch of historical anachronisms." ("Verdict on India", Beverly Nichols, 1944).

No objective and unbiased pen pusher could come out with such a sweeping and conclusive judgment on a country as vast and variegated as India after only a short visit to the metropolitan fringe. His visit and interaction with a chosen few like Jinnah were too flitting to enable any journalist worth the name to form any opinion about the country, its history and social structure, much less such a definitive and altogether negative opinion. Keeping aside the background of the writer, it appeared at the outset to any reader that much of the book was written even before the writer set his foot on India. The book aroused an uproar of protest in the print media not only in India but also in sympathetic circles in England. It was widely believed at that time that Beverly Nichols was sponsored by the imperialists in the British political establishment in order to denigrade the freedom movement then in its final stages. His singing of paeans to Jinnah and downgrading of Gandhiji in the wake of 'Quit India' stir speaks volumes about the Muslim League's British connection, the full implication of which was not realized at that time. Nor is it fully understood down to this day.

No doubt Pakistan was born, as commonly believed, out of the separatism of the Muslim League and intransigence of Jinnah. Separatism is latent among Muslim peoples all over the world because of the exclusivity of Islamic polity based on the concept of Islamic Ummah. To that extent, partition of the country may be attributed to the inherent separateness of the Muslim mind-set which refuses to integrate with non-Muslims to fully merge into a solid national identity. To the extent Jinnah almost single-handedly took the mantle of separatist Islam and steered it through to its goals, he can take the credit (or discredit from the Indian point of view) for creation of Pakistan. It would appear that innate Muslim separatism used Jinnah to achieve its ultimate objective and Jinnah used Muslim separatism to realize his personal ambition to be the sole leader of at least one part of the country. Both would appear to be in kind of an egg and hen relationship.

But that would be a superficial view of the matter. For there was a third dimension to the entire process which culminated in the partition of India and which has been generally overlooked by contemporary historians and political analysists of the events. It is the hidden and not so hidden hand of the British masters which was steadily and calculatedly guiding the entire show towards the inexorable climax of partition. All the dramatis personne-Gandhi, Jinnah, Nehru- and the parties-Congress and Muslim League- were unwittingly playing into the hands of the British who had their own long-term view about the future of the sub-continent.

The British strategy in respect of India went through two stages. The first stage which started during the last quarter of the 19th century was the well known formula of 'Divide and Rule'. After the first uprising of 1857, they felt concerned about the emerging Indian nationalism as a challenge to their rule. The only way to checkmate it was to prevent the two major communities – the Hindus and Muslims – from coming together to constitute a strong nationalist threat to their rule then and in future. And they started working slowly and steadily to keep them disunited. The strategy was to work overtime on community leaders of Muslims who could be vulnerable to their influence. The first among them was Sayyed Ahmad Khan who was keen to promote modern education, particularly among Muslims who were lagging behind. He had founded the Aligarh college with financial support from both Muslims and Hindus and had considerable presence of Hindu as well as Muslims. In 1884, he told a gathering of Muslims and Hindus: "Do you not inhabit this land? Are you not buried in it or cremated on it? Surely you live and die on the same land. Remember that Hindus and Muslims are religious terms. Otherwise, Hindus, Muslims and Christians who live in this country are by virtue of this fact one'Quom' (nation)". ('Communalism in Modern India' Bipin Chandra, 1987). And yet, after the formation of the Indian National Congress in 1885, the same Saiyyed Ahmad Khan made a complete U-turn to preach irreconcilable antagonism between Muslims and Hindus. He openly told the Muslims to oppose the nationalist platform of the Congress.

Among other notable Muslim leaders to be won over by the British to the separatist ideology later during the first half of the 20th century was Allama Iqbal, the great Urdu poet, who started off as an enlightened nationalist. The strongest testimony to his nationalist credentials is his famous patriotic poem "Sare Jahan Se Achha Hindustan Hamara", which continues to be a very popular patriotic song in India even now. It has been tuned into fine martial music by Indian Army and Police bands to be played on ceremonial occasions. But the same Allama Iqbal said at a meeting in the British House of Commons in 1932 that it was impossible for Hindu and Muslim social and political interests to merge together into one and that the British rule was the best option for India. Later he became one of the originators of the concept of a separate Muslim state comprising the Muslim majority areas of India.

Jinnah was the last and the most important leader to be roped in by the British in their game of fanning Muslim separatism and leading it to its logical conclusion from behind the scene. The idea of Pakistan may have originated in the minds of Muslim idealogues like poet Iqbal or Rahmat Ali of the Muslim League and given shape late in the day by Jinnah, but its foundation was laid by the British in 1905 when they brought about the partition of Bengal to carve a separate Muslim majority province in that part of the country. (The partition of Bengal was however subsequently revoked·after the storm of protests by the nationalists giving rise to the Swadeshi movement). Since then, the British kept pursuing the separatist agenda from behind the scene, keeping one Muslim leader or the other in front. From the stage-managed Aga Khan delegation waiting upon Lord Minto in October 1906 to the formation of the Muslim League by Nawab Samaullah of Dacca through the Minto-Morley Reforms introducing the pernicious measures of Muslim reservation and separate electorates in 1909, reinforcing these measures in the Montagu-chelnsford Reforms of 1919 and communal Award of 1932, the British kept moving steadfastly and on the single track leading to a permanent divide in India's body politic on religious lines. The nationalist and Muslim leaders kept shuffling across, uniting and disuniting alternately, without making any difference to the one point programme of the British which they pursued single-mindedly.

This policy was carried through unwaveringly right up to the partition of India in 1947. Even when the British sought to secure the cooperation of Indian people during the second world war and sent a mission under Stafford Cripps in March 1942 to bring round the nationalists, they did not stray from their set agenda of promoting communal divide. The Cripps proposal of freedom under the British commonwealth after the war contained the vital separatist provision of permitting any province to secede from mainland India and negotiate its future independently with the British. That was an open invitation to Jinnah and his Muslim League to opt for Pakistan. And finally, when the new Labour Prime Minister of Britain made an announcement in British Parliament on 20 February 1947 fixing 30 June 1948 as the dateline for British withdrawal from India, he made a provision that if the Muslim majority provinces did not join the proposed Indian Union by then, power would be transferred to more than one central government in India. That was no less than a declaration of creation of Pakistan after the impending British withdrawal. It was the culmination of a process started by the British way back in 1905 and 1906.

The implication of the announcement was evident to some British parliamentarians themselves, who minced no words in course of the debate on it in the British Parliament. Godfrey Nicolson said: "If ever there was a speech which was a direct invitation to the Muslim League to stick their toes in and hold out for Pakistan, that was one." (Quoted in 'India's Struggle For Independence", Bepin Chandra and others,1990). The Congress leaders in India were gloating in the sight of freedom near at hand, still hoping against hope that the Muslim League would join hands to usher in an independent united India. But Jinnah knew better. He told a senior Journalist: "I am getting Pakistan (on a platter); Why should I settle for anything less?" ("From Curzon To Nehru", Durga Das).

That was it. The entire drama of India's partition was scripted from A to Z and directed by the British. Jinnah was their front man and Muslim League their frontal organization. It was the British who had fostered, nourished and sustained Muslim seperatism and harnessed Jinnah's political ambition and skill to bring about the "Vivisection of India", as Gandhiji called it, to carve a separate Muslim state out of their Indian empire. How was it that every Muslim leader of consequence from Saiyyed Ahmad Khan to M.A. Jinnah started as a liberal nationalist and ended up as a communal separatist? Evidently there was an invisible or not so visible hand that was prodding them. That hand was of the British. And the instruments they had used were reservations for Muslims, separate electorates and communal award.

Incidentally, it is highly intriguing that similar instruments of Muslim reservations and separateness have resurfaced in India over half a century after the unfortunate partition of the country. The founding fathers of the Indian Republic, having burnt their fingers with those kinds of instruments which the British had used to divide the people, scrupulously avoided providing for or permitting any preferential treatment to any community on the basis of religion. And yet, history seems to be repeating itself when reservations in this sphere and that and separateness of their educational institutions are being offered to Muslims almost unsolicited. Around mid 2005, a meeting of the anachronistic Jamat-e-Ulama was organized in Delhi which was graced by no less a person than Sonia Gandhi, the Congress President and chairperson of the ruling United Progressive Alliance. The main demand of the ulemas was reservation for Muslims in various spheres which the Congress President was gracious enough to agree to consider favourably. The whole show bore ominous similarity to the Aga Khan delegation meeting the viceroy Lord Minto at Shimla in October 1906 with similar demands and the Viceroy's gracious response to it. What followed is history, discussed earlier in this chapter. The British did it to divide and rule. What are the latter day protagonists of Muslim reservations doing it for? To secure a ghettoized vote bank for a stint in office?

That was a digression. One question remains to be answered regarding the British rooting for partition of India and creation of Pakistan. For it has been clarified above that Pakistan was a creation of the British and not of Jinnah and his Muslim League. But why did they do it while finally giving up the Indian empire? The answer lies in the contemporary world situation at the end of the Second World War. As the most clever and sophisticated empire builders of the modern world, the British had realised that keeping up the empire of India, as of empire generally, with the force of British arms was neither feasible nor profitable after the ravages of the war. The economies of the European countries lay in ruins with their destroyed industrial base and all round shortages and deprivations staring their people in the face. In case of Britain, this was clearly brought out in the elections of 1946 when the Britons handed a resounding defeat to the Conservative Party led by the wartime hero Winston Churchill. The Labour Party led by Altee was voted to power with a clear mandate to go about with post-war economic reconstruction of their home country rather than frittering away energy and resources on holding on to an empire which had nothing to offer except an empty name. The British therefore knew that they had to withdraw from India when they did. But they were determined to maintain a foothold in the sub-continent before they departed. And they knew that it was only a separate and weak Muslim state of Pakistan, created by them and very much dependent on them for many things, that could serve as their foothold. That was their parting kick to India which was too big and independent a country to allow them any quarter. They had followed the policy of divide and rule as long as they could. When they could rule no longer, they switched over to the policy of divide and keep a foothold in the sub-continent.

This was a time when the post-war world was getting divided into two power blocks led by two super powers-the U.S. and Soviet Union. Churchill's famous Fulton speech of 1946 referring to an 'Iron curtain' descending upon Eastern Europe which was fast being sovietised, was a waking call for America and its allies in western Europe to form a bull work against communist expansion ism in Europe and other parts of the world. The broad configuration of two mighty power blocks comprising the U.S. and its West European allies on the one side and Soviet Union and the communist Eastern Europe on the other had taken shape. In Asia, China was fast slipping into the communist camp. In the circumstances, Britain, as the closest U.S. ally and an important member of the western camp, had realized that only a breakaway state like Pakistan could stand up and be counted as a member of the Anglo-U.S. block, at a price. Pakistan thus represented Anglo-U.S. presence in the sub-continent even after British withdrawal for which it was created.

The Kashmir problem, which is supposed to be the causative factor behind the onslaught of Jihadi terrorism against India, is also largely a legacy of the British. Under the scheme of independence, the princely states, of which Kashmir was one, had the option of acceding to either India or Pakistan. Maharaja Hari Singh of Jammu & Kashmir was under intense pressure from Pakistan to accede to it, but he kept resisting it for as long as he did. In the light of massacres of Hindus in Pakistan on the eve and immediate aftermath of its creation, the Hindu Maharaja was least inclined to accede to Pakistan simply on the ground that a majority of his subjects in the Valley were Muslims. Even as he was resisting the Pakistani pressure and biding his time, Pakistan army personnel in the grab of tribal raiders from the North West broke loose into Kashmir, making mince meat of the ramshackle forces of Kashmir Raj. The Maharaja sent frantic messages to the Government of India to come to his aid through military intervention. For the Maharaja, the die had been cast and the moment of decision had come. India could have accepted the Maharaja's request forthwith, signed the document of accession and rushed its troops to Kashmir to defend the state. But it was Lord Mountbatten, who was still the Governor General of India, who advised caution. When the situation deteriorated and the Pakistani raiders were within striking distance of Srinagar, India accepted the accession of the state of Jammu & Kashmir "Provisionally", subject to some kind of confirmation by the people. The clause of provisionality was entirely uncalled for and it was believed to have been introduced on the advice of Mountbatten.

After one year of bitter fighting, the Indian Army succeeded in chasing back the Pakistani raiders from Kashmir Valley and was poised to clear them off the remaining one third of the state. But exactly at this point, India took the surprise decision to refer the case to the U.N. Security Council and lodged a complaint on 1 January 1948. That started a process of intervention by the U.N. in Kashmir leading to a ceasefire between India and Pakistan on 1 January 1949. India's decision to take the issue to the U.N. at a time when it was in a position to clear the remaining one third of its territory off the illegal occupation of Pakistan within a mater of weeks, not only surprised but also shocked the intelligentsia in India at that times. As a post-graduate student of economics and political science in 1948-49, this writer was involved in endless arguments and discussions about the rights and wrongs of that decision. It was widely believed at that time that the British through Mountbatten's influence over Nehru had got him to agree to take the matter to the U.N. in order to have a leverage over India in the context of the cold war then in progress. They had Pakistan already under their thumb and they wanted to rein in India also through the lever of Kashmir. The result is there for every one to see. The Kashmir problem still remains where it was on 1 January 1949 when the ceasefire came into force, inspite of three wars fought between India and Pakistan over the issue.

But the worst fall out of a hundred years old British policy of dividing India on religious lines is the build up of Pakistan into a Frankestein to keep India perennially under the sheath. For, pathological hatred of India and Islamism are the two foundational pillars of the Pakistani state and its core ideology right from the day it came into being. After partition, India left the past behind and proceeded to build up and consolidate its national identity irrespective of diverse religious faiths of its people. Muslims have since been considered as valuable a p[art of India's nationhood as Hindus, Sikhs and others. It is a testimony to India's secular or religion-neutral polity that the country has had three Presidents, two Vice-Presidents, a Chief Justice of the highest court, Chief Ministers and any number of other important government functionaries drawn from the Muslim community. Pakistan, on the other hand, launched upon a course of religious 'cleansing' right from the day of its creation through a ruthless process of liquidating and throwing out the Hindus and Sikhs and forcibly converting the remnants to Islam.

The pattern was set in the run up to the birth of Pakistan when Hindus and Sikhs were annihilated wholesale in one locality or another by rampaging

Muslim mobs in the North West. Larry Collins and Dominique Lapiarre narrate the devastation of one such locality-Kahuta-which the viceroy Lord Mountbatten visited in April 1947. It needs to be quoted in extenso: "For centuries, Kahuta's dirt had been shared in peace by 2000 Hindus and Sikhs and 1500 Muslims....Kahuta's citizens, as they had for generations, were sleeping side by side in mutual confidence and tranquility. By dawn, Kahuta for all practical purposes had ceased to exist and its Sikhs and Hindus were all dead or had fled in terror into the night....A Muslim horde had descended on the village like a wolf pack, setting fire to the houses in its Sikh and Hindu quarters with buckets of gasoline. In minutes, the area was engulfed in fire and entire families, screaming pitifully for help, were caught, tied together, soaked with gasoline and burned alive like torches.... Hindu women, hauled from their beds to be raped and converted to Islam, survived; others had broken away from their captors and hurled themselves back into the fire to perish with their families." ('Freedom At Midnight', Larry Collins and Dominique Lapiarre, 1976). That showed the shape of things to come.

The scene continued to be replicated after the creation of Pakistan in towns and villages of west Pakistan until it was cleared of the unwanted Hindu and Sikh communities. It was religious 'cleansing' par excellence, in comparison to which the ethnic cleansing in Bosnia would pale into insignificance. Pakistan had to be converted into a land its very name literally meant-'the land of the pure', the faithful'. It had no place for people professing different faiths-particularly Hindus and Sikhs. And it showed in the complete demographic transformation of the country. From around 30 per cent at the time of partition, the share of Hindu-Sikh population in the territory constituting Pakistan came down to barely 2 percent or so. The pre-natal seed of hatred which gave birth to Pakistan sprouted into a full-fledged forest of hatred against India, which has spread its dark shadows over its attitude and policy towards India for all times to come.

Pakistan's congenital hatred of Hindus is in the nature of Nazi's hatred of the Jews. It has shown time and again in most diabolical forms. When Sikhs in India were estranged after "Operation Blue Star" in 1984, thanks to monumental blunders committed by India's political leadership, Pakistan found its opportunity to hit India where it hurt most. Addressing a group of trainees in the Institute of Regional studies in Islamabad, Lt. General (Retd) A.I. Akram said:"Punjab of India provides Pakistan the last opportunity to settle scores with the Hindus of India who gave Pakistan a truncated part and later reduced its size further." (Quoted in the book `ISI Ka Atank' in Hindi meaning 'Terror of ISI' by Ram Naresh Pd. Singh, a former Intelligence Bureau officer who had watched Punjab terrorism from close quarters, 2001).

Pakistan grabbed this "last opportunity" with both hands. It launched upon the notorious 'K-2' plan of fomenting large scale terrorist violence in both Punjab and Kashmir to break up India, the code name for operation Khalistan and Kashmir. This was revealed to Indian intelligence agencies by some of the Khalistani Sikh terrorists arrested subsequently in 1988 and 1992. Under the 'K-2' plan, Pakistan organised a sustained Hindu-killing campaign in India through Punjabi terrorists sheltered in Pakistan. Terrorist groups openly nourished, financed and armed by Pakistan went on a killing spree during the second half of 1980's. Apart from selective killings of Hindus in buses, trains and market places, they also killed a number of prominent Sikh leaders and personalities supposed to be loyal to India. At one time, famous Sikh author and journalist Khushwant Singh was a prime target of terror strike for writing against any further break up of India.

At its peak, around a dozen terrorist outfits ensconced in Pakistan and pumped with money and weapons by it, ran one of the world's most lethal and bloodiest terrorist killing machines on Indian soil from across the border. In his preface to the book 'ISI Ka Atank', Om Prakash Sharma, then Governor of Nagaland, wrote:" During a decade of peak terrorism in Punjab, some 20,000 lives were lost at the hands of ISI sponsored terrorism. These figures are more than the combined casualties during all the wars India fought after independence."

The Punjab terrorism was eventually curbed, not because of any let up on the part of Pakistan, but because of other reasons. The basic fact about the Punjab situation was that Sikh anguish and anger against operation Blue Star and subsequent unfortunate events did not amount to alienation from Indian nationhood. They were deeply hurt but not alienated. Julio Riberio, the Police Chief of Punjab during the peak of terrorism in that state, writes:" An overwhelming majority of Sikhs, anyway, were not in favour of a separate state" ("Bullet For Bullet" by Julio Riberio, 1998).

Pakistan did its best or worst to bleed India by exploiting to the full the hurt Sikh psyche, but could do no more. In a fit of anger, the Sikhs were lured into thinking about a separate Sikh state of Khalistan, but they could never contemplate teaming up with Pakistan. How could they forget the annihilation of Sikhs, along with Hindus, at the hands of Muslims preceding and following the creation Pakistan? More so, how could they put aside the torture and killing of two of their revered Gurus by Mughal emperors who succeeded Akbar?

But Pakistan would never give up. When its game plan 'K-2' failed to click in Punjab, it turned attention to India's North East where a different kind of ethnic terrorism was already on. With bases in the Islamic state of Bangladesh, where Jamat-e-Islami was a major force, Pak ISI established links with regional terrorist outfits like ULFA to undermine India through terror in that part of the country. In March-April 1991, three top ULFA leaders visited Islamabad and established direct contact with the ISI at the latter's instance. After that, ULFA militants from India's North East started visiting Pakistan for training in handling rocket launchers and other lethal weaponry. They also began receiving training in subversive terrorist operations in camps in Bangladesh organised by Pak ISI.

Pakistan thus has turned out to be the principal factor in India's terror scenario across the board from North West to North East. It all forms part of Pakistan's unceasing Jihad against India. The twin ideologies of Islamism and anti-Indianism, which are the corner stones of the failed state of Pakistan, have merged to give rise to the hydra-headed monster of Jihadi terrorism which India has been battling for the last two decades or so. India's predicament is that it has had to cope with an inveterate enemy next door syndrome right since its inception as an independent nation. It is living with that even today. More of it in the next sub-chapter.

In The Thick of Jihadi Terror

It is commonly believed that the dispute with Pakistan over Kashmir is the cause of the eruption of Jihadi terrorism in India. That is an over simplistic view of the matter. In a broad sense, Jihad against India was inherent in the mind-set that gave birth to Pakistan in the first place. It is true that Pakistan was the product of Muslim separatism fostered, aided and abetted by the British from behind the scene and given practical shape by Jinnah and his Muslim League. But it was an outgrowth of the basic ideology of Islamism which guided the separatists and constituted the core value of the Pakistani state. Kashmir is not really the cause of Pakistan's unceasing Jihad against India but a result of it.

A slogan loudly raised by Muslim League crowds in the euphoria of announcement about the creation of Pakistan in June 1947 vouched:"Hans Ke Liya hai Pakistan, Lad Ke Lenge Hindustan". ('We have achieved Pakistan smilingly, that is with ease. We will conquer Hindustan by fighting a war') This writer was personally a witness to such processions jubilantly raising the above slogan in a district town of Bihar in June 1947 after the final announcement of the scheme of partition of India. Bihar, it may be noted, was one of the strongest citadels of the Muslim League at the time of partition. In the Assembly elections of 1946, all the reserved sweats for Muslims in Bihar (except those in what is now Jharkhand), under the scheme of separate electorates, were won by the Muslim League. The slogan, though dismissed as mere rhetoric at that time, was not so innocuous after all. It amply reflected the spirit of Jihad against India which Pakistan was born with.

This has been amply corroborated by what followed in the shape of Pakistan's unmitigated hostility towards India right from the day one. Pakistan's record in this regard will speak for itself, but before that, a glance at the mind-set of Pakistani academicians would be quite revealing. In the eyes of Pakistani historians, Aurangzeb, who is well known the world over for religious persecution of Hindus and Sikhs, was the greatest Muslim ruler of India. And as a corollary to that, Akbar was denounced as a ruler who undermined the morale of the Muslim people of India by his liberal policy towards the Hindus. The Pakistan History Board got prepared "A Short History of Hind-Pakistan" according to which Aurangzeb was quite justified in giving an Islamic character to the state. It was necessary, it is argued, to enlist the full support of the Muslims in order to strengthen Aurangzeb's empire. It goes to the extent of justifying the imposition of Jizya tax on Hindus in order to restore the institutions of Islam and destruction of Hindu temples on the ground that they had been built in an "unauthorised manner", whatever that might mean. Even the killing of Sikh Gurus has been justified in the name of suppressing political opposition to his rule.

Pakistan thus 'doctored' history also to justify Aurangzeb's Jihad against Hindus and Sikhs in the manner only Nazis and Fascists could do. It is like the fundamentalist Islamic President of Iran-Ahmedinejad-who, in his pathological hatred of the Jews, is out to prove that the Holocaust did not happen.

Further proof, if any proof is needed, of Pakistan's inborn itch for Jihad against India is provided by the nomenclature of the ballistic missiles it has developed. Evidently directed against India, these missiles capable of carrying nuclear warheads have been named "Ghouri" and "Ghazni" after the notorious Muslim conquerors of India in the Middle Ages. The havoc wrought by them in India, particularly against the Hindus, is well known, as already dealt with earlier. The point to note here is not what Mohammad Ghouri and Mohmud Gahzni did or did not do to India, but the brazen-facedness of Pakistani wish to demolish India. It is in the very texture of Pakistan right from its very inception. And it has been the cherished dream of every Pakistani regime, military or civil, to hand down a crushing defeat on India in the manner of Mahmud Ghazni and Mohammad Ghori someway or the other, someday or the other.

Pakistan's first attempt to brow beat India in a trial of strength over Kashmir failed, but its itch to defeat India someday somehow did not subside. For various reasons known to all, including the manipulations of international interlocutors to serve their own strategic interests, Kashmir became the focal issue on which Pakistan concentrated to realize its ambition of defeating India. Its opportunity came when a competent professional general like Ayub Khan assumed the reins of the country as the President of Pakistan. After consolidating his position in the country and legitimizing his military rule under the cloak of 'Basic Democracy', Ayub Khan launched Pakistan's second military offensive to take Kashmir by force in late July 1965. The timing of the launch was most opportune from Pakistan's point of view. India had been battered in the border war of 1962 by China which had become a close ally of Pakistan. The Indian colossus-Jawahar Lal Nehru-had passed away in May 1964 and the little known 'little man' of Indian politics-Lal Bahadur Shastri was in charge of the country.

And yet Ayub Khan did not take any chances. He was quite conscious of the ill organized manner in which the first Kashmir war was launched by Pakistan in 1947 resulting in its failure. "Soldiers and Officers were put on their own", he had recorded in his autobiography, "with little direction from headquarters and with considerable responsibility placed in the hands of junior officers."[4] This time round, the entire war strategy had been masterminded by the great General himself who was also the President of Pakistan. He had earlier tasted the political will of the new Indian leadership by making a probing military move in the Rann of Kutch. Shastri's gesture of buying peace in the Kutch sector was taken as his lack of will to fight a war with Pakistan if it came to that. To leave nothing to chance, Ayub Khan had also mended his fences with Soviet Russia to ensure its neutrality, even though Pakistan was a member of the American block. This was possible because of the growing détente in the

Cold war between the two super powers around the mid-1960's.

Having planned every move to perfection, armed with heavy American Patton Tanks to which India had no answer, Pakistani armour struck in strength at India's most vulnerable point. It was the Chhumb-Jauria sector of Jammu, India's chicken's neck, which served as its only narrow link with the Kashmir valley. If this link was snapped, the Indian troops trapped in Kashmir valley would have been swarmed by the full force of the Pak army from the Pakistani main-land resulting not only in the capture of Kashmir valley but also a decisive military defeat of India. And it seemed very nearly happening as the mighty Pakistani armour seemed unstoppable in the Chhump-Jauria sector.

Driven to the wall, the Indian military High command advised and Prime Minister Shastri decided to strike at a point where Pakistan least expected a military strike by India. 'The Big Little Man', as Shastri came to be called in India after the event, signaled the Indian army to cross the international border in Punjab and attack Sialkot and Lahore directly. The move was fraught with grave possibilities of a large scale war in which Pakistan could claim support from the American block of which it was a member. But India took that risk to defend Kashmir and also the country's honour under determined onslaught from Pakistan. And it paid India to take that risk which altered the entire complexion of the war and eventually brought about a ceasefire. The ceasefire was confirmed by the Tashkent Agreement brought about through Russian mediation in January 1966. Here again India made a territorial concession in the interest of peace by giving up the Hajipir pass which it had captured in course of the war.

Pakistan clashed with India for the third time in December 1971 over the issue of struggle for liberation of Bangladesh, Pak army's crack down on East Bengalese and India's support to them. In the light of the ultimate victory of India in this war and emergence of Bangladesh as an independent state. it was alleged by Pakistan and its close ally China at that time and is generally believed that India started the war to ensure the secession of Bangladesh from Pakistan. India of course was vitally concerned with the ongoing genocide of East Bengalese by Pak army leading to unceasing influx of millions of hapless refugees - both Hindus and Muslims - into India. The influx of such large numbers not only strained the resources of India beyond the tolerance limit and endangered internal peace and order but the rampaging Pak army next door also posed a threat to India's external security. Being aware of Pakistan's proclivity to embark on military adventures against India over Kashmir or otherwise, India did make preparations to fight a war if it was thrust upon her. Pakistan could be expected to flex its military muscles once again, supported as it was this time by both the U.S. and China, and embark upon an adventurist course against India. To guard against active American and Chinese support to Pakistan in case of a confrontation, Indira Gandhi concluded the Indo-Soviet Treaty of friendship in August 1971 as a cushion in case of need. India was also giving all moral and material support to East Bengalese groaning under the ravages of the ruthless Pakistani military machine.

But with all the support for the East Bengalese and military preparations, India did not actually start the war. From all available accounts and contrary to all the Goebbelsion propaganda by Pakistan, it was Pakistan which actually pulled the trigger and started the Indo-Pak war of December 1971. Here is a brief account of what exactly happened "Darkness had just fallen on the evening of 3rd December 1971 when air raid alert was sounded at 6 p.m. in most of the cities of India. President Giri was with some of the Union Cabinet Ministers and Members of Parliament, sipping a cup of tea in the lawns of Parliament House to celebrate the Goldern Jubillee of the Public Accounts Committee. In the Press Information Bureau of the Government of India, the newsmen had just assembled for the routine 6 o' clock briefing on the military situation in Bangladesh. With the sounding of sirens, all lights went off. Everyone including the President, the Cabinet Ministers, the Members of Parliament, the newsmen, was taken unaware and no one knew whether the air raid alert was an exercise or the sirens signaled a real alert. As minutes ticked off, the briefing officer told the newsmen that the air raid alert was a genuine one and that news had just been flashed to them that Pakistan had attacked our several airfields..... the street lights were never switched on,. The cities were plunged into darkness., The AIR then revealed the unfortunate incident of unprovoked aggression by Pakistan.

Pakistan Air Force, it turned out, had launched pre-emptive strikes at a dozen Indian Air Force Stations at 4.45 p.m. on 3 December 1971 all along the western sector ranging from Srinagar in Kashmir to Jodhpur and Jamnagar in Rajasthan. Coordinating with the air strikes, Pakistani ground forces launched massive attacks on Indian border posts all along the western sector in Jammu and Kashmir, Punjab and Rajasthan. After heavily shelling the Indian posts in the Poonch sector, Pakistani troops crossed the ceasefire line posing a serious threat to the Chhamb-Jauria 'Chicken neck'. The Indian retaliation was swift and effective.

The Indian Air Force counter-attacked by striking at Pakistani air fields in both the western and eastern sctors throughout the night. By the dawn of 4 December 1971, the IAF had struck eight PAF stations in the west and three Pakistan controlled air fields in what is now Bangladesh. The third Indo-Pak war had begun, started once again by Pakistan as on the earlier two occasions, thanks to Pakistan's fiendish ambition to hand down a military defeat to India which remains insatiated still.

For the consumption of those die-hard India-baiters who refuse to believe that Pakistan actually started the war, one remarkable fact about the political weather in India on 3rd December 1971 has to be brought to light or rather recalled. It was like any other day, with busines as usual in the political circles at Delhi. Prime Minister Indira Gandhi was away from the capital on a day's visit to Calcutta. After addressing a public gathering, she was meeting a group of artists when an aide walked in and gave her the news of the Pak attack on the western front. She treated the news with disbelief and wanted it to be re-checked. Her other senior colleague, Y.B. Chavan, the Finance Minister, had left Delhi on a scheduled tour just before the Pakistani attack was launched. And the most important political functionary in the prevailing situation, India's Defence Minister Jagjiwan Ram, was out on a tour of Bihar. By a rare chance, this writer in his capacity as the Police Chief of the area, had personally received the Defence Minister at Musaffarpur air strip at about 1 p.m. on 3rd December 1971. The Minister travelled by road to Pusa Agricultural Institute and addressed a gathering of farmers and agricultural scientists in the afternoon in the most normal sort of way. There was not a trace of tension or emotion which could be expected on the face of the Defence Minister of a country going to attack another. It would be preposterous to hold that the Prime Minister, Defence Minister and Finance Minister, the three topmost political functionaries of a country, would be out of the national capital attending to routine business on the day it started a war fraught with serious consequences.

Pakistan's misadventure in starting the war by attacking India all along the western front had an obvious motive. By opening the Kashmir, Punjab and Rajasthan fronts, it wanted to keep India bogged down in the western sector, allowing Pakistani forces to wipe out the Bangladeshi freedom fighters. It was rank bad political assessment and rank bad generalship to boot. Perhaps Pakistan banked upon military intervention on its behalf by its closest ally-China in the war. Zulfiqar Ali Bhutto had actually visited China at the top of a high level political and military delegation to solicit active Chinese support in the impending war. China had assured full support to Pakistan over the crisis in Bangladesh from outside just short of actual military intervention. In fact General Yahya Khan was to claim later that Bhutto had misled him into believing that China would actually join Pakistan in the war against India. Whatever might have passed between Bhutto and Yahya Khan, Pakistan and its leadership had none but themselves to blame for so decisively losing the war they had started themselves.

But the war cast a dark shadow on the future of the sub-continent. Bhutto, who came to power in Pakistan, minus East Bengal or Bangladesh, had already talked of fighting a "thousand years war" against India earlier. Pakistan's inborn and obsessive anti-Indianism reached an all-time high. There was a clear convergence of Pakistan's anti-Insianism with China's own strategic interests in South Asia. It was this close Sino-Pak convergence which eventually gave birth to the Pakistani bomb. In his hysteric cries after the Bangladesh war, Bhutto talked of producing an 'Islamic Bomb'. That was a camouflage to hide the secret nuclear deal which Bhutto was striking with the Chinese during this period. It was the Chinese bomb or Sino-Pak bomb which Bhutto meant when he talked of the 'Islamic bomb'. And he was to tell his countrymen later that he would be remembered by his countrymen for the deal which he had struck with China to help produce the Pakistani bomb. Pakistan's real opportunity came during Zia-ul-Haq's regime when Russia occupied Afganistan and America launched the Mujahideen resistance in a big way. The U.S. needed a conduit to fund and arm the Mujahideen resistance against the Russians inside Afganistan and Pakistan ideally filled the bill. General Zia not only acted the loyal bidder of the U.S. in Afganistan but also built Pakistan's own terrifying terrorist machine to launch a different kind of offensive against India this time round. Run by that notorious Pakistani agency—the I.S.I (Inter Services Intelligence), - Pakistan's terror machine got an ideal opportunity to hurt India mortally.

But before launching the terrorist offensive in a bigger and more sustained manner in Kashmir, Pakistan waited for another big thing to happen. In exchange for the services rendered in Afganistan, America, the doyen of crusaders for nuclear non-proliferation, had agreed to look the other way while Pakistan had been forging ahead with its clandestine nuclear bomb programme in collaboration with China. It reportedly tested its first atomic device at China's Lop Nor testing site in 1985 in secrecy. By 1987, its army generals openly boasted of having acquired atomic bomb capability. It was now time for real action to beat India and settle old scores. With a few vintage bombs beneath its basement, Pakistan mounted its real terrorist offensive in the more familiar grounds of Kashmir. It was an important contributory factor for Pakistan's most effective and sustained terrorist onslaught against India, as distinguished from sporadic acts of terrorism which had become endemic, from early 1980's. Having tested defeat in three successive wars, Pakistan knew it could not defeat India in a conventional war. Not to take any chances, it launched what has come to be called a 'proxy war' this time in the shape of virulent terrorist action organized and marshaled from within its borders. And it had its atomic bomb to blackmail and browbeat India In March 1987, General Zia, the Pak President, told the "Time Magazine": "You can virtually write today that Pakistan can build a (nuclear) bomb whenever it wishes. What is difficult about a bomb? Once you have acquired the technology, which Pakistan had, you can do whatever you like" ('The Time Magazine' 30 March 1987).

It is measure of Pakistani desperation that it not only flaunted its nuclear weapon capability in a bid to terrorise and blackmail India, but very nearly came to turning it into a real threat in 1990. It precipitated a crisis situation over Kashmir with implied threats of using nuclear weapons. But if Pakistan had, say 20 bombs fabricated out of its test explosion in 1985, India had around 40 or so based on its first nuclear test in 1974. And India did respond by putting its air force on the alert, ready to press the trigger in case. Dr. Raja Ramanna, India's Minister of state for defence, announced in the Rajya Sabha that while India would never use its nuclear capability first against a neighbor, but if the latter did so India would rise to the occasion. The U.S of course came to know and was alarmed. It sent the Robert Gates mission to warn of the devastating India retaliation if Pakistan actually launched a nuclear attack (K. Subramanyam 'Nuclear India', 1998).

Seymore Hersh, the noted American author, also knew and asserted that in 1990 Pakistan and India came close to using the bomb against each other causing a nuclear devastation in the sub-continent.

Having failed in its attempt at nuclear blackmail, Pakistan launched upon the most lethal phase of Jihadi terrorism against India which was not confined to Jammu & Kashmir but included India as a whole. As already mentioned earlier, one of the most destructive terrorist strikes against mainland India sponsored from across the border took place on 12 March 1993 when a series of high powered explosions rocked Mumbai, India's commercial capital. For nearly three hours, 13 big blasts tore through the heart of the city, devastating the Bombay Stock Exchange and Air India Buildings and prestigious hotels like the Sea Rock and Centaur. A lorry filled with high explosives was blown through remote control in the congested central Bombay locality of Dongri causing extensive loss of life and property. In all nearly 300 people were killed and 1500 injured.

Another sensational terrorist act that attracted international attention was perpetrated in July 1995 when five foreign tourists were kidnapped by terrorists in Kashmir. The terrorist group Al Faran responsible for the kidnapping was an affiliate of Harkat-UL-Ansar, a supra-national terrorist organization based in Pakistan. According to the U.S. State Department Annual Report on global terrorism, 1995, Harkat-Ul-Ansar had spread its tentacles not only to Kashmir but also to Burma, Tajikistan and Bosnia. Maulana Saddatullah Khan, leader of this organization, defined its goal as helping armed struggle against non-believers and anti-Islamic forces across the world.

Of the five captives, one was killed and his dead body was cynically exposed to public gaze; The remaining four were never traced. One of the lasting regrets of Wisner, the outgoing U.S. envoy to India, was that he could not secure the release of the hostages in course of his long tenure in India. It was no ordinary run-of-the mill case of kidnapping of tourists out on a pleasure trip to Kashmir to enjoy its salubrious summer. Its primary objective of course was to secure the release of hardcore Jihadis like Masood Azhar and Omar Sheikh then locked up in Delhi's high security Tihar Jail. But it was meant to deliver a blow to the western nations because the victims were all citizens of these countries including a Swede and an American. By this time, the Jihad in Kashmir had become a part of global Islamic Jihad. With Taliban, created, nourished and propped up by Pakistan running through Afganistan like a knife through a banana, Pakistan had come to be the hub of international Jihadi terrorism and India was caught in its vortex.

By now almost the whole of Afganistan except its northern fringe had come under the virtual control of Pakistan through its surrogate Taliban. It was around this time in 1996 that Osama bin Laden shifted from his roving bases in Sudan and elsewhere to establish a firm base in Talabani Afganistan. Pakistan was now in a position to harness international terrorists from other parts of the world to intensify its Jihad against India. This brought about a spurt in Pak sponsored Jihadi terrorism against India particularly directed against the Hindus of Kashmir and neighboring areas.

It was in this background that on the night of 21/22 March 1997; about 15 armed terrorists swooped on Sangarampur hamlet, 32 km from

Srinagar, inhabited by over 600 Kashmiri pandit families. They called out male members from their houses, took them some 15 mtrs away and showered bullets killing them on the spot.

This was no isolated event. In 1990 the local Urdu press in Srinagar had published a press release from the top terrorist outfit Hizbul Mujahidin demanding that Hindu Pandits should leave Kashmir. Since then, gangs of young terrorists carrying guns began random and indiscriminate killing of Hindu Pandit families. As a result of this sustained campaign of terror against them, the entire community of Hindu Pandits, once the cream of 'Ksahmiriat' or the harmonious Kashmiri style of life, were driven out of Kashmir valley. Today more than a quarter million Kashmiri pandit refugees have taken shelter in neighboring areas of Jammu, Punjab and Delhi. They are languishing in refugee camps in squalor and disease.

Simultaneously with killing of Hindu pandits in the valley, Pak sponsored Jihadi terrorists have been carrying out sustained killing of Hindus in different parts of Doda district bordering Pak-occupied areas which has a sizeable Hindu population. The objective behind this terror act is the same as in the case of killing of pandits in Kashmir valley. That is, to cleanse the area of the infidels so as to make the Doda district an overwhelming, if not exclusive, Muslim land. It may be noted that when Parvez Mushriff once talked about an out of the rut settlement of the Kashmir issue, he hinted at the idea of handing over Doda district or a part of it to Pakistan. The systematic killing of Hindus in this border district appears to be a part of this long term plan of Pakistan.

Another gory incident of killing of Hindus took place in 1998 when 35 persons, nearly all Hindus, were gunned down by Pakistan based terrorists in two villages of Himachal Pradesh adjoining Doda district of Jammu & Kashmir. All the victims were ordinary day labourers working on a road project in the area. They were shot dead by automatic weapons while sleeping during early hours of the morning.

The Taliban connection in Jihadi terror against India was clearly demonstrated in the hijacking of the Indian airlines plane from Kathmandu to Kandahar in December 1999, as already referred to earlier. The close linkage between the hijackers of the plane and Talibani officials dealing with the hostage release issue was quite evident in course of the entire negotiations carried out by the officials of Govt. of India. The freedom with which notorious Jihadi terrorists like Azhar Mahmood and Omar Sheikh walked away to Pakistan for carrying out the Jihad against India clearly showed that the Talibanis were acting as agents of Pakistan.

With the Taliban firmly established in Afganistan as its protégé, Osama bin Laden spreading his Al Quida network from there and the ISI actively associating with them, Pakistan was in a very strong position to indulge in acts of terrorism against India. And it made full use of this opportunity to bleed India at will. Then, by a quirk of destiny, came the Jihadi strike against America on 9.11.2001 that brought about a paradigm change in the situation. The world woke up to the serious threat posed by Jihadi terrorism to civilized life across the world. When an international coalition led by America took up the challenge and set about to demolish the Taliban and Al Quida in the wake of 9/11, a let up in Pakistan's terrorist offensive against India could be expected but, as it turned out, this did not happen. Pakistan promptly surrendered before America and joined the US band wagan, while at the same time carrying on its terror campaign against India. This was and continuous to be one of the rarest feet of duplicity, with hardly any parallel in the world. The Americans were satisfied with Pakistan's acquiescence in destruction of its own creation that was Taliban and also a show of helping them in the process. As for Pakistani Jihad against India, the Americans simply kept making some innocuous noises from time to time and nothing more. As a result, Pakistan continued its terror campaign against India after 9/11, which goes on unabated with the US looking the other way.

It was in this backdrop that even as the US forces were battering the Taliban in Kandahar beginning 7 December 2001, Pakistani terrorist struck at the Indian Parliament House on 13.12.2001. It was with the bold encounter and the ultimate sacrifice of their lives that the Indian security forces prevented a massacre of India's top political leadership and incapacitation of the Govt. itself. India reacted in a manner any state would react when the security and honour of the nation was at stake. As a tough message to Pakistan, India nearly snapped its ties with that country. The Indian Ambassador to Pakistan was recalled and Pakistan was debarred from using India's air space. On top of that, a grand mobilization was ordered of Indian armed forces all along the Indo-Pak border from Kashmir to Gujarat, throwing hints of hot pursuit of terrorists across the border. Alarm bells started ringing in Pakistan which got the right message. The US and its close ally Britain also got the message and started turning the heat on Pakistan to desist from its terrorist misadventure in India. For well over a year, the Indian armed forces remained poised for any eventuality along the border. The wily Pakistan President went about pleading with the world leaders to persuade India to start a dialogue. It was not until Pakistan gave reasonable assurance against promoting terrorism that India relented and armed mobilization was gradually called off. The evident outcome was Mushraff's open commitment to Vijayapee in January 2004 "not to permit any territory under Pakistan's control to be used to support terrorism in any manner".

But Pakistan being what it has been all through in the past, its assurances to India to end terrorism remained empty words, as subsequent events amply testify. Mushraff's record is no better than that of Hitler's. Before the start of the second world war, Hitler gave a firm assurance to England and France in terms of the Munich Pact of 1938 not to attack Sudetenland which was a part of Czechoslovakia and had a large German population. But within six months, he broke the promise, attacked Czechoslovakia and grabbed the whole country.

It took General Musharref about a year to probe India's vulnerability before launching upon a fresh wave of well calibrated terrorist onslaught.

Meanwhile, a change of guard took place in India's political establishment which was also factored as an input in framing Pakistan's new strategy of terror against India. The new political dispensation that emerged in India after May 2004 general election sent out signals indicating loosening of the leash upon terrorists of all varieties. The only specific legislation directed against terrorism - the Prevention of Terrorism Act (POTA) - was allowed to lapse. It was not as if POTA was an altogether new partisan law enacted by the previous Vajpayee government to deal with terrorism. It was only a more effective edition of TADA (Terrorist and Disruptive Activities) Act already enacted by earlier governments. It was ironical. The only special anti-terror legislation on the statute book was killed exactly when terrorism was at its peak the world over and country after country was enacting harsh legislation to deal with it. The message emanating from India was unmistakable and Pakistan took note of it.

As if that was not enough, India's new leadership virtually lost the ground gained by the previous government through its large scale Army mobilization in the wake of the attack on Parliament on 13.12.2001. In January 2004, as mentioned earlier, General Musharraf committed "not to permit any territory under Pakistan's control to be used to support terrorism in any manner." In April 2005, it was watered down to a commitment only to "not allow terrorism to impede the peace process" in the joint statement issued by the Pak President and Indian Prime Minister. In practical terms, it meant that Pakistan could continue to foment and export terror and India would continue to talk peace. That is what exactly started happening with a fresh spurt of terror in India in 2005.

This is clearly proved by the fact that no major terrorist strike on mainland India, apart from the chronic terrorist operations in Kashmir, took place for two years during 2003 and 2004. It was prevented first by the extensive Indian Army mobilization along the border during 2003. During 2004, Pakistan waited for the outcome of general election in India and the attitude of the new government that came to power. Once it was assured that the new political dispensation was soft on Jihadis inside the country, Pakistan got going again in its terror campaign against India along a different track though.

This time round, it is terror on the hub of economic and commercial activities deep inside India far away from the battlefield of Kashmir. And that also perpetrated not by foreign Jihadis but by India's own misguided sons of the soil, sponsored, motivated and remote-controlled by Pakistan's Jihadi network. This is the most sinister and diabotical aspect of the terrorist outburst in the heart of India during 2005 after a gap of over two years. And unless India sends a tough message to Pakistan and adopts a tougher policy in dealing with Jihadis, both inside and outside the country, more devastating terror strikes on the mainland are in the offing.

It is very much a part of the new Pakistani strategy of taking the war of terror right inside the heart of India. Pakistan has long been telling the world that Kashmir terrorism was the indigenous effort of the Kashmiri Muslims to secure the right of secession from India. Now by promoting Jihadi terror on mainland India, it is trying to hurt India deeply and blaming it on India's supposed maltreatment of its muslim people. In support of its effort, Pakistan has caused a wide network to lure Indian Muslims into its terrorist enterprise in the name of Islam. It is a measure of the secular democratic character of the Indian state that the vast muslim population of India has refused to fall in the trap and rebuffed Pakistan in this regard. The absolutely modern secular or religion-neutral character of the Indian state is testified by the fact that the country has a Muslim President, Sikh Prime Minister and a Catholic Christian as the chairperson of the ruling United Progressive Alliance today.

And yet, with an 'Islamo-Fascist' state like Pakistan next door, it is impossible to prevent an extremist or lunatic fringe of India's muslim population from falling a prey to Pakistan's evil designs in the name of religion. That has enabled Jihadi outfits like Laksher-e-Toiba, named by the UN as an international terrorist organisation and unabashedly sheltered by Pakistan, to recruit some extremist muslim elements in India to carry out terrorist operation on the Indian soil. That is the handicap of India in tackling terrorism inside the country by India's own Jihadi elements remotecontrolled by Pakistan. The basic fact remains that not a single act of Jihadi terror inside mainland India, or even in Kashmir for that matter, is perpetrated without active instigation, support and planning by Pakistan.

Here is an example of how Pakistani Jihadi organizations supported by the state recruit some vulnerable Indian muslims, including underworld

Dons, to carry on their operations in India. In Jan '2002 a gang of Jihadis made a deadly attack on the USIS building in the heart of Kolkata killing 5 policemen on the spot. One Aftab Ansari called a Kolkata Newspaper the same day claiming responsibility for the attack. Elaborate investigations into the case by the CBI brought to light some chilling facts about the Pakistan sponsored Jihadi terror network in India. Aftab Ansari belonged to Varanasi in U.P. and was a graduate of Law and Journalism from the Benaras Hindu University. But a career in journalism did not satisfy him. In order to become quick rich, he wanted to be an underworld. Don and his role model was Daud Ibrahim, the notorious Mafia Don hailing from Bombay and now living between Dubai and Pakistan. The rest was easy. After collecting crores of rupees by kidnappings for ransom between 1999 and 2001, Aftab Ansari shifted to Dubai alongwith his principal associate Asif Reza Khan. From Dubai, Ansari and Asif Reza Khan travelled to Karachi and were taken to Rawalpandi by Laksher-e-Toiba operatives. During 12 days that they spent there, they were told that Pakistani Jihadi organizations wanted to use Ansari's criminal network for Jihadi activities in India. Then onwards Aftab Ansari and Asif Reza Khan became part of Laksher-e-Toiba's terror network in India.

It was in pursuit of this deal that Asif Ansari's gang abducted Pratha Roy Burman, a big shoe marchant of Kolkata in July 2001. They collected Rs. 3.7 crores as ransom money for release of Burman, part of which was sent to Omer Sheikh who sent Rs.50 lakhs out of it to Mohammed Atta for 9/11 attack on America. The duoAftab Ansari and Asif Reza Khan harboured an army of Madarasa educated young muslims from the muslim pockets of Kolkata to initiate them into Jihadi terrorism. This is one of the modus operandi adopted by Laksher-e-Toiba, and other Pak based Jihadi outfits to harness underworld Dons as well as Islamic fanatics for terror acts against India.

It is through such sleeper cells established by Pakistani Jihadis in India that they are now indulging in terrorist acts in different part of the country with full connivance of the Pakistani state. In an encounter with police at Delhi in the night of 5th March 2005, three terrorists belonging to Laksher-e-Toiba were killed and large quantity of RDX, geletine sticks, arms and ammunitions were seized from the place of their stay. The documents seized and disclosures made by two of their associates revealed that they had planned to attack the Indian Military Academy in Dehradun and prominent Software Companies in Bangalore. The revelations shocked the country for two reasons. First they were only three days away from launching their attack on the Indian Military Academy at Dehradun. Second, they were now targeting the Software Companies in Bangalore which are the pride of India and have come to be the envy of the world.

There was actually a spurt in Jihadi activities in mainland India during the year 2005. Subsequent to the above encounter, one Haroon Rashid hailing from Bihar and a student of a Technology Institution in U.P. was arrested in Delhi. His interrogation revealed that he was plotting to blow up Hindustan Aeronautics Limited and Indian Air Force Base located at Kanpur. He is an active member of the Students Islamic Movement of India (SIMI) and a hardcore Laksher-e-Toiba militant. His timely arrest prevented a major damage to the Indian Air Force and Aeronautical industry. And then there was the aborted Fiadeen terrorist attack on Ram Temple in Ayodiya on 5th July 2005.

On top of all these, Jihadi terrorism returned to India in a big way with a lethal assault right in the heart of the national capital towards the end of October 2005. Three deadly bomb blasts ripped through the heart of Delhi on 29 October 2005 on the eve of Deewali festival. Even as the pre-Deewali shopping was at its peak, there were bomb explosions first at the busy Paharganj market at 5.39 p.m. the next at Govindpuri at 5.52 p.m and the third at the busy Sarojni Nagar market at 5.56 p.m. Thus within a span of 18 minutes, around 60 innocent men, women and children lost their lives and about 170 were injured in the blasts. Investigations revealed that Laksher-e-Toiba and its sleeper cells in India were responsible for this terrible terrorist attack on the capital.

A little earlier on 10 October 2005, just two days after the devastating earthquake in Kashmir and North Western Pakistan, Jihadi terrorists belonging to Hizb-ul-Mujahideen and Laskare-e-Toiba attacked a Hindu populated village in Rajauri district of Jammu & Kahsmir state. They carried out a selective killing of Hindu civilians of the place in pursuance of their program of religious cleansing. Evidently, not even the massive devastation wrought by nature in the area put a stop to the Jihadi's murder spree against the 'infidels'.

Interestingly, the Jihadis interpreted the disastrous earthquake in Pak occupied Kashmir and North Western Pakistan in their own way to intensify the Jihad against India. Talking to a Pakistani journalist, Hafiz Mohammad Saeed, the founder Chief of Markaz Dawa-al-Irshad, now renamed as Jamaat-ud-Dawa, attributed it to the wrath of Allah against Pakistan's supposed compromise with the U.S. and India. He observed: "They were not afraid of Allah but Bush. At his behest, they wanted to purge our school books from verses of Jihad, befriend India and recognize Israel. They blatantly ridiculed the commandments of Allah. Thus they invited the wrath of God in the form of the earthquake." (Quoted in the 'Frontline' magazine, January 14-27, 2006).

Jamaat-ud-Dawa, it may be noted, is the new name of the arch Jihadi organisation promoting terrorism worldwide since early 1990's under its original name 'Markaz-Dawa-al-Irshad (Centre for Proselytisation and Preaching). It was nominally proscribed in 2002 under pressure from the U.S. But in keeping with Pakistan's well known expertise in duplicity, it has been allowed to flourish under its changed name. It is the parent organisation of the deadly terrorist outfit Laskher-e-Toiba which is engaged in relentless terrorist onslaught against India. It is based on a 160 acre campus at Murdike near Lahore from where it openly conducts its terrorist activities right under the nose of Pakistani authorities. There is an old axiom of Political Science which says, "What the sovereign permits, he commands." That aptly describes the connivance of Pakistani political establishment with the ravages of Laskhar-e-Toiba, its armed wing, in India.

An ominous feature of resurgence of Jihadi terrorism in 2005 is its appearance in India's south, far away from the regular battleground of Jammu & Kashmir, where most of our strategic defence and related research installations are located. It was not a mere chance that the Lashkar terrorists killed in Delhi in March 2005 had planned to attack the Indian Defence Academy at Dehradoon as well as I.T. Companies at Bangalore. That brings out another sinister aspect of the latest phase of Jihad. The Jihadis extended their area of operation to the south in order to hit at both the defence installations and India's sunshine industrial hub at the same time.

In course of their operations in the South, the Jihadis caused the bomb blasts in the office of Andhra Pradesh Police Special Task Force in Hyderabad on 12 October 2005. One of them named Motasin Billa was killed in the blast while some others escaped 3 of them were subsequently arrested by Delhi Police and thoroughly interrogated. Further investigations revealed that the terrorists involved in this blast belonged to Bangladesh based terrorist outfit Harkut-ul-Jihad-e-Islami. One of them was trained in a camp run by Pakistan's ISI near Baluchistan border. They were assigned the task to attack the Bangalore software park, the Hyderabad Hitech city, certain politicians, Railway Stations and other busy places. What is more important, it was revealed in course of investigation that the Harkut-ul-Jihadi Islami of Bangladesh and Pakistan's ISI worked in close cooperation to launch terrorist attacks against India.

The most dastardly and symbolically devastating Jihadi attack took place on the evening of 28 December 2005 at an international conference of scientists being held at the prestigious Indian Institute of Science, Bangalore. Just as the delegates at the Operational Research Society of India conference were coming out of the Tata Auditorium of the Indian Institute of Science campus, at about 7.15 p.m. a terrorist started firing randomly from an automatic rifle killing one of the delegates on the spot and injuring at least 5 more. The eminent scientist killed on the spot was M.C. Puri, Retired Professor of the Indian Institute of Technology, New Delhi. This was the first time that Bangalore, India's most happening city and technological face to the world, was directly hit by the Jihadis. By striking at an internationally known scientific research institute in a South Indian city, the terrorists noticed India that nothing in the country was beyond their reach.

Perhaps the most virulent and venomous justification of Jihad against India came from a Pakistan based journal 'Voice of Islam' released in print and on the internet in December 2005. Authored by a Retired Pakistani Naval Commodore, Tariq Majeed, an article in the Magazine argues that retaliation against India should be made part of 'the expression of our national aims and military doctrine'. A long editorial in the 'Voice of Islam' argues against the ongoing peace process between India and Pakistan and claims that it is a part of a 'Conspiracy against Islam and Pakistan'. Instead, it pleads for supporting a war on India to make it bleed militarily and financially. Pakistan's rulers should 'understand that Jihad is the main stay of politics in Islam because it paves the way for the establishment of a Caliphate'. That sums up the mind-set of the Jihadis targeting a scientific research center located in South India.

'The 'Voice of Islam' it may be noted, is published by the notorious Jiahdi outfit Jamaat-ud-Dawa headed by Hafiz Mohammed Syeed referred to earlier. The Jihadi terror campaign in the south continued. Soon after the terror strike at Indian Institute of Science, Bangalore, the Hyderabad Police busted a terrorist plot aimed at blowing up the offices of Director General, A.P. Police, Commissioner Hyderebad Police and the Hi-tech city where a majority of I.T. software Companies are located. The police seized 2 Improvised explosive devices with an intricate detonation mechanism which could be activated by a cell phone. The terrorist group involved in this plot, needless to say, was backed by Pakistan's ISI.

Alongwith the South, the east of the Country has also become quite vulnerable to Jihadi terror with the emergence of Bangladesh as a major center of Jihad. It has become an international haven of fundamentalist Islamic groups from other parts of South East area. A large number of Jihadi terrorist camps are operating in Bangladesh which include members from Laskher-e-Toiba and Jaise-e-Mohammed of Pakistan and 'Jamaah Islamiah' of Indonesia. In June 2005 the Left Front Chief Minister of West Bengal, Budhdev Bhattacharya told the 'Frontline' magazine in an interview that the first major problem faced by West Bengal was 'Islamic fundamentalists backed by the ISI who are operating from Bangladesh'. According to local police, there is coordination and exchange of personnel among atleast 10 Islamic militant groups, including Harkut-ul-Islami –Jihad and the Laskher-e-Toiba, all along the eastern border of the country (The 'Frontline' magazine, January 27, 2006). The problem in eastern India has become alarming with large scale planned infiltration of Bangladesh muslims into the adjoining Indian states of West Bengal, Assam and Bihar. According to a report submitted by General S.K. Sinha, the former Governor of Assam, to the President of India, the number of Bangladeshi immigrants was 79 lakhs in West Bengal and 50 lakhs in Assam besides sizeable chunks in the adjoining areas of Bihar and Jharkhand.

Another area of concern from the point of view of Jihadi terror in eastern India is the mushrooming of Islami Madrasas in these parts, particularly in West Bengal bordering Bangladesh.

In the wake of the Jihadi attack on the USIS building in Kolkata in Jan '2002, the West Bengal Chief Minister had pointed an accusing finger at the Madrasas hosting what he termed as 'Anti-national elements'. For political reasons, he did not pursue the matter further. But the fact remains that Madrasas have been the fountain spring of Jihadi terror in the Sub Continent. In fact the bulk of Talibanis including the Taliban leader Mullah Omar were products of Islamic Madrasas located in Pakistan in N.W.F.P As mentioned earlier, Peshawar was once termed as the 'University of Jihad'

It is not so well known that the rise of Jihad in its present form in Kashmir Valley can be traced to the spread and complete Islamisation of Madrasa education in Kashmir from 1980s onwards. Kashmiri Islam, it may be noted, was quite tolerant of non Islamic faiths from the time it came to the valley in the middle ages until not very long ago. Islam was promoted in Kashmir by local Sufis, who were also called Rishis. Places of worship established by Sufis or Rishis were venerated by Muslim and Hindu worshipers alike. This was the foundation of the Kashmiri way of life involving mutual toleration and harmony between Hindus and Muslims. But during 1980s, this basic value of 'Kashmiriat' was dealt a blow from which it has not recovered. Moderate Kashmiri Muslims woke up to find that their Mosques and Madrasas had new preachers, many of them having been trained in Pakistan. They preached against the Kashmiri version of Islam and insisted that their own intolerant Wahabi strain must be adopted by all Kashmiri muslims. That was a major source of the rise of Jihadi spirit among the Madrasa educated younger generations of Kashmiris.

History is being repeated in West Bengal with the spread of Madrasa education among muslims. That is going to be a source of more visible Jihadi terrorism surfacing in Eastern India in not very distant future. It is true that West Bengal has been relatively free from overt Jihadi terror after the attack on the U.S.I.S building at Kolkata in 2002. This is because the Jihadis would not like to expose themselves by resorting to terror acts in an area which has come to be their safe sanctuary.

But this relative calm in West Bengal may not last long. For Bangladesh is fast emerging as a hot-bed of Jihadi terrorism in Eastern India in the same way as Pakistan has developed as a nursery of terrorism in respect of the rest of India. There has been visible increase in the number of Madrasas on the Bangladesh side of the border. These Madrasas are being used to train Jihadis recruited from West Bengal and other states of Eastern India bordering Bangladesh. They are being initiated into the tenets of Jihadi terrorism to be pushed into Eastern India for terror acts.

The Islamisation of Bangladesh under its present regime is proceeding unabated. The process which started with the brutal assassination of Sheikh Mujbur Rehman, founder of independent Bangladesh, in August 1975 and was consolidated by General Zia-ul-Rahman has picked up again under Begam Kalida Zia's regime. The process was sought to be reversed under the rule of Begam Sheikh Hasina, daughter of Sheikh Mujbur Rahman. But after she was voted out of power with the help of fundamentalists like Jamaat-e-Islami and Islamic Oikya Jote, Bangladesh is back on the path of fundamentalism. It showed in a big way on 21 Aug 2004 when there were high voltage bomb explosions at a public Rally of Sheikh Hasina killing 23 people and injuring about 200. Even before that, many secular politicions of Bangladesh including the former Finance Minister Shah.A.M.S.Kibria, progressive writers and intellectuals opposed to fundamentalism were assassinated in Bangladesh. The internationally known Bangladeshi writer Taslima Nasreen is leading a life in exile outside the country because of 'Fatwah' issued by the foundamentalists to kill her. Harkut-ul-Jihadi-Islami, as the counterpart of Laskher-e-Toiba in

Bangladesh, is the principal promoter of Jihadi terror in Eastern India.

Both these organisations - Harkut-ul-Jihadi-Islami in the East and Laskher-e-Toiba in the West are not only in close touch with each other but also with other Jihadi outfits in South East Asia like Jemmah Islamiah which is very active in Indonesia. It is reported that Laskher-e-Toiba has been recruiting south Indian muslims residing in Singapore and Indonesia for involving them with Jihadi terrorism in south India. In 2002, 13 Jihadis of Jemmah Islamiah were arrested in Singapore and they were all of south Indian oprigin. Al Quida of course is the global terrorist outfit which serves as the umbrella organization for Jihadi terrorism all over the world.

Between Harkut-ul-Jihadi-Islami in the East and Laskher-e-Toiba in the west with the Al Quida on top of them, India has been caught up in the vortex of the most lethal Jihadi terrorism ever faced by any country in the world. It is not really a question of secessionists in Kashmir or any grievances, contrived or otherwise, of muslims in India which has brought about the spate of Jihadi terror in India. It is very much a part of the eruption of Jihadi terror all over the world. The only distinguishing feature of Jihadi terrorism in India is the factor of Pakistan. It is the failed state of Pakistan which is the real midwife of Jihadi terrorism in India. Jihadi terror is the most lethal missile that Pakistan has let loose against India in course of its long war on India ever since it came into being. To that extent, relationship between India and Pakistan becomes a very important factor in understanding and tackling the problem of Jihadi terrorism as far as India is concerned.

Looking at the problem in the above perspective, it can be said that Indo-Pak affair has been a perennial saga of conflict and bitterness, with occasional episodes of normal good neighbourliness. The old communist dictum based on Lenin's elaborations of Soviet foreign policy in 1920 'One step backward and two steps forward', has been reversed in case of Indo-Pak engagement. Thus far, it has been one step forward and two steps backwards.

For the first time since the eruption of conflict in Kashmir on the morrow of independence, there was some hope of peace between the two countries when Tashkent agreement was signed in Jan 1966. With Soviet assistance, a breakthrough in the relationship seemed to have been achieved and cautious optimism prevailed. The Tashkent accord was followed by agreement between two countries on the second phase of Indus water treaty which came into effect in April 1966. But the brief romance between India and Pakistan soured too soon, with Pakistan back on the path of conflict.

The most radical phase in Indo-Pak relations came in 1971 over the upsurge of Bengali nationalism in erstwhile East Pakistan. Although it did not have much to do with India to start with, it developed into a situation which involved the two countries into conflictual positions. The Indo-Pak war that follow culminating in the defeat of Pakistan and birth of Bangladesh is recent History. In the post- Bangladesh situation, Shimla conference of

June 1972 provided an opportunity for Pakistan to break from the past and resolve the existing problems on the basis of realities of the existing situation. The two countries agreed upon a bilateral approach for solving all outstanding problems to the exclusion of outside powers. At Shimla, India insisted upon bilateralism in Indo-Pak relationship in order to keep it out of the ambit of cold war. It is believed in knowledgeable circles, though never openly admitted by either side, that the settlement of Kashmir question had also been worked out, based on acceptance of the existing ground reality with minor adjustments. That amounted to acceptance of the Line of Control as the final international border between India and Pakistan in Kashmir.

But, as in the case of Tashkent, the Simla accord ended sooner than anticipated. The Simla document was sought to be erased by Pakistan even before the ink on it had dried. The Field Commanders of Pakistan could not readily agree even on the delineation of the cease-fire line in Jammu & Kashmir.

Since then there were many abortive efforts initiated by India to bring peace with Pakistan in recent years. Indian Prime Minister Vijpayee made a bus journey to Lahore which was soon followed by Pakistan's misadventure in Kargil. Inspite of that, Vijpayee made even a bolder move by inviting General Mushraff for the Agra summit. That also failed. At Agra Mushraff, still gloating at his capture of power as the ruler of Pakistan, came like a conquering General, rigid and inflexible over Kashmir, made full use of the media to propound his case and walked away unrelently.

The Pakistani boom however crashed in the wake of 9/11 terror attack on America. It was a rare occasion which saw all the big powers, America, Britain, France, Russia and China, combined against Jihadi terrorism unleashed by Al Quida and Taliban. It was a moment of reckoning for Pakistan. And as discussed earlier, General Mushriff made no mistake. He promptly fell in line to be counted as a member of the international coalition in the war against terror, even though it meant abandoning Pakistan's own creation-the Taliban. What Pakistan did or did not do as a 'frontline state' in the war against terror has been discussed at some length in Chapter VIII before. To join the U.S. in the war against Taliban was a political compulsion for Pakistan. Right since its birth, Pakistan had lived on the oxygen provided by Britain and America, particularly the latter, thanks to the politics of cold war. Even after the end of the cold war in early 1990's, it continued to live off its American connection through benign indulgence of the U.S. for the old time's sake. How could it opt to lose its long-lasting support base by declining to align with the U.S. after 9/11?

But once again, Pakistan cleverly managed to join the U.S. led war on terror and continue to promote terror against India at the same time. It was like eating the cake and having it too. It is a rare feat which Pakistan alone is capable of. And now if it is engaging in a dialogue process with India, that is also at the bidding of America. For the U.S. does not want any conflict between India and Pakistan to distract the rest of the world from the on-going war against Jihadi terrorism. For that reason, America wants Pakistan to make peace with India and Pakistan has no option but to make a show of talking peace. But no more. Those in India and the world who are pinning their hopes in the dialogue process to bring about the end of Jihadi terror on the sub-continent are chasing a mirage.

The defining event of today is the scourge of Jihadi terrorism. It is posing a serious threat to all values of civilized life or modern civilization itself just as Nazism and Fascism did before the Second World War. The world stands clearly divided between the sponsors and perpetrators of Jihadi terror on the one side and the targets and victims of it on the other. In this sharp divide, Pakistan and India are standing on the two opposite sides of the fence. Pakistan, inspite of its fake alignment with the U.S. in the global war on terror, has come to be the very embodiment of global Jiahdi terror, with India as its special target. Terrorism, it may be noted, is indivisible. It cannot be held, as Pakistan seems to suggest, that terror against America is bad and that against India is good. In such a situation, there is no question of any convergence of interests between Pakistan and India. In absence of such a basic convergence, any dialogue process is a mere eyewash, as other such processes have been in the past.

If there is any clear convergence of interests and values, it is between India and the rest of the world led by the U.S. which is at war with Jihadi terrorism across the board. The war against Jihadi terrorism cannot be deemed to have come to an end until the last vestige of Pakistani terror structure is demolished. Till then India will have to face and overcome the full blast of Jihadi terror on its own, with or without support from the rest of the civilized world.

The interminable peace negotiations between India and Pakistan hold no prospect of end of Jihadi terror in India. More so because India has meekly agreed to carry on the process even with Pakistan continuing to actively sponsor terrorist operations inside mainland India. The insipid attitude of India's political establishment to grievous terror strikes against its civil population was evident in its response to the pre-Diwali bomb blasts in Delhi on 29 October 2005. The world leaders from the U.S. President to British Prime Minister and U.N. Secretary General expressed deep shock and anguish. But India's national leadership voiced no more than regulation protest or concern. The sense of rage or anguish that any responsive and responsible government would feel or express was totally missing, as if the ghastly tragedy was no more than a run-of-the-mill massacre carried out by a dacoit gang.

To rub salt to the raw wound of the victims and the nation at large, Natwar Singh, then India's foreign minister, promptly pronounced that the blood bath would have no effect on Indo-Pak dialogue. And the Indian Prime Minister had no hesitation in being convivial with the Pakistani leadership in the SAARC summit held at Dacca in less than a month after the Delhi blasts. For the Indian government, it was business as usual, no matter how many innocent Indian lives were lost. The routine reaction to all such blood spilling is to put the blame on Laskhar-e-Toiba or Jaish-e-Mohammad or any such terrorist outfit and let it rest at that. The intelligence and law-enforcing agencies routinely go about looking for their modules or agents in India and taking action under the ordinary criminal law of the land. The stalwarts of the media, political analysts, intellectuals and intelligentsia are content condemning the terrorist outfits and pouring all their criticisms upon the governmental agencies for failure to prevent the terror acts. But no one either in the political establishment or the intellectual fraternity has the gumption or the common sense to put the blame squarely where it lies – the super terrorist state of Pakistan.

The prime question any thinking mind would ask : who permits, promotes and allows outfits like Laskhar-e-Toiba to flourish, and to what purpose? Can they survive, much less go about killing people in India, without the connivance and active cooperation of the state of Pakistan ? How is it that the parent organization of Laskher-e-Toiba-Jamat-ud-Dawa (the new incarnation of Markaz-Dawa-al-Irshad referred to earlier) is able to build up a vast empire of Jihadi education in Pakistan with control over more than 200 schools, eleven seminaries and two colleges? The answer is provided by the fact that in April 2001, Lt. General Mahmood Ahmad, then the Chief of Pakistan's, I.S.I., attended its annual convention as its chief patron. A resolution was passed at the convention calling upon the Jihadi cadres "to capture Hindu temples, destroy the idols, and then hoist the flag of Islam on them". (Quoted in the 'Frontline' magazine, January 14-27, 2006).

Jamat-ud-Dawa is only one such Jihadi terrorist umbrella organization, albeit a very deadly one so far as India is concerned, flourishing in our neighboring country with blessings of the Pakistani state. There are many others raising an army of Jihadis. There is, for instance, the Islamic Seminary at Binori near Karachi, referred to earlier, where many Talibani big wigs were indoctrinated.

There is another notable Pakistani NGO Al-Rashid based at Rawalpindi with its offices in Lahore and other towns. It was set up in 1996 when the Taliban captured poswer in Afganistan and Pakistan was at the peak of the high tide of Jihad in this part of the wqorld. It collects 'Zakat' or Islamic tax from the faithful and sends money to Jihadis in Kosovo, Chechnya, Kashmir etc to carry on with terrorism. In Chechnya, it sends money to Sheikh Omar bin Ismail Dawood, a fundamentalist chieftain opposing the regime of Maskadov.

Al Rashid is a cog in Al Quida's terror machine financing it through its collection network in Pakistan. It publishes a weekly, Zarb-e-Momin, in which Masood Azhar writes every Friday appealing to Muslims to kill Jews, Hindus, Christians, Westerners.

Yet another international Jihadi umbrella organization Al Fuqra, referred to earlier, which has cast its net wide even in America training Jihadis in guerilla warfare, is also going strong in Pakistan. And then there is Harkat-ul-Mujahidin, one of the most radical and blood-thirsty Jihadi groups, spreading terror all around under the wings of the Pakistani state.

The world knows it, everyone knows it or should know it. And yet the entire intellectual and political establishment in India refuses to see or talk about it, not to speak of serving a stern notice on Pakistan to close its terror shops before joining the dialogue process. They have buried their heads under the sand ostrich-like to avoid having to look at it. The result is there for everyone to see.

Even as these lines were being penned, three powerful bomb blasts ripped through the holy city of Varanasi in Uttar Pradesh. The first explosion happened in the 'Sankat Mochan' temple adjacent to the world famous Kashi Vishwanath temple at about 6.30 p.m. on 7 March 2006. It was the evening pooja time and the temple was teeming with devotees. An ill-fated marriage party, with the bride and bridegroom in tow, was also present in the temple at the time of the blast going through the rituals of marriage.

Minutes later, another bomb exploded at platform number one of Varanasi Cantonement railway station. And a third blast occurred in a crowded coach of the Shiv Ganga Express train just as it was about to leave for New Delhi.

According to on the spot official estimates, around 21 persons were killed, eight of them being women, and over 62 were injured in the blasts. Of these, 10 were worshippers killed in the temple and 11 were train passengers who died at the railway station. The unofficial estimate of the death toll was higher.

Besides the three fatal blasts, two unexploded bombs were found by police at the crowded Dashaswamedh Ghat, the city's main cremation site on the banks of river Ganga. If these had exploded, as the Jihadis evidently had intended, many more would have perished.

And then followed the monotony of the familiar drill. The Chairperson of the ruling United Progressive Alliance came calling, the Home Minister of India and Chief Minister of the state descended on the scene and all the motions were gone through meticulously. Cash compensations were announced for the dead and injured, as if money could compensate for the lives lost and limbs dismembered. After that, it was business as usual, as if the ghastly tragedy was no more than a natural calamity. It is true that massacres perpetrated by Jihadi terrorists have come to be regarded as natural calamities by the people of India, thanks to the callous attitude of the national leadership.

Not a word was uttered by any dignitary against the unconcealed hand of the Jihadi State of Pakistan which was pulling the trigger from behind to spill the blood of Indians. For India's political leadership, blood of Indian civilians is easily expendable. They would keep on extending the hand of friendship to Pakistan whatever the cost in terms of Indian blood. This was the kind of confidence-building that India and Pakistan had been talking about. Blame it on the ill-famed Laskhar-e-Toiba or Laskhar-e-Qahar and keep 'building confidence' with the father of them all.

The massacre at Varanasi clearly fits into the strategy formulated by Pakistan to foment terror in mainland India, after a lull of around two years in 2003 and 2004, for reasons discussed earlier. It is very much a part of the well-crafted pattern of fresh terrorist upsurge beginning the year 2005. The terror acts in Delhi, Bangalore, Hyderabad and Varanasi are different scenes of the same macabre drama being staged by Pakistan from behind the stage. It is the state of Pakistan which has actually laid the landmine of Jihadi sleeper cells in India's heartland.

To focus all attention only on these sleeper cells or modules of terrorist outfits like Lashear-e-Toiba or any other, is like treating the symptoms and not the disease. In a vast country like India with wide religious and ideological diversities and myriads of problems including poverty, unemployment and religious conflicts, there are bound to be thousands of disgruntled individuals nursing one grievance or another. It is no big news that many of them fall prey to Jihadi propaganda and perpetrate terror acts. It is for the detective and law-enforcement agencies of the state to locate them and put them out of action according to the law of the land at the micro level. That is no big deal either.

The main task is to confront the agency or agencies which are on the prowl to pickup such disgruntled elements for terror operations and, most importantly, the state next door which has created, nourished and put these merchants of death on to the job. It cannot be done by talking sweet to a state which has been on a collision course perennially right from the moment of its creation. It is a colossal failure of India's political leadership to expose and confront Pakistan with a tough message to dismantle its Jihadi terror machine against India. The U.S. did it after 9/11 and forced Pakistan to go along with the destruction of its surrogate. Taliban and wind up Abdul Qadir Khan's nuclear proliferation 'walmart'. The Americans squeezed Pakistan hard in order to save American lives. They cannot be expected to do it to save Indian lives. It is for India's political leadership to take on Pakistan at the macro level and make it abandon the dance of death it is choreographing in India through its multiple agents. It is the failure of India to do something like what the country did in the wake of attack on Indian Parliament on 13 December 2001 which is responsible for spilling of so much Indian blood by Jihadis.

As for the ominous significance of Varanasi temple attack, it is worth pointing out that U.P. has been developing into a hub of Jihadi terror for quite sometime. It may be recalled that U.P. was in the center of agitation for creation of Pakistan and Nawabzada Liaquat Ali Khan of U.P was next only to M.A.Jinnah in the heirarchy of Pakistani leadership. It is in U.P. that the grand Islamic Seminary of Deoband is situated which is the fountain spring of the hard Sunni orthodoxy having sway over large parts of the Muslim world. The Saudis, both the ruling Sheikhs and their arch adversary Osama bin Laden, are all followers of Deobandi spirituality or Deoband school of Islam. What is not so well known is that the 'Fatwah' issued about a hundred years ago by the venerated Deoband Seminary to wage war against the infidels or non-believers is still valid since it has not been revoked. It is another matter that it has been kept in cold storage.

In such a background, the kid-glove treatment meted out to Jihadis by the political establishment from time to time has helped them to set up a strong base in this crucial state. In November 1994, Abu Baker, a hard-core agent of Pak ISI was nabbed in a raid on the hostel of Nadwa college at Lucknow. He had been using it as his hide-out for the previous eight years to carry out terrorist acts all over India. What followed was outrageous. The government of the day immediately intervened, set him free, apologized to the Rector of the college for the arrest and promised not to make such arrests in his institution in future. What is more, the government set up a high level enquiry and took to task the officials of the Indian Intelligence Bureau and U.P. state police who had conducted the raid.

With such soft treatment of Jihadis spreading their tentacles in the state, it is no wonder that U.P. has become a hotbed of modules of Pak based terrorist outfits. In May 2005, two Laskhar-e-Toiba operatives-Sadat Rashid and Masood Alam-were nabbed by police in the state. Their task was to recruit yound Madarsa students in Bihar and Jharkhand for initiation into the cult of Jihad. Subsequently, two more recruiters of Laskhar-Mohammad Hanif and Younis Ahmad-were arrested in U.P. on the basis of information provided by the Assam Police. Again a Dubai-based recruiter and fund-raiser of the Lashkar-Abu Razzak Masood-was also arrested in the state. The Jihadi operations in U.P. were not confined only to bringing in fresh recruits from neighboring areas. They were also planning and indulging in 'performance terrorism' in the state. This showed up in 5 July 2005 abortive fiadeen attack on the Ram temple in Ayodhya in which six terrorists were killed by the security forces. Investigation revealed that the attack had been facilitated by Jihadi cells run by fresh recruits from Deoband, Saharanpur and Delhi. This was followed by the bombing of Delhi-Patna Sramjeevi Express train two weeks later near Jaunpur in U.P. in which 12 persons were killed and 52 injured. The Varanasi bombing was a terror event in continuation of the fresh Jihadi outburst beginning 2005 in U.P.

After all, it was only in U.P. that a responsible minister of the state cabinet publicly declared to reward the killer of the Danish Cartoonist who drew up the cartoon of Prophet Mohammad with Rs.51 crores and gold equivalent to his weight. All concerned citizens in India, irrespective of their diverse faiths, roundly condemned the mischief of the cartoonist and the Danish paper that published it. Prominent among them was Swamy Nischalanand, the Shankaracharya of Puri. Even a 'Fatwah' by an Islamic cleric to kill the Cartoonist could be understandable in the circumstances. But for a responsible Minister of a government wedded to secularism to issue an open call to kill the cartoonist was nothing less than outrageous.

Contrast it with what happened in Britain in regard to the ignominious cartoon controversy. In the first flush of outrage, the British Muslims took to the streets in a rowdy protest against the cartoons. In course of the protest demonstrations, slogans were shouted and placards displayed glamorizing the London bomb-blasts of 7 July 2005 in which a large number of Britons had been killed. This gave rise to a strong counter protest by concerned British citizens including sober elements among British Muslims. The Muslim Council of Britain came out in the open to denounce the extremist elements among their co-religionists for lionizing the perpetrators of London bomb blasts, even while condemning the publication of the cartoons. The British government reacted too in a manner any government worth the name, which cared for the lives of its citizens, would react. Tony Blair brought about a tough legislation against those who even "glamourised" terrorism. And in this move, he got the support of the more liberal members of his party also who were usually opposed to such tough measures. In the light of the above, it can only be said that when it comes to caring for the lives of its nationals, India is a different proposition. And U.P. is more so.

In any case, it would be a mistake to consider the Varanasi bomb blast as only an U.P. centric event. It was just a part of Pakistan's new terror offence on India's mainland. Within a week of the Varanasi killing event, a major terror strike in Bombay was averted on 11 March 2006 with the timely detection of an improvised explosive device containing two kg of explosive ammonium nitrate at the Byculla Railway Station in central Mumbai. Apart from the explosive filled in a polypack water bottle, a pocket-size transformer was also recovered from the spot which could have provided the necessary current if a detonator had been attached to the explosive device.

Mumbai, of course, had long been on their scanner and a happy hunting ground of terrorist outfits. But their operation was no longer confined to metropolitan Mumbai only. It now extended to the neighboring tourist land of Goa also. On the evening of 10 March 2006, one Tariq Jalal, a terrorist belonging to Muzaffarabad-based Tehrik-ul-Mujahiddin, an offshoot of Laskhar-e-Toiba, was arrested by Goa police at the Margao railway station. One kg of RDX, two hand grenades and two electronic detonators were recovered from his possession. The hand grenades were of Russian make and highly sophisticated. He had been trained for over two years in Pakistan and also had been to Nepal and Bangladesh.

From U.P. To Delhi, Hyderabad, Bangalore, Mumbai and Goa, the internationally famed tourist resort of India, from railway trains to temples of worship, no place in any part of the country is beyond the reach of Pakistani terror network in India. The scene of terror war has shifted from Kashmir to the whole of India. And the target area has vastly expanded to encompass not only hubs of civil population like market places but India's prestigious commercial, scientific, strategic and even tourist centers. In Goa, for instance, the arrested terrorist Tariq Jalal was planted by a Pakistani terror outfit to set up a base for terror operations. For eight months, he was being maintained in Goa receiving funds from Pakistan through the hawala route.

After the Varanasi temple blast, the Home Minister of India observed that the government was considering posting of Central security forces to guard all important temples. That was talking like the head of a security or police organization and not the Home Minister of a vast country like India. One may legitimately ask, how many temples in the country can you protect Mr. Home Minister by cordoning them off with security forces? There are thousands upon thousands of them spread throughout the length and breadth of the country and each of them is vulnerable to terrorist strike. And temples are not the only targets. Railway trains, transport buses, vital strategic installations, commercial centers, high-tech compuses and now even academic and tourist centers have become prime targets of Jihadi terror. If all the vulnerable spots are to be protected by security forces, even the combined strength of all the police forces in the country would not suffice, apart from turning the country into a vast police camp. How long can India's political leadership indulge in that kind of self-deception?

As long as terrorism was confined to Jammu & Kashmir, people of the rest of India could look the other way. Now that it has come to encompass the entire country, how can the people of India as a whole ignore it? Especially when the state of Pakistan through its ill-conceal Jihadi front organisations has been relentlessly warring on India. Pakistan's flagship front organization Jamaat-ud-Dawa, the parent organisation of Lashkar-e-Toiba, minced no words when its chief Haliz Mohammad Saeed declared: "The Jihad in Kashmir would soon spread to entire India. Our mujahideen would create three Pakistans in India" And earlier, Sayed Salahuddin, head of Pakistan's another front organisation, had pronounced: "Almighty Allah, by his will and tactics, is bringing the Jihad movement of Kashmir on a track that will liberate not only the oppressed people of Jammu and Kashmir but also crores of Muslims and other minorities in India oppressed by Brahmin imperialists" (Quoted in 'The Week' magazine, 8 January 2006). That leaves nothing to imagination or conjecture about the objectives of the Jihadis and their patron state in their incessant terror assault on India.

As regards the Muslims of India, the Jihadis have only to take note of the spontaneous reaction of the community to the Varanasi temple blasts. Soon after the blasts, Muslim women of Varanasi, normally confined to their homes, took out a long march, with their viels on, protesting against the outrage on 9 March 2006. With their hands lifted towards the sky in prayer mode, they prayed to Allah to visit the terrorists with severe punishment. Moulana Tufail observed that the Muslims should push out the traitors hidden in their houses, failing which the future generations would never pardon them. Several Muslim youngmen donated their blood to save the lives of Hindu victims of the bomb blast. And the people of Madanpura locality of Varanasi, with 90 percent Muslim population observed 'bund' on the day following the blasts. Needless to say, the heart of Muslims of India is in the right place and that is the greatest cushion against Pakistan's terror war on India.

Yet, it would be impossible to prevent some extremist, disgruntled or lumpen elements on the fringes of the Muslim society from falling into their trap. And that is what had been happening over the years. Pakistan has now accelerated its terror engine to harness such elements to widen the area of its operations. Catching such strayed youngmen and putting them out of action, which is all that the Indian state machinery is doing, is no answer to the problem. That kind of micro level management of the problem is the job of the security and intelligence agencies of the state. But no intelligence apparatus can be or has ever been fool-proof anywhere in the world. The most glaring example of inherent limits of intelligence mechanism in preventing a well planned terror strike was the 9/11 strike at America.

When the mighty U.S., intelligence mechanism could fail to detect and check a non-state outfit like Al Qaida from mounting a massive terror attack, how can the Indian intelligence and security agencies be expected to prevent terrorist onslaught crafted, nourished and launched by the State of Pakistan? It is for the Indian state to stand up to take on the terrorist state of Pakistan to tackle the problem at the macro level. It was done by the Indian state after the attack on Indian Parliament on 13 December 2001 to good effect. The world rallied behind India to turn the heat on Pakistan to desist from its misadventure in India and seek for peace. The result was relative quiet on the terror front, that is absence of any significant terror act on the Indian soil, for two consecutive years in 2003 and 2004. But once the Indian state lowered its guard, terrorism in a more virulent form was back beginning 2005.

This time round, a massive armed mobilization on the borders like in 2002-2003 may not be necessary. It would be enough to expose the terrorist face of Pakistan before the world and mount an effective diplomatic offensive against it. The international situation is very much in favour of India for its diplomatic war against Pakistan. In fact, Pakistan has never before been internationally so isolated as it is today. It has been virtually abandoned by all its long-standing godfathers like China, America and Saudi Arabia. The Pak President visited China seeking a favourable response on the Kashmir issue and returned back empty handed. If anything he had to make a commitment to denounce terrorism. King Abdullah of Saudi Arabia visited Pakistan towards the end of January 2006 and scrupulously avoided espousing its case in regard to Kashmir inspite of President Musharrff's appeal to him in the name of Islamic Ummah. And the last but not the least, the U.S. President George Bush demonstrably cold-shouldered Pakistan in respect of solving the Kashmir issue. All of them told Pakistan in the quiet or openly to solve its problems with India bilaterally.

The reasons are not far to seek. Pakistan's close linkage with Jihadi terrorism worldwide has alienated all its old time allies. China, Pakistan's strongest piller of support in the past, is faced with separatist Islamic movements in its Xinjiang province bordering Pakistan. The Dulkan organization of ethnic Uighur Muslims is leading a separatist movement in China in the Xinjiang region. The result was that the Pakistan President had to make a commitment to fight against terrorism in the joint statement issued at the conclusion of his China visit. And the U.S.President Bush made no secret of his concern that enough was not being done by Pakistan against Al Quida and Taliban Jihadis hidden in its northern tribal areas. So far as Saudi

Arabia is concerned, the ruling Sheiks of the country are as much a target of Osama bin Laden as the American President. In such a situation, Pakistan stands completely isolated in the international arena on account of its terror connections.

On the other hand Afganistan is being seriously troubled by Talibani terrorists sheltered in bordering areas between Pakistan's Northern tribal region and Afganistan's southern areas. On 12 March 2006 Sibghatullah Mujaddedi, the head of Afganistan's upper House of Parliament and a Muslim cleric of repute, was attacked by Talibanis while traveling in his car. He escaped with burns on his hands and face in the well plotted suicide attack which killed four other persons in Kabul. Sibghatullah Mujaddedi straightaway accused the Pakistan's ISI for the attack and the Afgan President Hamid Karzai indirectly hinted at that.

Russia has long been a victim of Jihadi terrorism involving the Chechen terrorists supported by Al Quida and other terrorist organizations centred in Pakistan's northern areas.

The result is that Pakistan has developed as the main hub of global Jihadi terrorism and is looked upon as such by all countries adversely affected by terrorism. India can easily forge a powerful anti-Jihadi front with countries like China, Russia, Afganistan and the U.S. It will not only thoroughly expose Pakistan as the strongest support base of Jihadi terrorism in the world but also put a curb on its terrorist onslaught against India. A diplomatic offensive against Pakistan along the above line can be the real answer to the Pakistani challenge rather than wasting time and energy over interminable peace negotiations with Pakistan which India is indulging in. To live any longer in the make-belief world of buying peace with Pakistan through fruitless talks will be suicidal for India. How many more Indian lives will have to be sacrificed in Pakistan directed terror attacks before the Indian leadership rises to the occasion and puts Pakistan's terror machine out of action through a concreted diplomatic war outlined above?

Instead of an armed mobilization as organized during 2002-2003, what is needed is an aggressive international diplomatic mobilization to compel Pakistan to close its terror shops. One of the visible measures in this regard could be to work on the United Nations for removing Kashmir from the list of international disputes. As long as Kashmir remains on the list of disputes before the U.N., it gives Pakistan a handle to keep up the terror war against India in its name. In this connection it would be interesting to note that Kashmir had not been before the U.N. as a dispute since around the mid 1960s. The U.N. Secretary General, in fact, tried to remove it from the agenda of dispute in two successive years. But Pakistan lobbied hard to get it retained on the U.N. agenda, as a result of which it has been kept there to be reviewed from year to year. There had also been a proposal both in the U.N. and the U.S. Senate to do away with the U.N. military observation group in Kashmir and save the money wasted on it. Now that all the permanent members of the Security Council, including China, have clearly affirmed that the Kashmir issue should be solved by Pakistan and India bilaterally, India can easily succeed in getting it removed from the

U.N. agenda. The United States, which has been the strongest prop of Pakistan in the U.N., has repeatedly asserted that Simla agreement was the best framework for resolving the Kashmir problems. Pakistan today stands completely isolated internationally in this regard. If Kashmir is removed from the agenda of U.N. with a little extra diplomatic effort on the part of India, it will knock the bottom out of Pakistan's terror enterprise in the name of Kashmir.

It may be noted that the Pakistani state is not made up of the stuff that is Al Quida. Nor is the Pakistani political leadership, be it General Musharaff, Nawaz Shariff or Benazir Bhutto, of the mettle of Osama bin Laden. Once they are deprived of the support from their foreign God-fathers, they would have no option but to come to terms with India and desist from their unceasiong terror offensive.

References

1. *Glimpses of World History,* by J L Nehru.
2. *A survey of Indian History,* by K M Panikkar
3. India through the Ages, by Jadunath Sarkar
4. *Friends not Masters* ,by Ayub Khan.

Epilogue

The 'Clash of civilizations' between Islam and the West shows no signs of abating. This was painfully brought out in the recent cartoon controversy. Even as Muslim protestors all over the world were indulging in a raging and tearing campaign against the Danish cartoonist, the print media in western countries kept replicating the Danish cartoons which depicted the Prophet Muhammad as a terrorist. Some French, Italian, Swedish and Irish papers republished the cartoons in the name of asserting the right of freedom of expression. To the westerners freedom of expression is as sacred as the figure of the Prophet is to the Muslims. The divergent perceptions of sacredness apart, the persistence with which the cartoons were flaunted by the western media shows a toughening of attitude of the westerners against the Islamists.

That would go to show that the westerners are as much in a mode of war as the Islamists. The battle lines were drawn on 9/11 2001 with the Jihadi strike at the leader of the western world. The spontaneous outburst of an American soldier at a place in Afganistan on 5 February 2002 aptly reflects the western mindset. Standing in front of a pile of stones arranged as a tomb-stone over a piece of demolished World Trade Centre buried underneath, a battle-hardened American soldier said 'We consecrate this spot as an everlasting memorial to the brave Americans who died on Sept 11....... We will export death and violence to the four corners of the earth in defence to our great nation' (Quoted by Bob Woodward, 'BUSH AT WAR', 2003).

That brings us to the eternal issue of war and peace. Is mankind doomed to live either under the shadow or fear of war for all times to come? In 1990 when the cold war ended, it did not appear to be so. The vista of lasting peace was clearly in sight. The mood of optimism was reflected in the observations of Peter Millar, a newspaper columnist. In late 1989, he observed that "only now is the Second World War ending...... In 200 years from now, the 20th century may be seen as the era of the great 75-year war which began in 1914 and ended in 1989". For a few years beginning 1989 end, long standing strifes and conflicts in different parts of the world started ending with remarkable ease. Seemingly interminable civil wars and strifes in many troubled areas of the world were ending with remarkable speed like in strife-torn Nicaragua, El Salvador, Angola, Combodia and parts of the Middle East. A 36 years old civil war in Guatemala in Latin America, in which around 1,30,000 lives were lost, came to a smooth end towards the end of December 1996. But the vision of lasting peace in the world proved to be as illusory as ever before. Even as old war zones were being transformed into areas of peace, Jihadi terrorism had already started raising its head in different parts of the world. In the wake of 9/11, the world has again been turned into a war zone.

Does it mean that war is human destiny? Is mankind destined to live with war, which in the nuclear era can destroy human civilization itself ? Historical evidence points to that. History would seem to suggest that war is an essential attribute of humanity. But such a view would be untenable on two counts – the quality and quantum of history itself.

First, the quality. The recorded history beginning from Herodotus, or even proto history derived from epics and other literary works, is grossly deficient and imperfect. It is not an account of human activities in totality but of what the record-keepers, miscalled historians, chose to record in accordance with their own predelictions. Perhaps they were inclined to record only such activities of people of their times which were more describable or thrilling. What we know as history of ancient times is thus highly selective and therefore severely flawed.

So much about the quality of our known history. The angle of its quantum has two dimensions – Space and time. Taking up the space angle first, it may be noted that the big wars waged by the Greeks, Romans, Arabs, Mongols and Turks were all confined to West Asia, Europe, North Africa and occasionally central Asia. By and large, the Chinese in the east, Mayas, Incas, Azteks and the Caribbs in the American far west, Negro groups in southern and central Africa and numerous others in different parts of the globe lived in relative calm, even as the west Asians, Europeans and North Africans were engaged in relentless warfare. That would show that a major portion of the world remained outside the cycle of big wars that rocked a limited area for centuries. If still human history has come to be a story of perennial warfare, it is the fault of history and not of humanity.

Now about the time angle. The comprehension of the time frame encompassing the evolution of our kind of humans – the homo sapiens – would set the records straight. Fully modern humans, that is homo sapiens with big brains, were around by about a 1,00,000 years ago. This is supported by the discovery of parts of a human scull, 1,15,000 years old, in a cave in South Africa. And cave paintings from 40,000 years ago revealed a world of sophisticated European hunters and the animals they hunted.

With such a long past of humans, how old is human history ? By all accounts, our recorded history is not older than about 5000 years. Thus the earliest human species existed on this earth around a 1,00,000 years ago, while the history of wars is only about 5000 years old. That would show that man has lived 20 times more in relative peace than in perennial war. A holistic view of our past from beyond the frontiers of history would demolish the myth that war is a historical necessity or inevitability.

Nor is war a biological necessity, as the Darwinian postulate 'struggle for existence and survival of the fittest' would seem to suggest. Even post – Darwinian socio-biologists maintain that man has survived and multiplied because of 'reciprocal altruism', because he has been able to reason, compromise and cooperate with his kind. Man is an 'altruistic ape', with altruistic instincts and ability to reason and compromise being coded for, directly or indirectly, in his DNA. His self-interest in most cases is enlightened self-interest, which is the bed-rock of inter-personal, inter-social and international relationships. As one writer has put it, "if hamadryas baboons had nuclear weapons, they would destroy the world in a week." But humanity has lived with nuclear weapons for over half a century because he is endowed with that 'superior logic' or intelligence which, in biological terms, separates him from the ape.

Man's ability to cooperate and accommodate, stemming from 'reciprocal altruism' rooted in his DNA, is the surest guarantee of his living in peace in a complex society of 'reciprocal altruists', rather than committing mass suicide through an all pervasive war or series of wars. Conceptually, it may be close to the Freudian 'pleasure principle', in concert with the 'reality principle', which constitutes the human instinctual structure.

At the physical plane, so much has been created and is being multiplied so fast to add to the pleasures of living. The range and sweep of material goods and services which make life worth living and people's ever growing craving for them are fast eroding the sway of myths and cults which promoted the big wars of our history. The over-riding concern and principal aspiration of people in all societies are full enjoyment of benefits of modern civilisatrion. There is no space available in human mind today to entertain any cult or 'ism' worth dying for. Such mega, 'isms' as nationalism which plunged the world into history's most destructive wars and Marxism which threatened to do so, are falling by the wayside in man's evolutionary march. Marxism has evaporated in the land of its glory and nationalism is evaporating in the land of its birth-western Europe- in the wake of man's pursuit of pleasure in peace.

A word here about the current wave of terrorism which seems to be rocking the world today. It is no more than a flitting moment in the life of humanity. The terrorists of today are leftovers of history breeding in the back waters of societies which are still grounded in the Middle ages. They will be consigned to the dung heap of history sooner than later.

Selected Book References

A short list of books and documents referred to, consulted or relied upon in writing of this book, is given below. Many books from which notes had been taken in course of my studies during the past several years which came in handy at the time of writing have also been included in the list.

1) A study of history, Arnold J.Tonybee, Abridgement of volumes I to VI by D.C. Somervell.
2) An Unfinished History of the World, Huge Thomas
3) A History of India, Romila Thapar
4) A short History of the Muslim Rule in India, Ishwari Prasad
5) Among the Believers by V.S. Naipaul
6) Being Human - by Mary and John Gribbin.
7) Bullet for Bullet, An Autobiography of a police officer by Julio Riberio.
8) Bush AT War - by Bob Woodward, 2003
9) Europe since Nepolean, David Thompson.
10) Empire and Islam (Punjab and the Making of Pakistan), David Gilmartin, 1989
11) From Jinnah to Zia, Muhammad Munir Khan, Retd. Chief Justice of Pakistan, 1981

12) Friends Not Masters, President Muhammad Ayub Khan of Pakistan.
13) Freedom at Midnight, Larry Collins and Dominique Lappierre, 1976
14) Glimpses of World History, Jawaharlal Nehru.
15) Governments and Politics of South Asia, J.C. Johari, M.Nazrul Islam and others.
16) History of Medieval India – by V.D. Mahajan- 10th edition, 2005
17) History of Peleponnesian war—by Donald Kagen
18) Hellenism: The history of a civilization, Arnold J. Tonybee.
19) Introduction to the Constitution of India, Durga Das Basu
20) India from Curzon to Nehru and After, Durga Das, 1971
21) Indo-Pak War, V.P. Juneja,. December 1971
22) India Wins Freedom, Moulana Abul Kalam Azad.
23) Inside Pakistan, Jamal Nagvi, Shaukat Ali and Farz Ali, 1986
24) International Terrorism, edited by Charles W. Kegley Jr.1990
25) ISI Ka Atank (Terror of ISI) – by Ram Naresh Pd.Singh
26) 'Islam: The Arab National Movement' – by Anwar Sheikh, Cardiff, Great Britain.
27) "Islamic Threat: Myth or Reality? By Dr. John Exposito (Oxford University Press-1992)
28) India's struggle for Independence, Bipin Chandra, Mridula Mukherji, Aditya Mukherji, K.N. Pannikar and Sucheta Mahajan.
29) India's Freedom Struggle, Bipin Chandra, Amles Tripathi and Barun De, 1971
30) Jinnah of Pakistan' – by Stanley Wolpert

31) Jinnah as I knew him, an article by Dr.Sachchidananda Sinha Published in the Hindustan Review, September, 1949
32) Last Days of the British Raj, Michael Edwards
33) 'Last Days of the British Raj' by Michael Edwards
34) Mountbatten and the Partition of India – by Larry Collins and Doninique Lappierre
35) Mission with Mountbatten, Alan Campbell-Johnson, 1951
36) Modern India 1885-1947, Sumit Sarkar
37) Modern Europe upto 1870, C.J.H. Hayes.
38) Modern Europe upto 1945, C.D. Hazen
39) 'Nuclear India' – by K.Subramanium and others.
40) One Human Nature—by Edward O. Wilson
41) Pakistan Crisis, David Lashak, 1971
42) Politics in Pakistan: The Nature and Direction of Change, Khalid B. Sayeed, 1980
43) Pakistan: Birth and Early Days , Sri Prakash, India's First High Commissioner to Pakistan, 1965
44) Plan of Attack-by Bob Woodward, 2004
45) Pakistan: The Garrison State, Dr.K.L. Kamal, 1982
46) Religion and Peace, edited by Home A. Jack, 1966
47) Reports of the Court of Enquiry into Punjab (Pakistan) Disturbances of 1953, Justice Muhammad Munir and Justice M.R.Kayani, 1954
48) Roman Britain R.G. Collingwood and J.N.L. Myres
49) Social Background of Indian Nationalism, A.R. Desai

50) Speeches and Writings of Jawaharlal Nehru, (Four Volumes) (Selected parts)
51) The Hellenistic World, F.W. Walbank
52) The Global Conflict (The international rivalry of the great powers 1880-1970), C.J. Bartlett.
53) The Wonder that was India, A.L. Basham.
54) The Writings and Speeches of Edmund Burke, Volume V: India and Bengal 1774-1785 edited by P.J. Marshal, 1981
55) The Oxford History of India, Vincent A. Smith Edited by Percival spear, 1958
56) The Sole Spokesman: Jinnah, the Muslim League and the Demand for Pakistan, Ayesha Jalal, 1985
57) Terrorism in India, edited by S.C.Tiwari, 1990
58) The Terrorism Reader, Walter Laqueur
59) Terrorism: History and Facets in the World and in India, N.S.Saxena, 1985
60) Terrorism: World under Seige, S.K. Ghosh,1995
61) The Anarchical Society (A study of Order in World Politics), Hedley Bull, Second edition, 1995
62) 'The Clash of Civilisations and the Remaking of world orders'-by Samuel P. Huntington, 1996
63) The Future of Freedom : Illiberal Democracy at Home and Abroad – by Fareed Zakaria, 2003
64) 'The Concept of Hindu Nation' – by Abhas Chatterjee, 1995
65) Visions of the Past, Christoppher Taylor and Richard Muir
66) Verdict on India, Bexerly Nichols, 1944
67) War And Civilisation-by Arnold J.Toynbee (From A Study of History)
68) "War or Peace"-by John Foster Dulles, 1957

69) "Who killed Daniel Pearl?" by Bernard-Henri Levy in French translated in English by James X. Mitchell, published in France in 2003, by Rupa in Inida later.

Notes on Other Source Materials

This book is not a doctoral thesis or an academic work. Nor is it a purely journalistic work or factual reporting and instant opinionating. Writing it was of course like giving a running commentary on a cricket test match though, but one that lasted not only for five days but for five years or more. I started toying with the idea of doing it specially after the devastating terror strike at America, the lone Super Power in a unipolar world, on September 11, 2001. The sight of the twin towers of the World Trade Centre in New York crashing in flames on the TV screen left an indelible mark on my mind. How could they dare do it ? And what for ? This was followed by the potentially very lethal attack on Indian Parliament on 13 December 2001, which too came live on the TV screen. Those few anxious moments when the news reader kept the viewers guessing whether the Jihadis had entered inside the Parliament hall or not, shall ever remain embossed in my memory.

Ever since then, I kept keeping a tab on every terror event in India and the world, with the idea of analyzing and interpreting it in totality in historical perspective someday always at the back of the mind. Historical studies have always been a passion with me which provided the background. But with a phenomenon like Jihadi terrorism with not much of a history behind it and assuming new dimensions everyday, that was not enough. I had to keep a close look on it from day to day as it kept growing into a colossal threat. It could be done only by taking note of news reports and instant reactions and comments by people concerned over the last 7-8 years. Even though I was not quite sure if I would be able to write a book on the subject, the motivation was always there, which goaded me to keep piling up news papers and periodicals containing relevant materials.

I finally decided to take to writing this book only when certain broad conclusions emerged in my mind and I couldn't hold them back anymore. And when I did start writing, the pile of informations culled from the print media turned out to be the most important source material for this work. I have generally indicated the source of any striking piece of information or quotation in the text itself, but I would like to mention below some notable news magazines and periodicals which I have heavily drawn upon in my writing. These are :-

1) India Today, 15 May 1994, 'Pan-Islamic Fundamentalism: Exporting Terror; A Special Investigation by Shekhar Gupta and Rahul Pathak.

2) Outlook, 15 October, 2001, 'Islam In Crisis'.

3) Newsweek International, U.S.A, Special Issue December 2001 to February 2002 'The Age of Muslim Wars' by Samuel P.Huntington and

'Their Target: The Modern World' by Francis Fukuyama.

4) India Today, 25 February, 2002, 'The Dons of Terror' by Sayantan Chakraverty.

5) The Week, 8 January 2006, 'Terror's New Targets'- Bangalore, Pune, Hyderabad.

6) Frontline, 14-27 January, 2006, 'Jehad Without End', 'Unending War' by Praveen Swamy; 'Challenges in the East' by Subrid Shankar Chattopadhyay in Calcutta and Haroon Habib in Dhaka.

7) Newsweek International, 30 January, 2006, 'Predator And Prey' by Michael Hirsh, Mark Hosenbalt and Sami Yousafzai. (The Bin Laden Tape)

8) Newsweek International, 6 March 2006, 'Iraq War of the Mosques', by Babak Dehghanpisheh, Michael Hastings and Michael Hirsh.

These were some of the more notable news magazines which served as my best source materials on the latest developments on the Jihadi front. Some of the important dailies which I have drawn upon were 'The Times of India', Hindustan Times' 'The Hindu' and Hindi dailies 'Hindustan' and 'Dainik Jagaran'.

On the subject of terrorism in general, the professional journal of National Police Academy came in handy. And in regard to nuclear terrorism, I drew upon an article entitled 'Nuclear Security & Terrorism': A Hyped-up, yet credible Threat' by

Index

J

K

N

Q

R

S

T

U